PRAISE FOR *ENDA THE ROAD*

'Comprehensive and clear, Gavan Reilly chronicles an important period in recent Irish political history, charting the dramatic twists and turns, played out both in public and private, to provide an insightful explanation as to how and why Enda Kenny's career as Taoiseach and Fine Gael leader came to an end. The reasons why things happen often get clouded as events take place at pace; in this case attention quickly moved as to who would be Kenny's political successor. With the distance provided by time, Reilly has done a fine job in cutting through the fog and bringing us into the relevant rooms to tell the big story.' – *Matt Cooper*

'In *Enda the Road: Nine Days that Toppled a Taoiseach*, Gavan Reilly combines the observational skills of a Leinster House habitué with the insightful analysis of an experienced political journalist. Meticulously researched and full of intriguing detail, the book expertly pulls together the complex strands of a tangled tale which proved to be both a cock-up and a conspiracy. It is a comprehensive and enlightening textbook for anyone trying to understand how the breakneck pace of events in Irish politics – a rough and unsentimental gladiatorial arena – brought an early and turbulent end to the political career of Fine Gael's longest-serving Taoiseach.' – *Lise Hand*

ENDA THE ROAD

NINE DAYS THAT TOPPLED A TAOISEACH

GAVAN REILLY

MERCIER PRESS

MERCIER PRESS
Cork
www.mercierpress.ie

ISBN: 978 1 78117 655 9

A CIP record for this title is available from the British Library.

Printed and bound in the EU.

To Ciara,
my favourite person.

CONTENTS

AUTHOR'S NOTE

Enda Kenny declined to be interviewed for this book. That is entirely his own prerogative and, given the difficult time being described, completely understandable. Others – both inside and outside his administration – were happy to offer their insights and recollections into the tumultuous nine days that, eventually, resulted in Kenny stepping down. I am deeply appreciative that each of them did so, in particular to those whose interviews went on for far longer than either of us might have expected.

Not all of those interviewees, however, could do so on the record. Some preferred to remain anonymous out of respect to their former Taoiseach and party leader; others required their identities to be withheld due to ongoing professional relationships. Rather than tell the story without their contributions – or to have names alongside some quotes, and leave others orphaned – I decided to conduct all interviews on an off-the-record, unattributed basis. I know this principle can be frustrating for the reader; my hope is that granting anonymity to sources has encouraged them to be more frank in their recollections and analysis.

Aside from those interviews, this book is drawn primarily from contemporary reporting across broadcast, print and electronic media, including my own audio recordings of the time. It also leans heavily on transcripts and reports of the Disclosures Tribunal, and on transcripts of Dáil proceedings, which are also published by the Oireachtas. However, I have opted against using the 'official' transcript of parliamentary business – which is sub-edited in the pursuit of oratorical correctness – in favour of re-transcribing speeches from the original footage. The resulting copy, I hope, captures some of the imperfections that give the Dáil its true colour.

PROLOGUE

The Election that Nobody Won

It was never supposed to be like this. He had worked too hard, waited too long. It had taken four decades of toil to get to the summit of Irish politics, and the view was too rewarding to climb down so soon.

The 2016 election was supposed to be Fine Gael's to lose. Five years earlier, in February 2011, with the largest parliamentary majority in Irish history, Enda Kenny and his government had inherited a country close to bankruptcy and under the thumb of the 'Troika' of the European Commission, European Central Bank and International Monetary Fund – the international lenders of last resort, drafted in by the outgoing Fianna Fáil-led government when nobody else would lend Ireland the money it needed. Four painful, hair-shirt budgets had been followed by an October 2015 package that put €1.5 billion back into the Irish economy and took roughly €350 off the average worker's tax bill. What's more, unemployment was falling and 200,000 people had been put back to work. Emigration had stalled and Ireland was once again becoming an economic sanctuary for foreigners seeking jobs. Opinion polls after the Budget showed Fine Gael with over thirty per cent of voter support and a double-digit lead over any other party. Fine Gael readied its position and prepared itself for a snap general election in November – and stopped short only when the Tánaiste, Labour leader Joan Burton, lobbied Kenny to allow her party more time to prepare its campaign.

Still, when Kenny did finally dissolve the thirty-first Dáil on 3 February 2016, there was little reason to doubt that he would become the first Fine Gael leader to win two successive terms as Taoiseach. The economy was continuing to grow, and all the big-picture statistics were positive – so much so that Fine Gael sought votes with the message 'Keep the Recovery Going'. One poll gave Kenny's party a fourteen-point lead over its nearest rivals, 31 to 17. The initial theme of the election was not who would win it, but rather with whom Enda Kenny would govern after it was over.

Moreover, this campaign was to be Kenny's swansong: 2016 would be the last election campaign he would ever lead. The sixty-four-year-old, who had led Fine Gael for fourteen years, had already committed to bowing out after this term. A few months previously his chief whip, Paul Kehoe, had suggested Kenny would not only complete two full terms as Taoiseach, but might even seek a third. Kenny, disputing the media's cheeky comparisons to an African strongman dictator, dismissed the story – vowing instead that if he were given a second term, it would be his last.

But, somehow, Fine Gael's comfortable lead in the polls ebbed away. The party's campaign appeared to stutter even from the moment it began, when Kenny decisively announced to the Dáil that he wanted to dissolve it, but then seemed to immediately dither on whether to head straight to Áras an Úachtaráin or allow opposition leaders to speak first. His final act before leaving for the Áras was a photocall with Joan Burton – this was intended as a sign of unity, but instead left Burton cutting the figure of a lonesome war widow, alone on the steps of Government Buildings as Kenny's motorcade pulled away.

Hours later, at the campaign kick-off press conference, Kenny was challenged about the party's calculations on the 'fiscal space', the voguish term the government had used when talking about the extra money available for new purposes in future years. Kenny flubbed, tried to evade the question on the premise of avoiding 'economic jargon', and eventually drafted his finance minister, Michael Noonan, to answer it. The confused performance would have reached a great audience, if only the recording could have been broadcast; such was the haste with which the event was arranged, the hired hands had no time to configure the sound system and so the resulting audio was almost completely unusable.

The rickety opening day would set the tone, and what ought to have been a canter soon became a stumble. Sinn Féin quickly pointed out a €2 billion over-calculation in the 'fiscal space' figures, which was especially damaging given the disparaging 'Shinnernomics' brush with which Sinn Féin's economic figures were usually tarred. The party also harnessed the raw power of the campaign against water charges, which had become a lightning rod of anti-austerity anger. That anger put paid to Labour, which had gained power on the premise of softening the edges of Fine Gael's austerity, but was mostly seen as having merely enabled it instead.

Fianna Fáil, meanwhile, had become keenly aware that a campaign aimed at 'keeping the recovery going' would wear thin in the large swathes of the country where little or no recovery was being felt. The cost of housing had also become especially pressing, and while unemployment had fallen, many in precarious work still struggled with the cost of living.

Fine Gael pursued the full traditions of a leader's tour, but something was amiss. Kenny, while being whisked around the country, remained somehow cloistered off from the campaign on the ground. He would later grumble that all of his events were set pieces, choreographed so that he would only ever speak to Fine Gael supporters and was rarely brought into contact with average voters.

The frustration perhaps boiled over when, on the final Saturday of the election campaign, Kenny addressed a hometown crowd in Castlebar where, excited by the crowd, he described some in the town as 'All-Ireland champion whingers'. Kenny claimed the remark was aimed at 'locals' who found it 'very difficult to see anything good, anywhere, anytime' – 'some of them wouldn't know sunshine if they saw it'. But as the remark attracted increasing attention, Kenny ended up revising his explanation – saying it didn't specifically refer to locals at all, neither in his own county nor in his own town, but specifically to pessimistic Fianna Fáil politicians.

Eventually, after spurning three earlier opportunities to withdraw the remark, Kenny relented. 'Mea culpa,' he said – a prescient formula of words, given that he would repeat it at a pivotal moment in the drama that was to come twelve months later. 'I accept I should have clarified my remarks,' he conceded. 'This is strictly a local issue – it's nothing to do with any member of the public, and any offence taken by any member of the public, in Castlebar, I unreservedly withdraw that … what I was referring to here was a continuous stream of talking down our county's capital town by Fianna Fáil politicians … no offence should be taken by any member of the public, and I regret that.'

The episode was emblematic of the tone-deafness of Fine Gael's campaign, and in particular its mantra of 'keeping the recovery going'. Kenny had unwittingly exemplified the inability of Fine Gael to tailor its messaging according to the public mood. Local volunteers were reporting back that the 'recovery' was an easier sell in wealthier urban areas, but that it was falling on deaf ears in areas where there was no recovery to see. There were plenty of villages nationwide with new retail units, built during the post-millennium good times, which were now empty and falling into dereliction. Rightly or wrongly, Ireland had become accustomed to certain standards of living, and those standards were not being met. Kenny, with four decades of public service under his belt, was kept out of reach of the ordinary punter and so was powerless to diagnose these faults.

The cost to Fine Gael of this tone-deafness became clear when the votes were counted. Despite its restoring relative normality to a crocked economy, Fine Gael's lead over Fianna Fáil had shrunk to just 1.2 per cent, forty-nine seats versus forty-four. Kenny's coalition had disintegrated: Labour returned just seven seats in the new chamber of 158 – with twenty-six deputies losing their seats – while Sinn Féin claimed twenty-three.

It was not supposed to be like this.

This was the election that nobody won – with a result that produced a serious problem. Each of the largest three parties had campaigned on the promise of refusing to coalesce with the others. Labour, hoping to continue its coalition with Fine Gael, took such a beating that it instead decided it had no mandate to govern at all. Nobody had any path to a parliamentary majority, and while both Kenny and Fianna Fáil's Micheál Martin held talks with others to build up their Dáil blocs, neither came anywhere close to a majority coalition of eighty TDs.

In an honest bid to break the deadlock, after six weeks Kenny offered to form a full coalition with Fianna Fáil, telling Martin that a minority government led by either party would not work and only a full coalition, perhaps buffered by a few independents, would give Ireland the stability it needed. Martin rejected the idea almost immediately, believing a full coalition would frustrate both parties while leaving Sinn Féin with a near-monopoly on opposition. A second election now seemed a real prospect, though many doubted whether the public would vote any differently the second time around. Few had the appetite (or money) to go back to the electorate, when the make-up of the next Dáil would probably look so similar.

Kenny's audacious gesture did, however, plant a seed. The new thirty-second Dáil had met as scheduled, failing to elect a new Taoiseach, forcing Kenny to fulfil his constitutional duty of officially resigning as premier, though remaining in a caretaker capacity. Fianna Fáil's Seán Ó Fearghaíl was elected the new Ceann Comhairle, succeeding Seán Barrett, who returned to the Fine Gael benches. This tweaking of the blocs made Kenny's numbers slightly healthier and opened up the prospect of an unlikely solution.

If Fianna Fáil's TDs were to abstain in major Dáil votes and the Ceann Comhairle followed the usual convention by breaking any deadlocks in the government's favour, the threshold of a working majority would be reduced from eighty votes to fifty-seven. Kenny, now with fifty, could govern once more if he found seven others to join him – and if Fianna Fáil could be convinced to sit on their hands. Kenny had already declared his unhappiness at a minority government, but it now offered him a ticket back into power. All it would take was the burying of a ninety-year-old hatchet.

And so the talks began. Kenny nominated a team of negotiators to pull the arithmetic together, with five ministers from the outgoing administration part of the team: justice minister Frances

Fitzgerald, agriculture and defence minister Simon Coveney, health minister Leo Varadkar, transport minister Paschal Donohoe and junior finance minister Simon Harris. Harris's superior at the Department of Finance, Michael Noonan, would join in whenever fiscal matters were being discussed. Beginning in the Sycamore Room of Government Buildings, the team spent endless days negotiating in parallel with multiple different blocs, hoping to secure either their formal support for Fine Gael's return to power, or at the very least their complicit abstention when the government was being elected.

The Fianna Fáil talks proved the most difficult. Nine decades of enmity provided a natural stumbling block. Never in their history had either party required the explicit support of the other to govern, and nobody was sure how to create such a culture. The clear public verdict on water charges also proved a tough nut to crack, with the Fine Gael team refusing simply to roll over and accept a quick humiliation on a policy that had cost the jobs of so many colleagues. Talks endured for several weeks and regularly decamped to venues in Trinity College – first the provost's mansion at the top of Grafton Street and later some meeting rooms inside the biomedical faculty on Pearse Street.

Often, after a day of talks with Fianna Fáil, the Fine Gael team would retreat back to the Sycamore Room for further discussions with several tranches of independent TDs – in particular, with three self-organised caucuses. The 'Independent Alliance' had run as a slate of twenty-one candidates on a common platform of political regeneration and reform, with six being elected. The group had been co-founded and informally chaired by Shane Ross, a stockbroker-turned-journalist-while-senator-turned-TD. His role proved simultaneously to be both an asset, because of his standing and general clout, and a liability: he used his then-weekly *Sunday Independent* column to label Kenny a 'political zombie' during a running commentary on the talks, to the severe annoyance of the Fine Gael team, and risking the outright collapse of the negotiations. Ross was joined in the group by re-elected TDs Finian McGrath, John Halligan and Michael Fitzmaurice, as well as first-timers Seán Canney and Kevin 'Boxer' Moran.

Separate talks were conducted with a group of five TDs representing rural constituencies, convened by ex-Fine Gael deputy Denis Naughten. He, Galway West's Noel Grealish, Tipperary's Mattie McGrath, Dr Michael Harty of Clare and Michael Collins of Cork South-West sought concessions on the regeneration of rural Ireland in exchange for backing Kenny's administration. For them, the future of water charges was not a particular concern; the group was more irked by how little political attention was paid to the rural dwellers who had already paid for water, via group water schemes, for decades.

Discussions were also held with the Dáil's smallest mini-faction, Kerry's Healy-Rae brothers, Michael and Danny, the first brothers ever elected to represent the same constituency at the same time. Those talks quickly came to naught amid rumours that family tensions had come to the fore. The brothers were the sons of former TD Jackie, a lifelong Fianna Fáiler who ran as an independent TD only because the party would not add him to its ticket. The suggestion was that idealistic Danny, a novice TD, shared these leanings and could not bring himself to support a Fine Gael government – while pragmatic Michael, already four years in the Dáil, was happy to make the best deal with the best partner available. The rumours even suggested that, knowing Danny's support could never be secured, Michael had delicately collapsed the talks by asking to be named Minister for Transport, an ostentatious request that Fine Gael would quickly reject.

One other independent had been recruited early in the process. Katherine Zappone, a former senator who had now joined the lower house in Dublin South-West on the back of its 'respectable' liberal vote, signed up as soon as Fine Gael offered a guarantee that a new citizens' assembly would be established to consider the repeal of the Eighth Amendment, the constitutional clause banning abortion. It was an easy sell: the proposal already existed in Fine Gael's manifesto.

All the while, the Fine Gael negotiating team were mindful that the deals being struck were needed to appoint not only one government, but two. Kenny regularly reminded his team of negotiators that he was not destined to govern forever and that his pledge not to seek a third term meant he would have to hand over the reins sometime during his second. Constitutionally, whenever Kenny resigned, the whole government would technically follow him. The deals, therefore, could not be based on personalities but on policies, which would sustain the government of his successor whenever he chose to step away. 'I just want to put together the government, let it bed down, and I'll know when it's time to walk off the stage,' he told the team on several occasions, according to interviews conducted for this book. 'I'm not going to be around forever.'

Eventually, the deals were done. On the final Friday of April – nine weeks after the general election – Fianna Fáil agreed to facilitate Enda Kenny's return to power, in exchange for an agreed pseudo-programme for government. Fianna Fáil would agree to pass three budgets, as long as there were twice as many spending increases as tax cuts. Fine Gael in turn recognised that

Fianna Fáil was still an independent party, pursuing any policy it liked, and agreed a 'no surprises' clause where Fianna Fáil would be briefed on major government initiatives before their public announcement. A separate appendix was drafted to govern the retention of Irish Water as a State-backed utility, but with the concurrent abolition and refunding of the reviled water charges.

A week later the deals were tied up with some of the independents: five of the Independent Alliance agreed to a programme for government – Michael Fitzmaurice left the group over Fine Gael's refusal to challenge EU laws outlawing rural turf-cutters – while the rural independents group dissolved as Denis Naughten joined Kenny's new administration and Dr Michael Harty chose to support it from outside. Fine Gael's fifty, plus the Independence Alliance's five, Zappone and Naughten made fifty-seven – a bare bones working majority. The external support of Harty and the ex-Fine Gael minister Michael Lowry, whose backing was not solicited but granted anyway, brought the number to fifty-nine.

Enda Kenny was re-elected Taoiseach with the support of those fifty-nine TDs and the abstention of Fianna Fáil. Six of his seven independent backers were rewarded with ministerial jobs. Zappone was named the new Minister for Children and Youth Affairs. Naughten became Minister for Communications, with a reorganised brief in charge of climate change and environmental issues. Ross, who had devoted many column inches in books and newspapers to criticising the corporate largesse of the transport operator CIÉ, was handed the job of Minister for Transport, Tourism and Sport.

Jobs were also doled out to others in the Independent Alliance. Finian McGrath, with a particular personal interest in disability rights, was given the junior ministry for that field and the right to attend Cabinet meetings. John Halligan, whose Waterford hometown had especially struggled with unemployment, took a role responsible for training and skills. Another job responsible for public works and flood relief was made available, but nobody could decide whether Seán Canney or Kevin 'Boxer' Moran should take it, so the two simply flipped a coin. Canney took the job on the agreement Boxer would inherit it a year later.

It was an uneasy and rickety alliance – a one-party government topped up with seven independents, with the historical enemy now on the opposition benches empowered to pull the plug at any time. Ironically, Fine Gael's bruising election 'defeat' had left it holding *more* ministerial jobs than before – with more than half of its fifty TDs now holding a ministerial title of some sort. With no formal coalition partner, the role of Tánaiste was also kept in-house and given to justice minister Frances Fitzgerald.

Few expected this new arrangement to endure for one budget, let alone the agreed three. But it would suffice for now: the government was formed, the Cabinet table was packed and Enda Kenny was back in the second-floor office of Government Buildings from which the nation's levers of power are pulled.

Things would be different this time. Kenny's first government held the largest majority in Ireland's independent history, but his second would have the weakest grasp on power ever, with just over half as many TDs as its predecessor. The first had enough TDs behind it that it could afford to lose fourteen through various political rows, yet still have an iron-clad majority. It could effectively enact whatever laws it liked, and once Fine Gael and Labour were agreed on a policy, passing it into law was a relative formality.

This time there would be no such luxury. Defeats in votes – a complete non-feature of the thirty-first Dáil – would be commonplace in the thirty-second. Fianna Fáil was now signed up to facilitate some specific measures, including budgets, but retained its right to propose its own legislation and to vote against the government on any other unplanned bills or motions. The government could no longer control the schedule of Dáil business and had to secure the consensus of opposition parties before it could even allot time for its own bills to be discussed. Defeats, at first a novelty, soon became so common that journalists simply stopped reporting on them. The political culture shock even came with a semi-disparaging new name: 'New Politics'.

Governing now would be different in other ways too. The five-year marriage of Fine Gael and Labour had been largely stable. Each party had a formalised command structure, with a specific leader on top. The two ministers running the now-partitioned Department of Finance, Michael Noonan and Brendan Howlin, had such a collegiate relationship that they regularly mediated in otherwise intractable policy disputes, always with success. Now, though, there could be no command structure like that: Fine Gael would raise issues within its own ranks, but the fate of the nation was equally controlled by outsiders in Fianna Fáil and seven independent colleagues (both inside and outside any umbrella grouping) who could not be managed as a collective and who, individually, could bring the whole administration to a screeching halt.

'There was enormous adaptation, particularly for the Alliance people,' one Fine Gael minister later said of their non-party colleagues. 'They'd no experience, they were very tense around it … some of them weren't sure they wanted to be in government at all. This was all brand new for them. They hadn't any idea how to be ministers.'

This improvised administration had plenty on its plate. The green shoots of economic recovery were delicate and needed careful management. The UK's vote to leave the EU on 23 June 2016 – just seven weeks after the new Irish government took office – posed massive diplomatic and economic challenges, not least for Northern Ireland. Hospitals remained overcrowded. Demand for housing continued to drastically exceed supply. Gangland crime, after an audacious daylight shooting in the middle of the election campaign, had exploded back onto the front pages.

With his feet back under the desk, the Taoiseach would inject himself directly into his government's response to those issues. Kenny took a personal interest in the fate of Dublin's north inner city, believing that organised crime was flourishing largely because the underprivileged community left impressionable people with few alternatives. Faced with calls to appoint a special minister to take specific responsibility for Brexit, Kenny pointedly refused, instead planning to exploit his own status as one of Europe's longest-serving (and therefore best-connected) party leaders. 'There already is a Minister for Brexit,' his spokesman would sometimes explain. 'His name is Enda Kenny.'

In time, party colleagues would wonder if the Taoiseach was spreading himself too thinly. The eternally youthful man was still sustained by the enjoyment of his job, but the mammoth workload would only continue to get bigger. None of his colleagues doubted his honest commitment to meeting that workload, but plenty feared that Enda Kenny might just have been trying to make himself indispensable.

It was the election nobody won – yet still Enda Kenny had managed to come out on top.

Many within Fine Gael, however, still lamented their new circumstances. Sure, their party had retained power – but being reliant on the acquiescence of its historic rival meant there was little chance to enjoy it. An enormous lead in the opinion polls had not translated into the runaway success that the party felt it deserved. It wasn't, to put it simply, supposed to be like this.

DAY 1

Tuesday, 7 February 2017

It was a chilly morning in Dublin, clear but frosty. It was due to stay dry, but that was the only comfort; Met Éireann's weather forecast was promising a 'bitterly cold' day ahead.

Ministers thumbing through the morning papers would have had plenty to occupy their minds. Many pages were devoted to an RTÉ documentary, broadcast the previous night, about the lives of children waiting to get surgery for scoliosis, a debilitating curvature of the spine. Others outlined a growing class divide in Ireland's colleges and universities, the prospect of 1.3 million Internet users facing restrictions over illegal downloading, and the arrest of two Irishmen over an alleged gangland hit in the Netherlands.

There were thoughts of matters further afield, too. Northern Ireland had been plunged into a snap election after the resignation of Martin McGuinness as Deputy First Minister, in a row over a so-called 'cash for ash' scandal. Arlene Foster had introduced the botched scheme – an incentive to install more sustainable heating systems – while she was enterprise minister, but now refused to stand aside as First Minister while the scheme was investigated through a public inquiry. The ideological gap between green and orange was widening; Sinn Féin was also aggrieved at the DUP's persistent refusals to entertain issues like gay marriage or an official Irish Language Act. Many feared the next Assembly would face similar trouble.

In London, MPs were debating whether to receive Donald Trump, resident in the White House for only three weeks, as a guest speaker in parliament. It seemed an unwelcome distraction, as in Brussels (and in Dublin) everyone was waiting with bated breath for Theresa May to formally trigger the 'Article 50' process, giving two years' formal notice of the UK's departure from the European Union. The social protection minister, Leo Varadkar, may have stirred the pot by saying Northern Ireland should be given the option to remain within the EU's single market, which would further offend the sensibilities of Northern Ireland's unionist population.

As per usual, Tuesday morning meant an early start for ministers and their closest advisors. The Cabinet was due to meet at its usual time of 9.45 a.m., with the Fine Gael ministers holding their own separate 'pre-meeting' at 9 a.m. While the full Cabinet was in session, ministerial advisors would hold their own weekly 'shadow cabinet' to brief each other on upcoming developments and policy issues, agree a timetable for announcing their own initiatives, and generally knock heads around the week's political agenda.

For the Department of Justice it was lining up to be a sensitive and delicate day. Four months previously, Minister Frances Fitzgerald had received two 'protected disclosures' – the bureaucratic term for whistleblowing complaints – which, if proven true, would unleash a mammoth scandal within the ranks of An Garda Síochána, Ireland's national police force.

Ireland's relatively young whistleblowing law placed strict limits on the degree to which Fitzgerald could share the contents of the complaints. Some details had already made their way into the public domain, though not via the Department of Justice. But after today's Cabinet meeting, the cat would be out of the bag.

A domino effect would require Fitzgerald to release some of the details of these explosive claims. A State inquiry could not be set up without the approval of both houses of parliament, but neither house could approve an inquiry unless they knew exactly what was being investigated. Fitzgerald and her colleagues would accordingly have to tell the Dáil, and therefore the public, exactly what allegations had been made.

Everyone involved knew this would be a delicate process. Even releasing the allegations into the public domain, without any comment on whether they were true or not, could ruin the chain of command within the Gardaí and make it almost impossible for the force to function. But there was simply no other option: the claims had to be investigated, and that meant announcing them to the world.

Deep down, many ministers had an uneasy feeling in the pits of their stomachs. *What is it*, they wondered, *about Maurice McCabe?*

* * *

For a relatively low-ranking member of the force, Maurice McCabe had managed to cast a long shadow across both policing and politics. In the latter end of the previous decade, McCabe – the sergeant-in-charge at Bailieborough Station in Co. Cavan – had raised a series of allegations around maladministration of policing in his Cavan–Monaghan district. The crimes to which he was referring were no minor matter: they included the force's local handling of a violent offender who had murdered a mother-of-two at a Limerick hotel in December 2007. At the time of the murder, the same man was already on bail twice, for two separate incidents: an assault on a taxi driver in Cavan that April and a violent attempted abduction of a child from her home in

Tipperary in October. McCabe felt his Cavan colleagues had not properly prosecuted the first case; if they had, bail would not have been granted after the second and the murder would never have happened.

An internal investigation within the force dismissed McCabe's allegations, generally upholding the standard of policing in the district. Senior Gardaí distributed a note, to be displayed on the staff noticeboards of each station in the district, clearly stating that the allegations – for which Sergeant Maurice McCabe was named as being specifically responsible – were without foundation.

Around the same time, an allegation of serious wrongdoing emerged against McCabe himself. The daughter of a colleague came forward with a story about a Christmas party in the McCabe family home at Christmas 1998. The girl, who was only six or seven years old at the time, had been playing hide-and-seek with Maurice and some of his children when Maurice found her hiding behind the sitting-room sofa. At the time the girl – known only as 'Ms D' – believed McCabe had simply tickled her, but by 2006 the now fourteen-year-old was interpreting the incident in a different light. Distressed, she went to her parents and told them that the encounter involved 'dry humping'. Her parents duly referred it to the Gardaí. (As it happened, this allegation resurfaced not long after the girl's father had been disciplined within the force after McCabe complained about him attending the scene of a suicide while drunk and off duty.)

McCabe told the investigating Gardaí he completely rejected Ms D's allegation, insisting he knew nothing about it, that this was the first he had heard of it, and rejecting vigorously any suggestion that he had acted in any way inappropriately. Ms D's allegation was eventually brought to the Director of Public

Prosecutions, James Hamilton, who found no grounds for action: it was simply one person's word against another, and even if the claim could be substantiated, there was no evidence of a crime being committed. The allegation appeared to dissolve away.

By late 2012 McCabe was once again on the radar of Garda HQ. He had become aware of suspicious behaviour in how motorists' penalty points were being quashed, citing examples of public figures, sportsmen and celebrities who had had penalty points removed from their licences. While it was always possible to have points quashed, motorists were supposed to make a compelling case to someone of inspector rank or higher – arguing that there was a fair and legitimate reason why the points should not be applied, or why the corresponding fine should be waived. McCabe suspected that not every cancellation was legitimate; some private vehicles had points cancelled up to seven times. Some beneficiaries named under Dáil privilege included journalist and broadcaster Paul Williams, District Court Judge Mary Devins, and Ireland's leading all-time rugby union points scorer Ronan O'Gara.

Hoping the full depth of the scandal could be exposed, McCabe and fellow whistleblower John Wilson began sending examples to individual TDs – including members of the Public Accounts Committee (PAC) – and to the Comptroller and Auditor General, the official public auditor. The PAC decided the matter justified further investigation and so asked the Garda Commissioner Martin Callinan to give evidence. It even considered inviting oral evidence from McCabe himself.

This put Callinan on a collision course with both McCabe and the PAC. He insisted McCabe had illegally shared records from the Garda PULSE computer system without authorisation and that the PAC had an obligation to return the documents under data protection law. A tug-of-war followed, leading to McCabe giving evidence in private, behind closed doors, and Callinan giving five hours of evidence in which he referred to the actions of McCabe and Wilson as 'quite disgusting'.

But again, just as McCabe was becoming a problem for Garda headquarters, the previous allegation arose once more. Whispers began to circulate in media and political circles that perhaps McCabe was not to be trusted – that this man was not so perfectly motivated. There was a suggestion that McCabe had an allegation of sexual assault on his record, against a minor, and that anything he said now would have to be taken with a pinch of salt.

Those whispers appeared to stop when Martin Callinan suddenly resigned in March 2014. The Commissioner was already under huge political pressure for his seemingly insensitive and brazen handling of the McCabe allegations regarding the ticket cancellations, especially when the transport minister Leo Varadkar – who had become aware of the allegations via the Road Safety Authority, and who shared the concerns about the points system being abused – described the actions of the whistleblowers as 'distinguished', as opposed to 'disgusting'. Once a separate scandal arose, of illegal tape recordings of phone calls at Garda stations, Enda Kenny communicated his disgust and Callinan 'retired' abruptly on 25 March.

He was replaced – first on an interim basis, but then permanently – by Nóirín O'Sullivan, his Deputy Commissioner, who had occupied the office next to his own and who had sat beside him during his five-hour grilling at Leinster House. Despite her ties to her predecessor, O'Sullivan insisted she wished to make An Garda Síochána a warm and welcoming environment for whistleblowers, whose bona fides could not be challenged and whose allegations deserved full scrutiny.

***

Barely two months after Callinan's departure, another head would roll. Within weeks of appearing before the PAC – behind closed doors, but in full Garda uniform – McCabe revived his 2008 allegations of wrongful policing in Cavan–Monaghan, handing over a dossier of his claims to the Fianna Fáil leader Micheál Martin. Martin in turn raised the issue in the Dáil and passed the claims on to Enda Kenny, who commissioned a report from barrister Seán Guerin.

One of McCabe's complaints dealt with the former Commissioner himself, on the premise that Martin Callinan had made a 'serious error of judgement' by considering the Cavan–Monaghan district officer for promotion when there were serious concerns around policing in his area. As there is no internal manager for the Commissioner to answer to, any complaints against them are passed to the Minister for Justice. McCabe's complaint about Callinan was therefore referred to then-Minister Alan Shatter.

Guerin's subsequent assessment was that Shatter had mishandled some of McCabe's allegations – including the complaint against Callinan, by immediately sending it back to Callinan himself for investigation. Shatter, given a few hours to resign or be sacked after Guerin's assessment came to light, quit on 7 May 2014. (Furious that Guerin had considered the allegations without actually speaking to him, Shatter eventually got some of these findings overturned at the Court of Appeal.)

Maurice McCabe had already been warned he would face Shatter's wrath for drawing public attention to his complaints.

Oliver Connolly, the 'confidential recipient' for internal Garda complaints, had told him: 'If Shatter thinks you're screwing him, you're finished ... he'll go after you.' (Connolly himself was sacked by Shatter after his comments emerged in the press, saying such commentary 'had undermined the office' Connolly had held.) The fallout from McCabe's complaints had not only claimed the Garda Commissioner's job, but now also that of a government minister – all while a national image emerged of McCabe as simply an honest Garda, loyal to the uniform, whose rightful concerns had unfairly brought him into harm's way.

Guerin's report resulted in another full State inquiry, the O'Higgins Commission, which, eventually, vindicated Alan Shatter's handling of the allegations. It turned out that, despite Guerin's finding to the contrary, Shatter had indeed acted correctly by seeking a report from Callinan on McCabe's complaint about him. O'Higgins found that Shatter was not asking Callinan to investigate himself, but simply to give a defence of his actions.

But O'Higgins also upheld many of Maurice McCabe's complaints. While noting that the whistleblower had an occasional tendency to exaggerate, it found that his concerns were well grounded and that there had been systematic examples of policing failures in Bailieborough and beyond. Once again, McCabe was publicly vindicated after a difficult and bruising public inquiry.

It was only after O'Higgins' final report that the public were to find out just how difficult it had been for McCabe to make his case. Partial transcripts from the commission were leaked to the press, which appeared to suggest that Nóirín O'Sullivan's legal team had set out to question McCabe's integrity, motivation and credibility 'right the way through'. This seemed to shatter the credibility of O'Sullivan, who had presented herself as a vocal supporter of McCabe and other Garda whistleblowers. While she denied any such allegation, publicly the suspicion was growing that the Garda machine had conspired against the country's most feted whistleblower.

* * *

One of Nóirín O'Sullivan's first acts in office was to remove the head of the Garda press office, Superintendent Dave Taylor. Taylor was well known to journalists as an accessible spokesman for the force, and always seemed to enjoy his job. He took it as a personal slight and a perceived demotion when O'Sullivan moved him instead to the Dublin traffic unit.

Ten months later, in April 2015, Taylor was arrested – accused of leaking details to journalists about a sensitive operation almost a year earlier, in which two Roma children were removed from their families – and suspended from work for almost two years while he was investigated. Responsibility for this inquiry, which resulted in many of Taylor's mobile phones being seized, lay with Chief Superintendent Jim McGowan, who happened to be O'Sullivan's husband.

Sidelined from the force and with time on his hands, Taylor began to dwell on the fallout from the Callinan–McCabe row, which had partly triggered the Commissioner's resignation, and decided that there were, indeed, some things in his past that he was not proud of. Sixteen months into his suspension, in September 2016, he invited Maurice McCabe to visit him at his home in north Dublin and made a devastating revelation. He told McCabe he had been ordered to smear him, on the orders of Martin Callinan, by drawing attention to the previous allegation of sexual assault against him. Whether this allegation was true was beside the point; the fact that the DPP had investigated and dismissed the allegation was also irrelevant. Furthermore, he claimed an intelligence file had been compiled on McCabe within Garda headquarters, a measure usually reserved only for serious criminals. For good measure, Taylor also alleged that Nóirín O'Sullivan was aware of the whole campaign – and that he would be able to prove his claims, if only he still had access to his mobile phones.

McCabe, shocked at this torrent of information, stewed on the revelations for a few days before telling Taylor he would send a protected disclosure to the new Minister for Justice and Tánaiste, Frances Fitzgerald, to inform her of these fresh allegations. Taylor decided to do likewise, recruiting help from a solicitor in committing his allegations to paper. Letters from both men landed on Frances Fitzgerald's desk in the first week of October 2016.

Taylor's disclosure was stunning in its bluntness: 'I can confirm there was a campaign at the highest level in An Garda Síochána involving the Commissioner, Martin Callinan, and the then Deputy Commissioner, now Commissioner, Nóirín O'Sullivan, to discredit Maurice McCabe.'

Frances Fitzgerald knew these allegations were dynamite and that she needed to act carefully. After consulting with Attorney General Máire Whelan, the Tánaiste opted to set up a low-profile scoping inquiry, handing the allegations to retired High Court Judge Iarfhlaith O'Neill. He was asked to review the allegations, make whatever preliminary inquiries he deemed appropriate and report back to Fitzgerald with recommendations for what to do next.

If the idea behind this was to keep the allegations out of the public sphere, it didn't quite work. Although Fitzgerald was assiduous in ensuring the information did not leak from her side, word made its way into the public domain anyway. Only two weeks after the protected disclosures landed on her desk in October 2016, the *Sunday Independent* carried details of the allegations made by both men, along with a colourful report of the three-hour meeting at Taylor's home (even reporting the sole thought that was running through McCabe's mind: '*I'm going to hit this guy.*') In fact, the leaking of the information only compounded a perception that Fitzgerald was trying to suppress the information, rather than investigate it – a difficult claim to refute when she was still legally constrained from talking about it.

'She did absolutely everything by the book,' one colleague lamented. 'The new law completely protected the whistleblower – but if the whistleblower got public attention in other places, Frances was totally hamstrung. The whole country was talking about this thing but legally she couldn't say a word. It only added to the paranoia.'

Importantly, though, the details published by the media didn't include the most damaging aspect: the fact that Taylor's smear campaign revolved around an allegation of sexual assault against McCabe, even if it had already been discredited and rejected. The reports discussed attempts by Garda HQ to undermine McCabe's credibility, but never made any mention of the hide-and-seek incident or anything of the sort. Those details were simply too sensitive, and far too legally troublesome, to ever find their way into print.

In early December, O'Neill reported his findings. He told the Tánaiste he had spoken to both Callinan and O'Sullivan, and sought observations from Taylor and McCabe. While it was impossible for him to determine which side was telling the truth, he recommended a full commission of investigation – a State inquiry with the power of compellability – to get to the bottom of it. Helpfully, O'Neill also drafted his own 'terms of reference', the legally binding parameters laying out the potential scope of this commission's mission.

All it would take to set up this State inquiry into the smearing of Maurice McCabe was the approval, granted swiftly and quietly, of the Government of Ireland.

***

Little was said of the O'Neill report when the Dáil got going that afternoon on 7 February 2017. Leaders' Questions was dominated by the fallout from the RTÉ documentary on scoliosis, and only a passing mention was made of the public inquiry that was now to begin. Enda Kenny told Fianna Fáil's John Curran that the matter had indeed been discussed at the morning's Cabinet meeting, and that the proposed commission of investigation had been approved.

Word subsequently emanated that Peter Charleton, a serving judge of the Supreme Court, had been picked to run the inquiry. It seemed a wise choice: before joining the bench, Charleton had served as a counsel for the Morris Tribunal investigating Garda corruption in Donegal. Asking for a Supreme Court judge to chair an inquiry also seemed a significant gesture, indicating just how seriously these matters were being taken.

Mindful of the government's reliance on Fianna Fáil, Frances Fitzgerald briefed her counterpart Jim O'Callaghan on the morning's discussions. O'Callaghan later issued a statement welcoming the new inquiry. 'Fianna Fáil has been clear in saying that such an investigation is needed,' he said. 'We now look forward to Judge Peter Charleton working towards a speedy conclusion to his investigation so that we can get to the truth of these matters as soon as possible.'

Sinn Féin also welcomed the inquiry, but insisted O'Sullivan had to stand down in the meantime. The party had demanded Arlene Foster stand aside during a public inquiry in the North; for the sake of consistency it had to now seek a similar temporary abdication from the Garda Commissioner.

Out and about at ministerial engagements in Dublin, Frances Fitzgerald was asked if O'Sullivan would indeed be asked to stand aside. 'These are allegations,' came her reply. 'There is no *prima facie* case against anyone. Tomorrow, when the terms of reference are published, clearly then it will become obvious, the scale of this commission.'

Fitzgerald could not have predicted just how prescient that final sentence would be.

DAY 2

Wednesday, 8 February 2017

The forthcoming State inquiry had not quite captured the public imagination. While a brief reference to it was carried on RTÉ's morning news, the nation's attention was fixed on other matters. The loss of 500 jobs at technology firm HP in Leixlip was attracting the most attention – worldwide redundancies had been flagged and the Irish operation would not escape the knife. Elsewhere, attention was still focused on the scoliosis scandal (one paper reporting that a bespoke orthopaedic operating theatre was lying idle due to lack of staff) and the continuing cold weather, with tokenistic coverage of how Michael D. Higgins was beginning a twelve-day visit to Latin America, starting in Peru before moving on to Colombia and Cuba.

Wednesday's newspapers contained only fleeting references to the forthcoming State inquiry, with the front-page stories of both *The Irish Times* and *Irish Examiner* focusing instead on the fate of Nóirín O'Sullivan and the support declared by Frances Fitzgerald. The former report, penned by Sarah Bardon, cited government sources who simply said there was 'no question' of asking the Commissioner to stand aside, possibly because of the time it would take for the inquiry to conclude. Her report also revealed the new commission would be asked to report within nine months, which almost certainly meant it would take a year or more.

The *Irish Examiner* report, meanwhile, revealed that although the draft terms of reference would be published later that day, the full text of Iarfhlaith O'Neill's assessment would not be released. As Kenny had said the previous day, 'the report will be published in redacted form, because it has to be published in redacted form'.

But even before the terms of reference could be published – and the government would publicly acknowledge the scandal facing its top police officer – the lid would be dramatically lifted on the whole affair.

***

Labour's Brendan Howlin was in Dublin when his parliamentary assistant, based back at the office in Wexford, took a phone call from Alison O'Reilly, a journalist at the *Irish Mail on Sunday*. She told the assistant she had information that was pertinent to the current Garda scandal, and asked that Howlin call her back if he had an opportunity. The message was passed up the food chain to Howlin's Dublin-based chief of staff, Neil Ward, who ensured his boss returned the call.

O'Reilly told the Labour leader she had been following the McCabe story within the paper and had heard the whispers about aspects of the whistleblower's supposedly unsavoury past, which were supposed to be taken in debit against him. Specifically, she named her colleague, crime correspondent Debbie McCann, whom she believed had been in direct contact with Nóirín O'Sullivan. O'Reilly said the Commissioner had given McCann information about the allegation from McCabe's past. McCann, after this conversation, was purported to have told her colleagues that McCabe was a 'dirty fucking bastard'. (McCann, for her own part, strenuously rejects this account.) This backhanded undermining of McCabe, O'Reilly said, had weighed heavily on her conscience and she wanted attention drawn to this perceived tactic to smear an honest man.

Howlin weighed up what he had just heard. He had a rostered slot on Leaders' Questions that day – a prime, live-on-TV opportunity to raise the matters in the public domain. With a public inquiry into McCabe now on the cards, the timing would be opportune. The terms of reference were due before the Dáil that afternoon, which would set the agenda (and limits) for the new commission. If some new material were left out of those terms of reference, the inquiry would likely be blinkered into ignoring it.

Eventually the decision was made: Howlin would raise these allegations on the Dáil floor. Shortly before midday he rang O'Reilly back to tell her of his plans, and to run over the text of the speech he proposed to give.

***

Inside the chamber, TDs were discussing more routine matters. Fianna Fáil's Micheál Martin was rounding on the government over the HP redundancies – it appeared ministers had not acted upon the earlier signals of global redundancies in any effort to save its local jobs. Sinn Féin's Gerry Adams followed up on the RTÉ scoliosis documentary, reporting that some children were missing out on transplant surgeries because the air corps unit did not have enough staff to transport them at the short notice required.

At twenty-three minutes past noon, Howlin rose to his feet, beginning with a complaint about the forthcoming inquiry. The charges laid at the feet of Nóirín O'Sullivan were evidently 'incredibly serious', he said; if they weren't, the government would not have agreed to set up this new formal inquiry. 'I cannot think of another walk of life where, if allegations of this nature had been made against a person in a position of power, he or she would not be placed on administrative leave until the outcome of the investigation is known,' he said. 'This would be true of a school principal or even a shop manager. That it is not true for the head of An Garda Síochána is troubling.' Nonetheless, if a commission was to begin, it was important that the inquiry enjoy popular political support – which would only be available, he suggested, if the Dáil was given some time to debate the proposed terms of reference.

Then, after a moment's pause, Howlin unveiled his new information.

'Taoiseach, this morning I was contacted by a journalist. The journalist told me that they have direct knowledge of calls made by the Garda Commissioner, to journalists, during 2013 and 2014 – in the course of which the Commissioner made very serious allegations of sexual crimes having been committed by Garda Maurice McCabe.'

The Dáil's TV feed cut to a view of Kenny, who seemed nonplussed by these new comments, as he leafed through his paperwork. Heather Humphreys, in the seat beside him, betrayed no reaction as she watched Howlin continue.

The Labour leader further claimed that Nóirín O'Sullivan had personally instigated the arrest and investigation of 'a Garda officer' (Dave Taylor) who was under suspicion of leaking sensitive material to the media. 'If it was a fact that the Garda Commissioner was in direct contact with the media making allegations against one of her own officers at around the same time,' Howlin correctly observed, 'it would be quite extraordinary.'

The Wexford veteran, by way of a prelude to his next point, admitted he had no idea whether this new allegation were true or not. This drew an intervention from the Ceann Comhairle, Seán Ó Fearghaíl, who felt it was unfair to recite a second-hand tale with damaging claims about an outsider with no parliamentary right of reply. Ó Fearghaíl went so far as to describe the tale as a '*dúirt bean liom go ndúirt bean léi* story': a woman-told-me-that-a-woman-told-her recitation of little more than pub gossip. Howlin, looking slightly wounded by this scolding, defended his position: if opposition parties were not being consulted about the terms of reference for Charleton's new inquiry, the Dáil floor was the only forum available to him. Eventually he settled for reasserting his original point, insisting that O'Sullivan should be asked to stand aside while subject to a State inquiry. 'I ask the Taoiseach to agree with me on that.'

However the Ceann Comhairle might have felt, most in Leinster House were simply aghast at what Howlin had just put on the record. Those who knew of the underhanded undermining of Maurice McCabe were stunned that it had now been so dramatically blasted onto the airwaves; any who didn't must have simply been flabbergasted. The general public watching idly on RTÉ One could only have been agape. The first scripts for lunchtime news bulletins, largely based on the job losses at HP, were now being quickly revised.

But if this was the general reaction amongst the public and those in Leinster House, it did not appear to be shared on the government benches. Enda Kenny, rising to his feet, betrayed no reaction whatsoever.

'I don't agree with you,' the Taoiseach said, entering a dispassionate defence outlining the procedures of how the protected disclosures were handled, how certain confidentiality still applied and how the Tánaiste had already set up a scoping inquiry to lead her to this point. 'These are all allegations, and they are vehemently denied by the two people against whom these allegations are made,' he insisted.

In fact, the only hints that Kenny had actually *heard* what Howlin said were in a brief preface ('The matter that you have raised is of the most serious import, and I know you understand that') and a passing reference to 'hearsay'.

The format of Leaders' Questions is that each opposition leader gets to solicit two replies from the Taoiseach. Howlin had used his first question to seek a guarantee from Kenny that, irrespective of whether the Taoiseach already knew about this bombshell allegation, opposition TDs would get a chance to contribute to the terms of reference. In the absence of getting such a guarantee, there was little else he could do with this second question, other than to restate his main call: that O'Sullivan should be stood down from the job in the meantime.

Another feature of the format of Leaders' Questions is that, knowing the opposition leader has no opportunity to follow up any further, the Taoiseach will often volunteer a more salient answer to the second question than the first. True to form, Kenny offered a slightly more substantive response to Howlin's new information. He told Howlin it wasn't possible to put Iarfhlaith O'Neill's report into the public domain simply because the allegations it investigated were far too sensitive. 'The House will appreciate that there is an obligation, including a general constitutional obligation, to protect the names and reputations of persons who may be the subject of untested allegations, and in that regard, it's not appropriate to comment any further on that.'

And with that, Dáil business moved on.

* * *

There was no putting the genie back into the bottle now. The lunchtime news bulletins on radio and TV were alive with the sudden suggestion – augmented by the veneer of Dáil privilege – that the country's best-known whistleblower was being smeared by his bosses as some kind of sex criminal.

Or, at least, some of them were. Some editors perceived the allegations as simply so overwhelmingly sensitive they simply could *not* be further sent into the public domain. Although the claims had been broadcast live on RTÉ's TV coverage of Leaders' Questions only an hour earlier, some editors decided not to propagate them further. Clips of Brendan Howlin and Enda Kenny were aired on both the television and radio news, but only ones in which Howlin called on Nóirín O'Sullivan to be temporarily stood down, and in which Enda Kenny defended her entitlement to a fair hearing. Both bulletins carried live reports from political correspondent David Davin Power, who alluded only to 'serious claims' that Howlin had made to bolster his case. The clip was not aired on TV3's lunchtime bulletin either, though this was most likely because the bulletin aired at 12.30 p.m., too soon to turn around the sensational material.

Their omission from lunchtime TV news did not stop Howlin's revelations from getting out more widely. Audio from the exchanges aired on radio: Today FM and Newstalk, the second and third largest radio stations, carried reports of a similar strain ('The Dáil has heard claims that the Garda Commissioner directly called journalists, making claims of sexual misbehaviour by Maurice McCabe …'). Importantly, as Newstalk doubled as a wire service for almost all of the country's local radio stations and for several commercial websites, the same content aired nationwide.

The Internet was ablaze with the story too, with domineering headlines on the major websites. 'Commissioner leaked McCabe "sexual offences" claims, Dáil hears', announced the website of *The Irish Times*; 'Dáil hears claims Garda Commissioner contacted journalist making allegations of "sexual crimes" against whistleblower Maurice McCabe', ran a similar headline on the *Irish Independent*'s site. Both *TheJournal.ie* and *Broadsheet.ie* – which had won a reputation for in-depth coverage of Maurice McCabe's travails – published videos and full transcripts.

Labour's press officer Cathal McCann, meanwhile, busily fielded phone calls and texts from nervous hacks looking for assurance on one major point. Howlin hadn't been clear on which Garda commissioner he meant: was it the departed Callinan or the incumbent O'Sullivan? It was the latter, McCann assured them. It was Nóirín O'Sullivan against whom the claims were being made.

Phones were also busy in the Garda press office at the force's headquarters in the Phoenix Park, with a response being sought from the under-fire Commissioner. There had already been calls for her to stand aside while her position was scrutinised by a public inquiry. Now those suggestions were mutating into calls for her to walk out the door and never come back. Similar calls were lighting up the switchboard at the Department of Justice, where the idea of protecting the protected disclosure, however obligatory by law, now seemed to be something of a lost cause.

One departmental source later labelled Howlin's actions as little short of 'barmy', ruining the 'fanatical' work of Fitzgerald to keep such damaging rumours about McCabe out of the public arena. 'Anyone with any knowledge of that issue would have been incredibly protective of McCabe,' they said, 'and made absolutely sure that it wouldn't have been in the public arena. What Howlin did was crazy. And explosive.'

* * *

With Howlin's claims dominating the news bulletins, further pieces were added to the jigsaw when Fitzgerald published the proposed terms of reference for the inquiry later that afternoon. Although news of the protected disclosures (and who had submitted them) had long made its way into the public domain, this was the first time that the Department of Justice had been able to confirm certain details. Before this, the law required Fitzgerald to maintain the confidentiality of the whistleblowers and the issues they were raising. Now, though, the formal announcement of a commission of investigation meant the details could no longer be stifled. So it was confirmed: yes, Maurice McCabe and Dave Taylor were the men behind the complaints – and yes, they were making pretty astonishing claims about their bosses.

In fact, if the very first item on the agenda for this new inquiry hadn't made it clear, the second one would.

[a] The allegation made in a Protected Disclosure made under the provisions of the Protected Disclosures Act 2014, on the 30th of September 2016, by Superintendent David Taylor, wherein he alleges that he was instructed or directed by former Commissioner Martin Callinan and/or Deputy Commissioner Nóirín O'Sullivan, to contact the media to brief them negatively against Sergeant Maurice McCabe and in particular to brief the media that Sgt McCabe was motivated by maliciousness and revenge, that he was to encourage the media to write negatively about

Sgt McCabe, to the effect that his complaints had no substance, that the Gardaí had fully investigated his complaints and found no substance to his allegations and that he was driven by agendas.

[b] The allegation of Superintendent Taylor in his Protected Disclosure, that he was directed to draw journalists' attention to an allegation of criminal misconduct made against Sgt McCabe and that this was the root cause of his agenda, namely revenge against the Gardaí.

Among other issues for Peter Charleton to investigate were the electronic and paper files held in Garda HQ about Maurice McCabe; Dave Taylor's phone contact with his two commissioner bosses; and the circumstances surrounding a hotel car park meeting between Martin Callinan and Fianna Fáil TD John McGuinness in January 2014, just as McCabe was beginning to attract attention at the PAC under McGuinness's chairmanship. It even proposed to investigate whether Nóirín O'Sullivan had any role in an *RTÉ News* item in May 2016, in which a few segments from the O'Higgins Commission report – including some passages that were relatively more critical of Maurice McCabe – were leaked ahead of their official publication.

Only a few hours earlier Brendan Howlin had gone public with his claim that the Garda Commissioner was calling reporters to label Maurice McCabe as a criminal. Now the government found itself acknowledging the sensational claim, from the force's spokesman, that he too had contacted reporters to share stories about the whistleblower. When all this was aggregated, most would simply have concluded: there's no smoke without fire.

Some in Fine Gael, the self-modelled party of law and order, reached the same conclusion too. 'It was pretty shit,' one TD said, 'having to entertain the idea that this might actually have happened – but we had to take it seriously. Every journalist we spoke to had heard about this rumour. It was pretty hurtful, to think that a Garda Commissioner was using black propaganda, but that's where we were. It was Catch-22: we couldn't afford to believe it, but we couldn't afford to dismiss it either.'

If Nóirín O'Sullivan had been hoping to quell Brendan Howlin's claims through sheer silence, the release of Peter Charleton's terms of reference made it virtually impossible. The formal announcement of a public inquiry, in which she was to be a protagonist, at least required the Commissioner to issue a pro-forma public declaration that she would cooperate with the inquiry. It was simply untenable that she could do so without also addressing the more explosive allegation made in the Dáil chamber. Close to 6 p.m. – a little over five hours after those allegations were first made – O'Sullivan broke her silence with a press release.

'The Commissioner notes with surprise the comments made by Deputy Brendan Howlin in Dáil Éireann on this date,' her third-person statement began. 'The comments made under Dáil privilege relate to allegations of the most serious nature against the Commissioner and other members of An Garda Síochána. The Commissioner has no knowledge of the matters referred to by Deputy Howlin and refutes in the strongest terms the suggestion that she has engaged in the conduct alleged against a serving member of An Garda Síochána. This is the first occasion on which the Commissioner has been made aware of the allegations made by Deputy Howlin and to her knowledge no report having been made to the Garda Síochána Ombudsman or elsewhere relating to the specific allegations.'

In short: not only was Nóirín O'Sullivan denying Brendan Howlin's allegations, but also insisting she'd never even heard of them before.

***

Fianna Fáil, realising the seismic importance of the story now unfolding, began some backroom machinations. Micheál Martin called Maurice McCabe to check on his mood and sound out whether he was happy with how Brendan Howlin had chosen to use his Dáil speaking time earlier that day. McCabe told him that while he was a little surprised, and hadn't expected the rumours to become public quite that way or quite so quickly, he was at least happy that the broader public now knew how he believed his name had been dragged through the mud.

But, McCabe said, even the slew of details revealed that day did not tell the full truth. More was coming, the whistleblower said. The Garda press office wasn't the only office responsible for blackening his name – another State body also had a role to play in circulating devastating claims about him. Details of this second agency would be revealed the following night on RTÉ's *Prime Time* programme – a programme which would further underline the personal toll Maurice McCabe had endured for trying to tell the truth.

Martin understood the need for discretion with this sensitive new development, but, equally, this new information presented some political issues. The Dáil's Business Committee, which was responsible for setting the parliamentary agenda, had already met to make arrangements for a debate on the proposed terms of reference for the new public inquiry, which would likely take place the following afternoon. If some salient new information had emerged, it was vital that the terms of reference accommodate it. Just as Brendan Howlin had information which needed scrutiny, now Micheál Martin too had issues requiring investigation.

Martin consulted with his chief lieutenant, his chief of staff Deirdre Gillane, about a course of action. Gillane opted to call her opposite number, Enda Kenny's chief of staff Mark Kennelly, making him aware that a TV programme was coming and that the commission's terms of reference would need to accommodate the issues it would raise. Kennelly agreed that these matters seemed significant, but said he was the wrong man to speak to; the query would be better raised with the Department of Justice, where the terms of reference were actually being drafted. He directed Gillane to Frances Fitzgerald's special advisor, Marion Mannion, but the two women could not agree whether the existing terms of reference would accommodate the issues Martin had just learned of.

Martin decided to proceed further. At around 7.30 p.m. he rang his justice spokesman, Jim O'Callaghan, summoning him to his office on the fifth floor of Leinster House's newer, northern LH2000 wing. O'Callaghan, already a well-known senior counsel before his election to the Dáil, understood exactly the sensitivities and immediately rang Frances Fitzgerald, asking to meet with her. The two had already been in fairly close contact as a result of the 'no surprises' clause in the confidence and supply pact, so direct consultation from one to the other was not as unusual as it might have been in a more typical government–opposition dynamic.

Fitzgerald was at the opposite end of the complex, attending the weekly meeting of the Fine Gael parliamentary party in Leinster House's southern wing where its TDs were based. The two agreed to convene in one of the areas where discretion was absolutely guaranteed and it simply wasn't possible for a journalist to happen upon them: the Leinster House members' bar, on the ground floor of the southern wing, into which only TDs and senators were permitted to enter.

The two agreed that there should be no question of Nóirín O'Sullivan having to stand aside. O'Sullivan had become a political problem; of that, there was no doubt. The government might even have liked her to quietly stand aside, were it not for Martin Callinan having already done so within recent memory. To lose one Garda Commissioner might have been seen as unfortunate; to lose two would be seen as careless – especially for Fine Gael.

O'Callaghan defended O'Sullivan for less politically loaded reasons. Sensitive and damning as the allegations were, they were only that – mere allegations – and had not been proven. Asking someone to stand aside simply because an allegation might be made against them was unfair. Even if the allegation were later disproved, the reputational damage would be done.

Moreover, both were anxious that this could become a dangerous path to tread. Even if it were only to facilitate an inquiry into her actions, any temporary abdication by Nóirín O'Sullivan could quickly set a worrying precedent. If a Garda Commissioner could be forced out simply because of an unproven allegation, why couldn't the same be true of a minister, or indeed any TD? Couldn't an opponent simply invent an allegation if they wanted rid of them? The institutions of State needed to be robust, and both agreed that there was a constitutional risk to the functions of State if a seat in Dáil Éireann or at the Cabinet table could be vacated by a malicious lie.

This shared view on Nóirín O'Sullivan's future would, for the time being, ensure the Commissioner's position. But this was one of the few points on which Fitzgerald and O'Callaghan agreed. That meeting, and their differing accounts of the other matters discussed, would turn out to be the source of even more angst in the days that followed.

DAY 3

Thursday, 9 February 2017

If the previous day's news agenda had been fragmented, with no single story dominating the headlines, Thursday's morning broadcasts were an almost wall-to-wall coverage of the McCabe controversy. Brendan Howlin's comments in the Dáil were understandably massive news, as was Nóirín O'Sullivan's claim of innocence. Between them, the Labour leader and the Garda Commissioner accounted for the lion's share of the morning news broadcasts. They would certainly cast ripples on the Dáil's debate on the terms of reference for the new public inquiry, which had been pencilled in to take place that afternoon.

The story also accounted for almost every front page of an Irish newspaper: *The Irish Times* splashed with O'Sullivan's claim of innocence; the *Irish Independent* focused on how RTÉ's coverage would now come under the inquiry; the *Irish Examiner* went into depth about Fianna Fáil's support for O'Sullivan and the sensational use of parliamentary privilege by Brendan Howlin.

The latter point was one for which Howlin himself accounted on *Morning Ireland*, where he met with trademark caustic scepticism from presenter Cathal Mac Coille, who reasonably inquired whether Howlin had investigated these allegations himself before relaying them to the wider world. Howlin said he didn't ask for the names of any journalists who had received these supposed calls from Nóirín O'Sullivan, but his source had volunteered one such name anyway.

'Did you call them?' asked Mac Coille.

'I most certainly did not,' came Howlin's indignant reply.

'Why not?'

'The whole nature of whistleblowers – and I have constructed the whistleblowing legislation in this country – [is that] it is not up to me to conduct this inquiry,' Howlin reasoned. 'If I believe there are serious matters of public importance to be inquired into, then [it's my role] to ensure that they are inquired into.'

That was all well and good, Mac Coille suggested, but Howlin had still gone public with explosive and sensitive allegations without appearing to make any effort to stand them up. Wasn't that just hearsay? 'The person who contacted me said they have first-hand knowledge of these matters,' said Howlin, appearing slightly rattled by this tone of inquiry. 'I believe that person … I believe what they told me to be their honest belief.' Moreover, he suggested, it was important to make this information public to justify Labour's demands that O'Sullivan stand aside during the inquiry.

But did that justify going public with such sensitive information? Even the Ceann Comhairle had expressed major misgivings about Howlin's use of privilege to recite a second-hand story of questionable provenance.

Howlin insisted that he took the subject of Dáil privilege very seriously, and though he agreed it was not to be abused, it was 'not to be not used. The easiest thing and the safest thing, always, is to say nothing and be silent.'

Ultimately, as Howlin saw it, Maurice McCabe was a 'follower of truth' and wanted the full truth to be revealed for all to see. 'We can edit them, we can talk about serious crimes, or we can give the facts as we know them.'

Jim O'Callaghan was not quite so convinced. On the same programme he argued that Howlin's use of parliamentary privilege was unfair, not only to O'Sullivan, but to McCabe too, as it arguably repeated the same smear on a national scale. 'If you look at the language used by Mr Justice [Iarfhlaith] O'Neill in his draft terms of reference, he refers to an allegation of "criminal misconduct" against Sergeant McCabe. I think it would be far preferable if language like that is used all the time when discussing this allegation.'

O'Callaghan illustrated further division within the opposition when he publicly asserted that Fianna Fáil would not add its voice to the demands for O'Sullivan to step aside. There were two reasons why: if someone forced aside was later acquitted of any wrongdoing, their personal good name would be tarnished nonetheless, and because the whole ethos of impartial State inquiries would be undermined if there were to be a new precedent forcing their subject to abdicate in the meantime.

* * *

This all formed the backdrop to the day's debate on the proposed terms of reference. There could be little accusation of political bias in the terms, given that they had been drafted by the former High Court Judge Iarfhlaith O'Neill, who had been the first to scrutinise the spectacular claims of McCabe and Dave Taylor, and who had voluntarily fleshed out his own suggestions for what needed further inquiry.

That notwithstanding, there were still concerns that some items might be left out. Michael Clifford, the *Irish Examiner* special correspondent with the ear of McCabe, relayed that there were two major shortcomings with the current draft. Firstly, it didn't examine the sensitive issue of whether anyone in Garda HQ had briefed anyone in the government about these allegations surrounding McCabe. Had there been any surreptitious contact about it, and if so, had it influenced the government's approach to dealing with him?

Secondly, Clifford observed, the new inquiry would also not delve into matters that arose inside the last one. The final report of the O'Higgins Commission had unreservedly accepted McCabe's bona fides in acting as a force for positive change within the Gardaí, without pointing the finger at anyone who might have suggested otherwise. Just days after this report was released, media reports emerged to give the background to this statement from O'Higgins: on 15 May 2016 the *Sunday Independent* revealed that McCabe had submitted 'up to 20 secret recordings', 'several of which contradicted allegations made against him by senior Gardaí'. One such tape had disproved the allegation that McCabe was driven by ulterior motives when first complaining about policing errors in Cavan–Monaghan. Several senior Gardaí claimed that McCabe had openly admitted to these motives during a meeting in 2008. It was only when McCabe himself produced a recording of the meeting that this allegation dissolved into nothing and was dropped entirely. Was this a simple error on the part of the Gardaí, or had this claim of malice been invented and perpetrated as part of a conspiracy against McCabe? As it stood, Clifford said, this would not be scrutinised.

The convention in Leinster House is that although Leaders' Questions is scheduled to take place three days per week, on Thursdays the business is handled by the deputy leaders from each side – with the Tánaiste taking the place of the Taoiseach, and with the opposition party leaders making way for their seconds-in-command. Often, to round out the set, the Ceann Comhairle would leave his deputy to preside over the business.

This arrangement left Frances Fitzgerald herself in the hot seat, though it was a role to which she was now accustomed. Fitzgerald had been Tánaiste for nine months, and opposition TDs regularly used the opportunity to raise queries about justice matters, in which Fine Gael was clearly now developing a chequered record.

Just before Leaders' Questions began, Chief Whip Regina Doherty rose to announce the revised Dáil agenda, as agreed by the Business Committee earlier that morning. There would be a three-hour discussion on the proposed terms of reference for the commission of investigation, but, importantly, TDs would *not* be asked to sign off on them at the end. Opposition parties had not been consulted about the exact scope of the investigation, so the three-hour debate would offer a chance for TDs to make suggestions on the floor, with Frances Fitzgerald then dwelling on the contributions and examining whether changes would be needed.

Following the previous evening's accord between Fitzgerald and Jim O'Callaghan, Fianna Fáil decided to raise other issues. Michael McGrath (Fianna Fáil's finance spokesman; the party did not have a deputy leader) raised concerns about the state of hospital waiting lists, which remained a hot-button topic after the TV documentary on children awaiting scoliosis surgeries.

When her turn came, Sinn Féin's Mary Lou McDonald had no such reservations and happily exhibited her usual skill of articulating what Joe or Josephine Punter might feel about the situation. 'This is, to borrow the phrase, a truly terrible vista,' she said. 'The idea of the forces of law and order turning on an officer of the law – a man who has done the State some service, a citizen prepared to step forward and speak out – is an outrage. It's an outrage that begs the most fundamental questions about the fair administration of justice and the authorities entrusted with upholding the law.' McDonald inserted a passing reference to what Brendan Howlin had put on the record, saying such tactics to ruin a man's character were 'quite frankly evil'. In that light, surely Nóirín O'Sullivan would have to stand aside – even without prejudice – while these grave issues were given a full investigation?

Fitzgerald wasn't buying it, echoing the general position on which she and Jim O'Callaghan were agreed. 'There's a general constitutional obligation to protect the good names and reputations of persons who may be the subject of untested allegations, and that constitutional protection applies to everybody involved in this situation – not [just] the two people you've mentioned, but everybody.' The Tánaiste said this was exactly the reason why she hadn't even confirmed out loud, even with Dáil privilege, what exact allegations had been made against O'Sullivan or Callinan in the first place. As if to underline the point, with an extra note of dismissal, she added: 'That's how we do things in this country.'

McDonald labelled this answer as 'astonishing on many levels' given that nobody was yet declaring O'Sullivan guilty of anything, but used her second question to nail down one other issue. We now knew of alleged high-level contact between Gardaí and the media, she said – but was the Tánaiste, by any chance, aware of any contact between Gardaí and other State agencies in relation to Maurice McCabe?

This time, looking a little baffled, the Tánaiste took a moment to get back to her feet. 'In relation to contact between Maurice McCabe and other agencies …'

No, corrected McDonald from across the floor: she was asking about contact initiated by the Gardaí themselves.

Fitzgerald furrowed her brow. 'The ones I would be aware of would obviously be contact with, for example, GSOC [the Garda ombudsman] in the normal course of events, whatever would be appropriate there. But no, I'm not ... I'm not in possession of any other contact ...'

'No other State agency?' clarified McDonald.

'I'm not in possession of information that they've initiated contact, other than what would ever be in the normal course of the work that they would do.'

With the Dáil due to debate Charleton's terms of reference within the next hour, there was little appetite for anyone to focus too closely on the matter any further: there'd be plenty of time for that later. Catherine Murphy of the Social Democrats did raise Garda issues, but merely added two further lines to the charge sheet facing Nóirín O'Sullivan: firstly, her claim not to have heard these allegations circulating around Maurice McCabe was preposterous, given they had been circling in media and political circles for several years now; and secondly, there were separate issues surrounding the handling of funds at the Garda training college in Templemore, Co. Tipperary, which in any other week would pose serious questions of their own for a Garda Commissioner.

* * *

The Dáil debate on the terms of reference began just after 1 p.m. The Tánaiste's opening speech contained little of note, and largely reasserted her previous positions: these were hugely sensitive allegations involving a major institution of State; a scoping inquiry had already been conducted; a full inquiry was warranted and now being organised; and everyone remained innocent until proven otherwise. 'It is very important that in addressing one injustice we do not create others,' she summarised.

Jim O'Callaghan was next, and opened with a declaration of impartiality. 'In one corner we have the superintendent and the sergeant,' he said, his gaze low and his fingers pressed together in a diamond shape. 'In the other corner we have the Commissioner and the former Commissioner. Members of this house are perfectly entitled to affiliate themselves with either corner, and to advocate on behalf of either corner. I will not be doing that, however. I believe the most important thing is to stand in the middle and try to establish the truth.'

O'Callaghan made a few vocal suggestions about issues to address. The clause in the terms of reference, examining whether Dave Taylor had been asked to draw attention to a criminal complaint in Maurice McCabe's past, was not broad enough – it should also include the extent to which Callinan or O'Sullivan were aware of it. Separately, the clause around Callinan's meeting with John McGuinness also needed to be broadened – because what if Callinan had also tried to hold similar meetings with ministers and other TDs?

His counterpart within Sinn Féin, Jonathan O'Brien, shared his views. The inquiry had to get to the bottom not only of the smear campaign, but also of the extent to which commissioners past and present were aware of this alleged criminality and used it against McCabe.

Up next to speak was Brendan Howlin, who equally had concerns about that aspect and had already made a submission in writing to Fitzgerald on how to address it. With that out of the way, the rest of his ten minutes was spent defending his dramatic use of parliamentary privilege.

'The word "hearsay" has been bandied about aplenty since,' Howlin said, clearly still aggrieved at Enda Kenny's characterisation of his allegations a day earlier. 'This was not idle gossip, or pub gossip. I received information which I believe to be credible and which is absolutely germane to a matter about which the government, in its own careful deliberation, has determined to establish a commission of investigation, thereby acknowledging the significance and importance of these matters.' Howlin added that both he and his source were willing to give the same evidence to Charleton's new inquiry, if the judge saw fit to seek it.

There was more. Howlin was clearly bruised from the suggestions he had abused his position and that this recklessness had done more harm to McCabe than good. 'I've spoken to Maurice McCabe today. He confirmed to me that he is of course aware, in specific detail, of all the allegations made against him. He has been aware of them, and he and his family have tried to live with them, for a number of years – and I am glad to be able to inform the House that he has expressed gratitude for my intervention yesterday, and in no way regards it as having been damaging in any way to him.'

Solidarity's Ruth Coppinger took another view, identifying a consistent strain in the terms of reference: an unhealthy nexus between the media and Ireland's elites. 'Essentially what we're seeing is the media as a propaganda arm of the Gardaí in manufacturing consent in society.' Specifically, she said, this loyalty to Gardaí had also showed up in coverage of the anti-water charges protests. One such example was that the criminal charges against several protestors over an infamous demonstration in Jobstown, near Tallaght, were described as 'kidnapping', when the charge was actually of false imprisonment. In Coppinger's eyes, this was because Enda Kenny had once used that phrase, giving licence to the media to use the same wording. (In fact, the crimes are one and the same: kidnapping is prosecuted under the same 'false imprisonment' clause.) Moreover, the media had happily reported how one minister's office was subject to 'bomb threats' – in air quotes – while another had received a bullet in the post, when the offender turned out to be an individual with mental health issues who had 'nothing to do with the water charges' (despite both communications, however frivolous their true threat, mentioning water charges as a motivation).

Next on the roster for speaking time was Independents-4Change – a formalised alliance of left-wing independent TDs founded by maverick Wexford socialist property developer Mick Wallace. He made the case for broadening the inquiry to include the travails of other whistleblowers, as McCabe was not the only one to face an internal rebellion.

One such case involved Nicky Keogh, a Garda based in Athlone, who had made claims in 2014 that a colleague in the drugs squad actually had links to the heroin trade in the midlands. The case allegedly involved the Garda giving advance warning of drugs raids, so that evidence could be destroyed beforehand. In other circumstances, undercover Gardaí had allegedly coerced people into selling drugs, arranging sales to other undercover officers who would immediately arrest the seller in a ruse to boost their overall conviction rates. 'It was May 2014 when Nick Keogh made his first allegation,' Wallace said. 'In that year alone, he faced five internal investigations. There was not one before that but five at that time.'

Wallace donated a few minutes of his time to his colleague Clare Daly, who further argued that Nóirín O'Sullivan needed to go – not least because Peter Charleton could hardly be expected to run a full and fair inquiry while still relying on O'Sullivan and her subordinates to share huge volumes of documents. She furnished Wallace's point about other whistleblowers: the likes of Keogh and Keith Harrison, another internal complainant who said he had endured difficulty after arresting a member of the drugs unit for drink-driving, had only met trouble after Callinan had left and O'Sullivan had taken over. The present Commissioner could not simply write this off as the fault of her predecessor.

At the very end of the Dáil debate – so late that it interrupted the chairman's attempts to close the proceedings – Fianna Fáil's John McGuinness made a final inquiry: 'Is the Tánaiste saying she believes other agencies of the State – y'know, departments and that – are excluded from this? For example, is Tusla excluded from this? Or will it be part of the commission's work?'

Fitzgerald seemed somewhat taken aback, not appearing to understand the pertinence of the question. 'I think,' she replied, hesitantly, 'that would be up to, eh, the Commission to decide. But I see no reason why if there is a relevant agency – for example the one that you mentioned – that it wouldn't be included in the work of the Commission.' The camera briefly cut back to McGuinness, betraying no emotion at this reply.

The Kilkenny man's contribution pricked the ears of some watching journalists, as he was known not only to be a major McCabe sympathiser, but also to have a fairly close relationship with him. McGuinness had chaired the PAC in the previous Dáil term (under a long-standing convention that the PAC be chaired by a non-government TD) when McCabe had prompted a major inquiry into the quashing of penalty points. Further, McGuinness had previously used the Dáil record to reveal details of a clandestine meeting with Martin Callinan in a hotel car park on the Naas Road outside Dublin – just as the PAC was investigating the penalty points issue – where the Commissioner had spread 'vile rumours' about indiscretions in McCabe's past.

It was public knowledge that Callinan had mounted a sustained attempt to stop McCabe from appearing before the PAC, arguing that it would be an act of insubordination for a sergeant to appear at a separate hearing to the Commissioner himself. He also claimed McCabe had broken data protection law by handing over thousands of records from the Garda IT system. It had not been known, at the time, that Callinan might also have tried to quietly brief the PAC chairman in a hotel car park. (McGuinness's reference to 'vile rumours' being spread by Garda HQ also now, suddenly, took on greater prominence.)

With all of this taken into account, there was good reason for journalists to sit up and take notice. Here, a TD with clear inside understanding of McCabe's predicaments had introduced the name of a new State agency into the mix.

Tusla? they wondered. *What does Tusla have to do with all of this?*

* * *

Tusla was a fairly young State agency, having only been set up in 2014. It was formed through spinning off some functions from the HSE and dissolving two other organisations, the Family Support Agency and the National Educational Welfare Board. The overall premise of the agency was to centralise the State's responses and interventions in family situations. If a child were in some danger at home, for example, it would fall to Tusla to take the appropriate measures and ensure that child's safety. The idea that Tusla might, therefore, have something to say, or some fleeting role in the Maurice McCabe story, was something to cause serious alarm.

A couple of hours later, Michael Clifford cast light on the claim. 'A file containing a false allegation of child sex abuse against whistleblower Maurice McCabe was sent by Tusla, the child and family agency, to Gardaí and widely circulated in 2013,' he wrote on the *Irish Examiner*'s website. 'However, no effort was made to substantiate the claim.'

The piece went on: 'The abuse claims were made by a young woman in August to a counsellor, who contacted Tusla and Gardaí. However, no attempt was made to contact Mr McCabe and put the allegations to him. In 2014, Tusla admitted a mistake had been made and attributed the false accusation to a "clerical error".

'It was only last year that Mr McCabe became aware that the highly damaging false abuse allegation had been widely circulated. He is to take a legal case against Tusla and has met with Minister for Children Katherine Zappone. She has indicated a public apology will be forthcoming.

'The allegation surfaced on a file in August 2013, and the "error" was detected the following May, a period during which Sergeant McCabe's claims of malpractice were causing major political and Garda-related controversy.

'The allegation was known among senior officers in the force. Despite this knowledge Sergeant McCabe was not informed about it, either after the initial file was created, or once it was discovered to be an error. He was not arrested or questioned about the initial allegation, and neither was he informed by the Commissioner, his employer, about the error after May 2014.

'Today's revelation puts in context the rumours and propaganda that has [*sic*] been swirling around Sergeant McCabe since he brought forward his claims of malpractice in the force.'

In other words, a false allegation of sexual abuse was made against Maurice McCabe, and seized upon by senior Gardaí as an opportunity to blacken his name, just at a time when he was making their lives awkward. The sexual claims against the whistleblower did not appear to have been entirely invented within the force, but they were still entirely baseless.

Not only that but, as Clifford explained that evening on Today FM's *The Last Word*, the institution had happily seized on this allegation and used it to defend its own position, without first meeting the primary duty of a police force: investigating a reported crime. 'No investigation happened ... it was in the possession of Tusla, it was in the possession of the Gardaí, no investigation happened, and then, eight months later, it turned out it was false. The whole thing was false.'

Clifford also told presenter Matt Cooper that while McCabe did not know of the allegation at the time, the same could not be said of those at the top of the force. 'There's a reference in the [Tusla] file to the Garda Commissioner in June '14 being informed about it, or having a meeting with the Superintendent in the jurisdiction about it. The extent of the knowledge of Nóirín O'Sullivan is, as of yet, unknown.'

The skeleton of a scandal was now exposed for public view. Meat would be put on those bones – as Micheál Martin had been told to expect – by RTÉ's flagship current affairs programme *Prime Time* that evening. On it, reporter Katie Hannon explained that the genesis of the original allegation against McCabe lay in 2006. In January of that year, McCabe made a serious complaint about the conduct of a Garda colleague, resulting in a disciplinary sanction against that colleague. Hannon's report did not discuss the circumstances, but the complaint related to a claim that this colleague ('Mr D') and two others had shown up drunk to the scene of a suicide.

Eleven months later, in December 2006, Mr D made a complaint of his own, about McCabe, on behalf of his teenage daughter, Ms D. She believed McCabe had rubbed against her in an inappropriate manner during a game of hide-and-seek at the McCabe home at Christmas 1998. The file was sent to the DPP, James Hamilton, who accepted the recommendation that no prosecution be taken. The allegation would continue to cause disharmony and aggravation between the McCabes and the D family, but from the State's perspective, that was where the matter rested.

That was the case, Hannon outlined, until August 2013. Then, a counsellor submitted a report to Tusla outlining how one of her clients – the aforementioned Ms D – had told her about an incident of sexual abuse in that client's childhood, at the hands of Maurice McCabe. The counsellor's report, however, now contained much more serious allegations. It included a claim that Ms D's reported abuse included 'digital penetration, both vaginal and anal'.

Tusla, acting correctly, took immediate action. A social worker contacted the Gardaí to seek a meeting. For some reason, however, it took eight months for a formal Garda notification form – in effect, an official complaint of criminal action committed to paper – to be sent to the superintendent in charge of the relevant Garda district. Only then would the Gardaí consider the allegation to be a criminal matter and begin a formal investigation.

In those intervening eight months, McCabe had risen to major public prominence and caused unprecedented headaches for Garda HQ. The whispering campaign against him had already begun. Some journalists had picked up rumours that there were shady elements in McCabe's past – a blemished history that perhaps ought to be debited against his glowing profile now. The reports never made it to press or the airwaves, most obviously because they could not be substantiated, and it was impossible to say whether they caused journalists to moderate the tone of their reporting on McCabe's courageous efforts.

McCabe himself didn't know that, throughout this time, false claims of the most grievous sort had been levelled against him. The country's best-known whistleblower had no idea that, at some internal levels, the State was entertaining allegations that he was a child rapist.

While the failure to lodge the formal Garda paperwork was inexplicable, social workers in Tusla had quite properly continued their own response to these new allegations. In April, files were opened on four of McCabe's five children, on the premise that their safety might not be assured. Those files each restated the central allegation that their father had digitally penetrated, vaginally and anally, a six-year-old girl.

It was not until the following month that the most sensational part emerged: the counsellor who reported these allegations had made a simple but catastrophic error. On 14 May the counsellor contacted Tusla to tell them she had accidentally 'copied and pasted' the allegation from one client's file into another's. Ms D was not the client concerned and Maurice McCabe was not the aggressor: the horrific allegation of digital penetration was made by someone else completely, and related to another man entirely.

To make this error clear, an internal Tusla email stated explicitly that the line, 'this abuse involved digital penetration, both vaginal and anal', should never have been included. The counsellor's client had indeed been discussing an allegation against Maurice McCabe, but the reference to digital penetration was entirely an error. A passage of this email, shown on screen by *Prime Time*, outlined how the claim was actually 'a line from another referral on another adult', made by another of her clients, 'that has been pasted in error'.

The allegation that Maurice McCabe was a child rapist was simply untrue, and created entirely through a simple mistake.

The Tusla social worker, again acting correctly, immediately set about updating the Garda notification, so that the mistake would be amended as quickly as possible. A revised notification was quickly sent to the superintendent in charge, clarifying the allegation against McCabe – stating clearly that 'at the time of the incident, both [Ms D] and the alleged were fully clothed and the incident involved inappropriate contact, as the alleged rubbed himself up and down against [the child] in a sexual manner'.

Any Garda investigation into this claim would quickly have concluded that these were the same allegations Ms D had made in 2006 – over the hide-and-seek game at McCabe's home at Christmas 1998 – which had already been examined and dismissed by the DPP. The story Ms D had given her counsellor in summer 2013 was, in fact, nothing new at all: she was simply telling her counsellor what she had already told Gardaí seven years earlier, about an alleged childhood incident which continued to traumatise her once she had grown old enough to interpret it through an adult's lens.

Up to this point, the only error had been the incorrect copy-and-paste mistake, for which the social worker accepted complete responsibility. Remedying that ought to have put an end to the matter – but Hannon's report explained that, for no evident reason, the wrongful allegation arose again a year and a half later.

A few days after Christmas 2015, a Tusla social worker wrote to McCabe to tell him the agency was investigating an allegation that he had digitally penetrated a child in the late 1990s. It was now over two years since the allegation had been mistakenly made to Tusla in the first place, and over eighteen months after the error had been remedied. Yet here, at Christmas, for the first time, this false allegation was now being put to the man himself. In cold and clinical language, befitting the magnitude of the allegation in question, McCabe was told he would have to be interviewed and was informed: 'We will have to decide if you pose a risk to children.'

It was clear to McCabe that the allegations were somehow related to the 1998 encounter, which had already been put to bed by the DPP. Alarmed, he wrote back via his solicitors explaining that this new report (which he did not yet know to be a mistake) was 'wholly untrue' and that prosecutors had already dismissed the genuine allegation. Inexplicably, it took Tusla six months to confirm what it already knew: that McCabe had never been accused to begin with, and that there had been 'a mistake' in the previous letter.

All of this left Maurice McCabe and his family highly perplexed and very concerned. He had been a Garda for thirty years, and his determined pursuit of fairness and justice had already taken a major toll. The suggestion that he was a criminal himself was anathema; the gravity of the claims was simply abhorrent.

He had known for ten years about the allegation made by Ms D, and that the DPP had already said no criminal act had ever taken place. But he also knew the allegation had crept into local knowledge: in October 2007, after learning that no prosecution would be taken, Ms D had publicly accosted McCabe on the street outside his Garda station. It was quite a fuss, and word of her claims against McCabe quickly got round.

But all of this was supposed to be water under the bridge, and McCabe had other things on his plate. His allegations on penalty points had made him an unlikely celebrity; his subsequent claims of policing failures had prompted a formal State inquiry and indirectly forced the resignation of a Minister for Justice. All of this had made him an unwitting thorn in the side of his superiors and granted him a level of notoriety amongst the Gardaí that he had never wanted. It now appeared that, in the midst of all the notoriety, someone had accused him of being a child rapist.

McCabe got to work and made a Freedom of Information request to Tusla, seeking a full copy of all its records relating to him and his family. Only in January 2017 would those records be handed over, revealing to him how a simple clerical error by a social worker had led to an appalling allegation landing on his doorstep. The thick file also revealed, for the first time, that the false allegation against McCabe had been copied into files on four of his children. As if to assert that the allegation was a genuine error, the file even carried a certification that Ms D, the original (genuine) complainant, wanted to move on with her life and had no interest in pursuing her own allegation any further.

The overall sense of shambles had a final coda in the closing sentences of Hannon's report on *Prime Time*. Within the fortnight prior to this sorry scenario being revealed to the public for the first time, Tusla's chief operations officer, Jim Gibson, had written to the Department of Children and Youth Affairs, informing its top civil servant Fergal Lynch of the whole affair. 'Mistakes were made in the management of this matter,' Gibson wrote, in a passage shown on screen. 'I regret that the management of this case did not reach the high standard we have set for the service, and it is our intention to issue an apology to Mr McCabe for the failings.'

Two weeks later, as *Prime Time*'s report aired, the McCabe family had yet to receive this apology.

Quite aside from the emotional toll that these allegations would have claimed, suddenly some jigsaw pieces began to fall into place. The rumours of dark deeds in McCabe's past had begun to surface in late 2013 and early 2014, just as his work on penalty points was garnering enough attention to cause problems for his bosses. It now turned out that, at the same time, a previous discredited allegation had re-emerged and been overstated to a gross proportion.

But was there a link between the two? Had Garda headquarters become aware of this wrongful allegation and seized upon it at a crucial moment? Was this the specific claim that Dave Taylor was allegedly told to bring to the attention of journalists and politicians? Or was this campaign from Garda headquarters simply an opportunistic chance to rehash the same allegations from a decade earlier, even though the DPP had decided there was no case to answer?

How had this gargantuan mistake been allowed to happen? Was it, as suggested, a simple clerical error on behalf of a lone counsellor? Or, given the level of the potential State campaign against McCabe, might it be possible that these new claims had come to life through some other means?

No matter their origin, was it simply the case that these allegations had conveniently fallen into the lap of Gardaí at a time when they could be deployed with maximal damage? Or, at some level of the Deep State, was there a chance that they were concocted deliberately, to destroy the man who was rocking the boat? If so, then who was behind it?

DAY 4

Friday, 10 February 2017

Late breaking news is a double-edged sword for newspapers. A massive story, breaking late in the day, offers an extra incentive for a curious reader to pick up a paper the following day – they will want to see extra context, sensitive analysis, informed reaction, or the development of some new information that moves the story further forward. A late breaking story is, in some ways, the currency of newspapers.

It is also, however, a disruptive inconvenience. From late afternoon the editorial staff will have a rough idea of what their leading stories will be, and the major pages of the title will be designed accordingly. A huge story emerging late in the evening means a headache not only for journalists trying to analyse or advance the news, but also for the editing and design staff who have to reshuffle the actual content. Moreover, while the larger circulation of British titles can justify repeated front-page updates and a much later deadline for concluding a paper's contents, most Irish titles prefer to have their content filed by 10 p.m., with the goal of sending the paper 'to bed' (in industry parlance) by 11 p.m. at the latest.

This was one such disruptive occasion. Even though the Tusla story had been carried late in the day on TV, it made front-page news for many of the following morning's papers. *The Irish Times* had learned that McCabe not only intended to pursue Tusla for an apology, but to sue it over its handling of the allegation and its failure to determine whether the claim in its file was actually true to begin with. It also alleged that Gardaí 'at the highest level of the force were aware of the claims made against the Garda sergeant but never informed him'. This would only add to the pressure on Nóirín O'Sullivan, who would either have to claim she was still somehow unaware of the file, or explain why she had declined to inform McCabe about it.

The story also made the front page of the *Irish Daily Mail*, which recounted the events from *Prime Time*, and the Ireland edition of *The Times*, which focused on Enda Kenny's steadfast support for Nóirín O'Sullivan. The only quality title to shun the story was the *Irish Independent*, which led with comments from Simon Harris, who had conceded that underperforming HSE or hospital managers could not be sacked – an especially sensitive admission given the ongoing scoliosis controversy.

The one title with some advance warning of the Tusla story, the *Irish Examiner*, elaborated on its previous evening's report with first-hand commentary from McCabe himself. 'They have destroyed us,' he told Michael Clifford. 'I find it hard to believe that it was an honest mistake … how can I and my family be on the system since 2013, and not be told about it?'

It was a very fair question.

Katie Hannon appeared again on Radio 1's *Morning Ireland* to add one other morsel of information to her report from the night before. She said the Tusla file handed to McCabe included one interesting claim: around the time the clerical error was discovered, the counsellor responsible showed serious anxiety to remedy the error – not just because the allegation was untrue, but also because she believed the superintendent in the relevant Garda district had been asked to meet the Garda Commissioner to discuss the case.

The counsellor was therefore keen to ensure that the corrected, amended report made its way to the superintendent before the incorrect details were passed further up the line.

In the ordinary course of events, a criminal allegation involving a serving Garda would not only have been passed to the superintendent, but probably also delivered further up the food chain, to chief superintendents and perhaps even to assistant commissioners based at headquarters in the Phoenix Park. Given McCabe's significance and profile within the force by this time, it was natural to assume that knowledge of this particular claim would go all the way to the very top. Counter-intuitively, however, the Garda press office had told Hannon that Commissioner O'Sullivan had requested no such meeting. It remained her position that she was unaware of the allegations connected to McCabe, or any smear campaign to further them, until the allegations had entered the public arena only a couple of days earlier.

The overnight allegations had left politicians in a tricky spot. There was a natural, reflexive desire to spring into action, full of fury and righteous indignation, demanding immediate accountability and for the appropriate heads to roll. But which heads? And how could accountability be pursued? There was already a commission of investigation in the works, which was set to investigate many of these claims. Frances Fitzgerald had, somewhat accidentally, speculated that those terms of reference would also cover the circumstances of this new aberration within Tusla. Where else, then, could political anger turn?

No sooner had Katie Hannon completed her radio appearance than an answer emerged. The next guest was Fianna Fáil's Dara Calleary, who pointed out some curious gaps in the government's apparent knowledge of the story thus far by referring to two overlooked lines in the previous evening's reports: Clifford's revelation that Katherine Zappone had met with the McCabes, and Hannon's detail about how Tusla's chief executive had written to the most senior civil servant in Zappone's department to discuss the agency's failings.

Calleary reasoned if the Department of Children and Youth Affairs were aware of this scandal, it was odd that the Tánaiste wouldn't have made any reference to it in the previous day's Dáil debate when TDs discussed a State inquiry into McCabe's treatment. Surely the Minister for Justice of the day would have known about these things before the general public? Surely – *surely* – Katherine Zappone would have shared this bombshell information, relating to a hugely sensitive public figure, with her colleagues in the government? If she hadn't, she could rightly be accused of withholding pertinent information from her colleagues at the precise moment when it was more relevant than ever.

An hour later, on the same programme, Sinn Féin's deputy leader Mary Lou McDonald focused her ire elsewhere. It was important that Justice Peter Charleton be able to conduct his inquiry without any possible impediments, and contacts between Gardaí and Tusla were now likely to be significant, she argued. Similarly, it was important for rank-and-file members of the Gardaí to uphold their own morale and not live under a shadow while that inquiry went about its work. For that reason, she said, 'Nóirín O'Sullivan must – without prejudice, because she is entitled to her good name – step aside and allow the Commission of Investigation to do its work.'

The McCabe saga had occupied acres of newsprint and hours of airtime since the whistleblower had first come to public prominence in late 2013, but only a handful of people – in policing, political and media circles – had ever heard his voice. As a matter of course, he did not grant interviews – indeed, no Gardaí ever did so without the legally required approval of the Commissioner. McCabe was especially wary of being cajoled into making sensitive – or insensitive – comments about his Garda superiors. Michael Clifford, who later wrote a book (*A Force for Justice: the Maurice McCabe Story*) about the whistleblower's struggles, was the only journalist who had ever quoted him directly in an article.

With McCabe now suddenly in the midst of another bona fide national scandal, but unavailable for direct interview, it fell to his solicitor, Seán Costello, to reiterate McCabe's viewpoint on air on Radio 1's *Today with Sean O'Rourke*, where he discussed his client's travails and the legal options available to him, including the possibility of suing Tusla. But his most notable comment, as it turned out, concerned the single aspect of McCabe's story he couldn't discuss.

'Has Sergeant McCabe met Minister Zappone?' asked O'Rourke, referring to the reports of the previous evening.

'I believe that he has,' came the clipped reply.

'Your answer suggests you were not at that meeting.'

'No.'

'Do you know anything about it, or how he got on?'

'I'm afraid I don't.'

'Or when it took place?'

'It would have been close to two weeks ago, I think.'

'Okay. And was he assured, or in any way reassured, by her?'

'I think that after the meeting he was happy that he had been met by the minister.'

Although news of this meeting between McCabe and Katherine Zappone was already in the public domain, the significance had been lost in the previous night's milieu of new information, and diluted by the sheer enormity of the scandal involving Tusla. With political correspondents now desperate to move the story forward, this point suddenly caught the imagination.

One factor in this was the fact that ministerial comments were thin on the ground. Enda Kenny, returning from a day in Warsaw with his Polish counterpart, fulfilled an obligation to open the new offices of the professional services firm Accenture, but managed to enter and exit without passing the sole journalist waiting outside in the continuing miserably cold weather. The only minister within reach of the political correspondents in Dublin was Simon Harris, the health minister, who called on Tusla to make a public statement outlining its position.

By that lunchtime, Tusla had done so. It said that it was unable to comment on individual cases, because of the need for discretion and to protect personal data. While citing data protection issues and the need to investigate any allegations of child abuse reported to it, 'it is clear to us that mistakes have been made'. Its statement continued: '... we can confirm that we are in the process of apologising fully to the individual involved.' The agency also pledged to give its full cooperation to any public inquiry that might get underway.

Tusla's chief executive, Fred McBride, also showed up on RTÉ to announce he had issued a written apology to the McCabes, and offered to meet them to restate it personally. Though admitting that Tusla had clearly made some serious mistakes, he absolutely denied that the agency had actively colluded with Gardaí to advance the allegations. 'I would never knowingly allow that to happen, so I absolutely refute that,' he insisted, adding that Tusla had notified the Department of Children about the error within days of realising it.

Nonetheless, in the midst of this sudden whirlwind, the woman now at the heart of the drama was nowhere to be found.

***

Katherine Zappone was rare among her Cabinet colleagues on several fronts, as one of only four women running full departments of State (out of fifteen), and one of only two members of Cabinet who were openly gay. Though she had been a long-standing activist for women's rights, it was her sexuality that inadvertently led her to wider public prominence, via a long-running and landmark legal battle to have the Irish government recognise her 2003 Canadian marriage to Ann Louise Gilligan.

By their own admission, while obviously grounded in the desire to have their love recognised by the State, the legal case was also grounded in financial concerns. When the couple were drawing up their wills, they realised the tax implications of leaving half a home to someone who would not be legally recognised as their widow. These concerns were crystallised by the fact that Zappone had no pension and that the couple had bought a second home hoping it would provide for a retirement income. Zappone declared this tax discrimination, in a 2008 interview with the *Sunday Independent*, as 'out-fucking-rageous'. Their unsuccessful High Court claim proved, for the first time, that the Irish Constitution could not provide for a same-sex marriage. This legal battle had won many liberal sympathisers, including within the Labour Party, at whose behest Enda Kenny appointed her to the Seanad in 2011, making her the first openly gay woman to hold office in Leinster House.

There was a certain poetry to how Zappone's legal initiative proved the illegality of gay marriage, and how she was now part of the parliament that triggered a referendum to permit it.

Zappone's unlikely path into Irish politics was sometimes lauded as an example of how the industry was not a closed shop, but privately some of her colleagues felt she was held to a lesser standard than other Cabinet ministers. 'When the media evaluate me,' one Dáil colleague explained, 'they evaluate me as a politician. She very much gets away with being seen as "not a politician", but she *is* a politician. It's like when Shane Ross and Finian McGrath criticise the establishment, when they both sit around the Cabinet table.'

Perhaps the most visible (or rather, audible) sign of Katherine Zappone's outlier status was her accent. She was born and raised in Seattle on America's west coast, and her life only led her to Ireland after she enrolled for a PhD in theology in Boston College in 1981. Zappone, who said she first felt attracted to girls at age five, and Gilligan, a former nun who had never had a lesbian relationship, were the only students pursuing the programme. The pair moved to Ireland in 1983 and had remained ever since. Zappone secured Irish citizenship through naturalisation in 1995, but often journeyed home for family occasions.

Through sheer coincidence, this was one of those occasions. Now at the centre of an erupting political volcano, Zappone was eight hours behind, 4,500 miles away, spending the weekend at a long-arranged family occasion in Washington State – out of the reach not only of journalists, but also of her own press officers, whose phones were now ringing incessantly.

Those press officers had to take matters into their own hands. Zappone had only flown over the previous afternoon and would naturally be jet-lagged. After lunch they began to draft a statement, on Zappone's behalf, setting out exactly the minister's handling of events – but, crucially, without being able to get hold of Zappone herself. Drafts were exchanged with the Department of the Taoiseach, where some of Kenny's most senior officials sounded the alarm. An element of dispute had arisen about the contents of the statement, and Kenny's team were keen to have the Taoiseach speak directly with his absent colleague before any statement was issued.

But the whirlwind of calls and texts from journalists was not abating and, with the urgent need of putting a response into the public domain, Zappone's handlers decided they could wait no longer. Just before 3 p.m. that afternoon – over four hours after Seán Costello's radio exchange drew attention to her knowledge of Tusla's unwitting involvement in the smearing of Maurice McCabe – the statement was issued, against the wishes of their counterparts on Merrion Street. The only change to the original draft was to modify the language so that it was no longer issued in the first person. Katherine Zappone still hadn't picked up any calls, and so the statement was rewritten in the third person and issued on behalf of a departmental spokesperson instead. (The hasty rewrite was incomplete: a single reference to 'my' department was left behind, four paragraphs from the end.)

> Minister Zappone has met with Mrs Lorraine McCabe and Sgt Maurice McCabe. She has heard first hand of the devastation caused to them by the false allegations against Sgt Maurice McCabe.
>
> The Minister became aware of the circumstances when Mrs McCabe contacted the office of the Minister for Health on 18 January 2017.

As the matter related to the Department of Children and Youth Affairs, the Private Secretary of DCYA was requested to call Mrs McCabe.

The private secretary did this on 18 January.

Minister Zappone met Mrs and Sgt McCabe on Wednesday 25 January.

Since then her office has been in regular contact with Mrs and Sgt McCabe and Tusla – which has led to the offer of a public apology.

The Secretary General of the Department of Children and Youth Affairs held a meeting with Senior Tusla Personnel on Friday 27th January.

Tusla provided DCYA with a chronology and analysis of the case – which my Department gave to Mrs and Sgt McCabe on Saturday 28th January.

Tusla informed the Secretary General that they have instituted a case review to extrapolate all relevant information in order to provide a more detailed analysis.

Minister Zappone informed relevant Government colleagues during the course of this period.

Minister Zappone was always of the view that Tusla would form part of the investigation by the Commission of Inquiry.

Kenny's team were profoundly displeased that Zappone's handlers issued the statement without their full agreement. The anger over perceived insubordination was compounded by the new political claims contained within it.

The first was where it suggested that Zappone was not in fact the first minister to be informed of the affair: Lorraine McCabe had first called the office of Minister for Health Simon Harris, which then passed the query on to Zappone's department. Harris himself quickly spread the word to newsrooms that Lorraine McCabe had called his office only mistakenly, thinking Tusla was a subsidiary of the HSE and not an independent entity in its own right. All his office had done was set her in the right direction – an interaction so fleeting that Harris was not told about it at the time. The minister himself – slightly mortified to have called for a Tusla statement hours earlier, only now to be named himself in connection with the agency's mishaps – had only found out about it when Zappone's spokesperson mentioned it in the statement.

The two final lines were where the real meat lay. 'Minister Zappone informed relevant Government colleagues during the course of this period,' it said. Oh? Who would those colleagues be? Surely the most relevant people to inform would be Frances Fitzgerald, the Minister for Justice whose tenure began and was engulfed by the fallout of Maurice McCabe, and Enda Kenny, the Taoiseach who had already lost one Minister for Justice (and, in essence, one Garda Commissioner) over McCabe's actions?

This new suggestion, that these two ministers might have been aware of the Tusla angle to the Maurice McCabe saga, was simply explosive. The country was still reeling from the idea that Garda HQ might have launched a whispering campaign including grievous sexual slurs to blacken McCabe's name. It was aghast at the possibility that a State agency set up to safeguard children had somehow entertained an egregious claim against him – either a conspiracy on a devastating scale, or an appalling confluence of misfortune that handed Gardaí a stick to beat the whistleblower with. *Liveline* – which many in Leinster House used as a yardstick of public opinion, even though only the most outraged would ever think to call it – was apoplectic, with Joe Duffy fielding calls from others who had been the subjects of false claims and who narrated the weary battles they fought to prove their innocence.

The final line, slightly overlooked, compounded the impression that two senior members of government had known about the Tusla problem all along. The department's statement said Zappone believed the issue of a Tusla file on Maurice McCabe was always going to fall within the remit of the new inquiry – but how did she know that? She wasn't the minister responsible for enabling the commission of investigation, but seemed very confident of what it would investigate. Did that mean she had discussed the topic with Fitzgerald, who therefore would have to have known about it too?

Unhelpfully, this was something on which one of Zappone's spokespeople could shed no light – as they were unable to confirm exactly *which* ministers Zappone had kept in the loop. As fate would have it, Zappone turned on her phone at 7 a.m. local time – just after 3 p.m. back at home – and made contact with her department only a few minutes after it had issued the statement.

* * *

Alarm bells were now ringing in Merrion Street and St Stephen's Green, where both ministers and their departments were acutely aware of the sloppy optics now at play.

Leinster House, too, was unusually busy. By Friday afternoons the building is usually quiet, with most TDs having retreated to their constituencies. In the wake of this scandal, however, the parliamentary complex remained abuzz, with journalists and politicians still plentiful. Fine Gael backbenchers, in particular, were openly seething. The idea that the government might have been able to get ahead of the story, but missed out because Zappone had failed to share pertinent information with colleagues, was causing pandemonium. Ministers quietly predicted some raucous scenes at the following week's Cabinet meeting when Zappone would have to account for her actions – or inactions, as the case may be.

Dublin-based Mary Lou McDonald had already taken advantage of the packed house to hold a morning 'doorstep' press conference, where she reasserted her wish for Nóirín O'Sullivan to stand aside. Such was the clamour for reaction now, to news unfolding at breakneck speed, that by late afternoon McDonald felt the need to call a second one. The claims of Zappone's statement had cast serious doubts over Frances Fitzgerald, she said. If the Tánaiste had been aware of this Tusla file all along, then why had she told McDonald a day earlier that she wasn't aware of any Garda contact with other agencies? At best, Fitzgerald had been 'less than forthcoming'; at worst, she had misled the Dáil outright.

The phones of other ministers were also kept busy. While officially the content of Cabinet discussions enjoyed the veil of confidentiality, ministers often sought favour with journalists by offering some insight into the nature of any discussions – in particular, if there was any dissent around the table. (This was becoming a more regular occurrence; Shane Ross always seemed to be demanding or critical of his colleagues.) Now journalists were keen to know if Katherine Zappone had betrayed any knowledge of a Tusla file containing false and damaging claims against Maurice McCabe.

No, came the answer. Not only had she not mentioned Tusla, she had barely contributed to the discussion at all. Some weren't sure if she had even opened her mouth.

The Independent Alliance was especially furious. There had

been a long-standing belief among its five TDs that Zappone's Cabinet behaviour was more akin to a Fine Gael minister than to an independent. If ever the Alliance would raise issues around the Cabinet table, expecting its independent colleagues to follow with vocal support, Zappone and Denis Naughten would be curiously silent. Some suspected that the non-Alliance independents were pointedly keeping their bibs clean at Cabinet, preferring to resolve their concerns in pre-Cabinet bilateral meetings with Kenny instead. The idea that Zappone was privy to hugely sensitive detail, but hindered them in their duty to act as a collective Cabinet because of her absolute discretion, caused plenty of rancour.

Zappone was not the only one about whom questions were now suddenly being raised. It was one thing – perhaps unforgivable – that the Minister for Children had allowed a Cabinet debate to proceed without sharing her extremely salient knowledge. But what about Enda Kenny or Frances Fitzgerald themselves? If the Department of Children's statement were true, it was almost certain that both were aware of Zappone's meeting with the McCabes in the first place. The idea that they, too, allowed the Cabinet to debate a McCabe-themed inquiry without inviting Zappone to pass comment, struck many in Leinster House as odd – and, indeed, as somewhat suspicious.

* * *

Just before the 6 p.m. news, Fitzgerald was able to issue a statement of her own. 'She [Zappone] informed me in January that she intended to meet with Sgt McCabe,' its second paragraph read, confirming that Zappone had not gone on a solo run. But Fitzgerald promptly added: 'She of course did not inform me about any details in relation to confidential Tusla records.'

This was an immediate contradiction. Zappone said she had kept her relevant colleagues informed 'during the course of this period'. Now the Minister for Justice, the most relevant colleague of all, was claiming she had known nothing at all of the role of Tusla. Phone calls to ministerial handlers confirmed this position: no matter how implausible it sounded, Fitzgerald knew nothing about the meeting other than that it was happening.

These handlers – and other Fine Gael ministers – also defended the Tánaiste's seeming incuriosity, in knowing about a Zappone–McCabe meeting but failing to inquire about it when it was now central to a Cabinet discussion. By now, State inquiries were commonplace and almost routine, and the established procedure was that the minister initiating the inquiry (Fitzgerald, in this case) did not have to actively solicit input from others. Cabinet discussions were supposed to be free-flowing and inquisitive, and other ministers would regularly chime in with questions and observations about the matters being scrutinised. In keeping with that principle, it would not be up to Fitzgerald to ask Zappone if she had anything to say – it would be up to Zappone to raise it herself. 'With the benefit of hindsight, do Enda and Frances wish they knew about it? Probably, yes,' one minister later lamented. 'But that's not the way things work: you presume people will bring to your attention what they need to bring to your attention.'

The fact that no new inquiries had been initiated since Zappone had been recruited to government appeared to have escaped them. In her nine months as a minister, Zappone could not have been privy to the established routine of how ministers dealt with the formation of a State inquiry: she'd never sat through the process before.

Soon after Fitzgerald's statement, Enda Kenny's press secretary, Feargal Purcell, also began returning calls to offer a similar explanation on behalf of the Taoiseach. Zappone had informed him that her meeting with the McCabes had been scheduled, but she had not indicated the topic. The Taoiseach, it appeared, was not especially curious to find out.

Not only were the two most senior Cabinet members now disputing the claims of a colleague, but they were both united on a separate point. Spokesmen for both Taoiseach and Tánaiste insisted they had only learned of the Tusla angle to this whole affair when it was reported on *Prime Time* and not via their Cabinet colleague who was responsible for that agency, who was aware of its damaging file on McCabe and who had claimed to be informing her 'relevant' colleagues all the while.

John McGuinness meanwhile had shown up on the *Six One* news, announcing that Tusla had sent someone to the McCabes' home in Mountnugent, on the Cavan–Meath border, to hand-deliver the apology of its chief executive Fred McBride ... and left it at the wrong house. McCabe had been at home all day, trying to cope with the fallout of the story ('He's trying to deal with it and he's not good,' his solicitor Seán Costello said), and his wife, Lorraine, was especially displeased at Tusla's latest error.

McGuinness also departed from the Fianna Fáil party line at this point – formally breaking ranks and calling on Nóirín O'Sullivan to stand aside for the duration of the forthcoming inquiry. The Garda Commissioner herself, at a function in Waterford, said what had happened to McCabe was 'a terrible thing to happen to anybody' and 'our thoughts are with Sergeant McCabe and his family'. No doubt the McCabes harboured some doubts about her sincerity.

Meanwhile, Katherine Zappone was barely able to get off the phone for the next few hours, dealing with the worried queries of colleagues and fellow ministers as she tried to fight fires from afar. It was unusual for her to spend so much time on the mobile: records released to the author under the Freedom of Information Act showed that, outside of her trip to Washington, she made only eleven calls in the entire month of February. On Friday 10 February alone, she made twenty-seven.

Among those to whom she spoke was Frances Fitzgerald, whose own role had been called into question as a result of the earlier statement from her departmental press officers. The Tánaiste, witnesses recall, was less than pleased, telling Zappone that there were now calls for her resignation and that significant pressure was being placed on the Taoiseach as a result of the statement. 'I'm sorry,' Zappone sighed down the phone, almost completely powerless to undo the mess.

By 8.30 p.m. – having been on the phone to various parties for over two hours – Zappone had her spokesperson release a follow-up statement.

'It would have been highly inappropriate for her [Zappone] to brief the Cabinet on confidential, highly sensitive and personal information which one could reasonably assume was the subject of a protected disclosure, which was leading to the establishment of the Commission,' that spokesperson said.

This was a climb-down. Having said she kept the relevant ministers informed at all times, Zappone's department was now admitting she hadn't told them of the Tusla detail after all – and, in fact, seemed to be confirming that she had told them virtually nothing. In order to cover the tracks of a U-turn, this was now presented as a virtue: Zappone had good reason to believe that the matters within the Tusla file formed part of the protected disclosures made by Maurice McCabe and Dave Taylor, and it would have been wrong to share the details in that case. It was obviously a pretty delicate balancing act: trying to ensure the most comprehensive response while sharing as little detail as possible.

But that only led to more questions. How had she arrived at that conclusion? McCabe and Taylor had sent their whistleblowing complaints to Frances Fitzgerald at the end of September 2016. McCabe himself didn't get full sight of the Tusla file, revealing the 'copy-and-paste' error of digital penetration, until January 2017. The Tusla file simply could not have been mentioned in the protected disclosure.

Had Zappone just taken a mental leap into the unknown, and prioritised McCabe's confidentiality over her duty to keep her colleagues in the loop? Or had this second statement – a late attempt to toe the line – accidentally given an insight into something more?

***

That evening, Katie Hannon appeared on the airwaves once more, on the 9 p.m. evening news bulletin. Tusla's involvement – accidental or otherwise – in this smearing scandal may not have been limited to Maurice McCabe.

'It turns out that this is not the first Tusla notification in relation to a whistleblower which has come across a minister's desk in recent months,' she revealed. 'I've seen correspondence today that shows that the justice minister, Frances Fitzgerald, has had correspondence from another whistleblower in relation to a child protection Tusla notification which was made about him by one of his Garda superiors.

'Now, in this case it was dealt with properly and speedily by the social workers – they found no evidence of abuse – but the whistleblower told the minister, in that correspondence, that this Tusla referral was part of a campaign of harassment against him by a senior Garda. And that complaint has been put into GSOC, and that has been put into a protected disclosure as well, that has been made by this whistleblower.'

Hannon stressed that this was an 'entirely different kind of complaint' to the one made about Maurice McCabe, which was thought to be legitimate because Tusla was unaware of the copy-and-paste error that generated it. In this new case, the complaint – allegedly made by a more senior officer – seemed to be entirely vexatious, and 'no evidence of impropriety' was found.

It would later turn out that this letter had come from Keith Harrison, the same internal complainant who had been named by Clare Daly the previous day. On the very same day as Katie Hannon revealed his letters to Frances Fitzgerald, Harrison wrote to Katherine Zappone appealing for his own case to be investigated in a similar manner to McCabe's.

Harrison saw massive parallels in his own case: he saw himself as an inconvenience for his superiors, having arrested an Athlone-based member of the Garda drugs unit for suspected drink-driving. He had told TDs that he was pilloried within the force as a result, office-bound for eighteen months while the man he arrested was allowed to continue on regular duty and holding a firearm. An internal inquiry had been instigated; Harrison claimed his superiors had actively solicited complaints from others with whom he had previous encounters. But, most significantly, he believed a malicious complaint about him had been passed to Tusla simply to discredit his standing in the community.

'The similarities are so alike it couldn't be coincidence,' he wrote to Zappone, 'and considering the geographical locations of us, such treatment had to come on orders from the highest level.'

However intolerable the McCabe case might have been, there was always a prospect that the complaint made to Tusla was just a deeply unfortunate error, without any Garda fingerprints on it – and that although the senior officers of the force might have exploited it, they were not responsible for generating it in the first place. This new instance, however, raised the prospect that maybe the ruse ran a little deeper.

That, in turn, raised a serious prospect of double standards. The view within the 'establishment' parties was that nobody could ask a Garda Commissioner to stand aside on the basis of a possibly malicious falsehood. But was the same principle being abused on the other side? Were senior Gardaí in the habit of making up allegations just to undermine people they didn't like? If a whistleblower was making the lives of their superiors too awkward, were senior Gardaí so intent on destroying them that they wanted to tie them up through any means necessary?

A grim new vista was emerging with each passing day. Just how deeply did this scandal run?

DAY 5

Saturday, 11 February 2017

Saturday is traditionally the quietest day of Ireland's political week. It is the sole day of rest for the daily newspapers, while those filing for the Sundays often have their stories lined up a few days in advance and spend the morning filing the copy. On Sundays, the daily editions are grinding back into gear, with journalists making calls and press officers fielding queries ahead of the next day's papers and events. Sunday also means RTÉ's *The Week in Politics* on TV, and current affairs talk shows across the radio spectrum. Saturday, on the other hand, largely means only one programme – the lunchtime talk show on Radio 1, with a single rostered minister put forward to represent the government position – but it is otherwise a political day of rest.

This was no such Saturday. The story of Maurice McCabe, Dave Taylor, Nóirín O'Sullivan and Tusla was now evolving at breakneck speed. It seemed that barely an hour would go by before another new angle would emerge, and evening news bulletins seemed to end with a different version of the top story than the one they had started with.

While the newspapers' online editions were red hot with the latest claims and counterclaims, it fell to the print editions to try to find some breathing space and summarise the lay of the land. Their verdicts were scathing, summing up the uneasy position of the minority government – now 'plunged into its worst crisis since taking office', according to the *Irish Independent* lead story under the headline: 'Web of deceit at heart of Garda smear probe'. The story spoke of how there was now a real prospect of the government losing its first minister, given both the internal rumblings and external dissent about Katherine Zappone's actions (or, rather, inactions).

'Cabinet at odds with Minister on McCabe', led *The Irish Times*, focusing on how the Taoiseach and Tánaiste had contradicted Zappone's first statement – and, indeed, how her second statement had contradicted the first. It reported how the terms of reference for the new Charleton inquiry had been 'discussed in detail' by the Cabinet on Tuesday, but that several sources confirmed the Minister for Children had not broached the subject of Tusla or whether the inquiry needed expanding in order to investigate it. While Zappone may have been confident that Tusla was already covered, few (if any) of her colleagues shared her certainty.

This was further explored by the *Irish Examiner*'s front-page story: 'Focus on Zappone over Tusla file'. Juno McEnroe reported: 'Rocked by the further grievances against Sgt McCabe, the Government said the Tusla blunder would be specifically included in the commission of investigation. The Cabinet will discuss this next week, before a Dáil vote on the terms on Thursday.' Implicit in this was a defeat for Zappone: surely, if Tusla were already being covered, there would be no need to expand the terms of reference any further?

If the vacationing minister had been awake early in Washington State and seeking consolation from the front pages, she would have found a single line of it buried within the *Irish Independent* story. 'Sgt McCabe has praised Ms Zappone's handling of the case,' it said, indicating that the whistleblower at least seemed pleased with how Zappone had followed up on their meeting.

Inside the pages of those papers lay another insight, which cast more doubt over Nóirín O'Sullivan's claims of ignorance over the smear campaign allegedly conducted beneath her feet. Inside *The Irish Times*, Miriam Lord – the doyenne of Irish political sketch-writing – devoted much of her Saturday digest column to an encounter three years earlier, in the anteroom of the LH2000 wing of Leinster House. Lord had been present at the infamous PAC meeting back in January 2014 – the one in which Callinan labelled the actions of Maurice McCabe and John Wilson as 'disgusting' – and, in the anteroom afterwards, remarked to another observer that she wasn't impressed by Callinan's bullish attitude and dismissive tone to the claims of McCabe and Wilson, his two seemingly insubordinate subordinates.

'I got back a tirade in the most colourful of language about Maurice McCabe and what an awful person he was and if I only knew the half of it I wouldn't be so quick to criticise the commissioner,' Lord wrote. 'The "half of it" included insinuations about inappropriate sexual contact with a minor.

'This didn't come as news – the rumours were already floating around … Nóirín O'Sullivan and her colleagues, one presumes, would have been outraged had they overheard what was said to me in their immediate vicinity on the day of the "disgusting" committee. It's hard to credit that, since then, not even a whiff of the disgraceful stories circulating about one of her own members reached Commissioner O'Sullivan's ears.'

Few could disagree.

* * *

Simon Harris had already endured a busy week with the scoliosis and waiting-list crises, before then being dragged into the

Zappone/Tusla scandal. He was given the job of defending the government after a difficult week on Radio 1's *Saturday with Claire Byrne*. Just minutes before the show was due to air, a statement landed from the HSE, claiming that the McCabe allegation had been reported to the State before Tusla was spun off from the HSE and that the copy-and-paste error had originated with a paid HSE employee; therefore the health service had to carry some responsibility. Although it was satisfied that it had done everything necessary to ensure the McCabe files were corrected, and had trained staff to ensure a similar error in future would not wreak such havoc, it nonetheless apologised 'unreservedly' to McCabe and his family.

Harris, having summarised the statement for Claire Byrne, went about immediately suggesting that the Charleton inquiry should be expanded even further. 'I'm very clear also that this piece must be included as part of the work of the Commission of Investigation. I've spoken to the Tánaiste about that this morning and I believe that that can happen.'

He was joined on the panel by the now ubiquitous Brendan Howlin, who revealed yet another lengthy conversation with Maurice McCabe from earlier that morning. 'He actually is of the view that what we need is something much broader ... what is required now is an external criminal investigation, headed by police officers from a force outside of Ireland.' Columnist Fintan O'Toole had broached this prospect in that morning's *Irish Times*, lending a plausible veneer to what was otherwise a daft idea. Given the circumstances, it was understandable that nobody wanted the Gardaí to end up investigating themselves. But anyone with a grounded understanding of the law – and, certainly, anyone who had served within the force – would understand how offensive it was to invite a foreign police force to investigate if Irish laws were being broken in Ireland.

Given the absurdity of that proposition, conversation quickly turned to the position of Katherine Zappone. Simon Harris revealed that he had overcome the eight-hour time difference and spoken, by phone, with his absent Cabinet colleague the night before. 'We've got to accept Minister Zappone's integrity here,' he insisted. 'We do need to acknowledge that Minister Zappone was genuinely trying to acknowledge the truth for the McCabes.'

But that wasn't the issue, Claire Byrne pointed out. The real question over Zappone's head was this: how had she concluded that the aspect of the Tusla file would actually fall within the terms of reference? (The same terms of reference which, according to the morning's papers, would now be extended to incorporate it?)

'When I spoke to Minister Zappone last night,' Harris answered, 'I asked the Minister that very same question. How were you satisfied, after having your engagement with Sergeant McCabe, that the terms of reference were going to address that? She clearly said that when she viewed the terms of reference, it was clear to her that the terms of reference were capturing the issue that was discussed.' ('That's extraordinary,' guffawed Howlin.)

How so? Well, Harris said, she only had to read them. If the inquiry was examining the claim that Taylor was drawing attention to a criminal allegation, it was self-evident to Zappone that the allegation held by Tusla would fall within its net. That seemed equally sensible to Harris himself, and indeed to others in Cabinet: 'The Tánaiste has also made it clear that the terms of reference will capture all of these issues,' he added, citing Fitzgerald's improvised response to John McGuinness in the Dáil two days earlier.

Attention then turned to Zappone's first ill-fated statement the previous afternoon. 'I thought it was unhelpful, the first statement, because it added to the confusion at a time when the last thing Maurice McCabe and his family need is any more confusion,' the Minister for Health admitted. He said he was 'crystal clear' that he had no personal knowledge of Tusla's involvement in the McCabe saga until it appeared on *Prime Time*; while his office had been called, an official had redirected the call to Zappone's department and Harris was not himself informed.

Also on the panel was Katie Hannon, who seemed at this point both indefatigable and omnipresent, and who queried Zappone's second statement – the idea that, contrary to her first, Enda Kenny or Frances Fitzgerald *hadn't* been told. If Zappone had made a point of informing Enda Kenny and Frances Fitzgerald that she was meeting with the country's best-known whistleblower – and then heard simply jaw-dropping details of how a false allegation of sexual wrongdoing had come close to ruining his life – how could she *not* bring that information to Kenny and Fitzgerald afterwards? Or how could she not raise her voice to contribute such salient information when it came to organising a public inquiry?

As Hannon saw it, this curious silence worked both ways. 'I cannot imagine any circumstances, if you were framing terms of reference about a smear campaign about Maurice McCabe, that you wouldn't inquire what that meeting was about. It is incomprehensible to me, on any level,' she explained.

Howlin and another guest, Sinn Féin health spokesperson Louise O'Reilly, hummed approvingly. The latter said both ministers had a case to answer. Fitzgerald had been 'less than forthcoming' two days earlier when Mary Lou McDonald had stunned her with an unexpected Dáil question – but Zappone's silence was also inexplicable. Even if Fitzgerald had a legal obligation to keep quiet over the sensitive allegations surrounding Maurice McCabe, there was no such obligation on Zappone.

'There was no protected disclosure made to Minister Zappone,' O'Reilly reasoned. 'There was no reason to prevent her from having a discussion with the Minister for Justice. I am not the only person who finds it utterly incredible that she wouldn't have brought those matters to the attention of the relevant people. One of them most certainly – most definitely – is the Minister for Justice.'

On the basis of that confusion, O'Reilly said her party's whip, Aengus Ó Snodaigh, had already written to the Dáil's Business Committee asking for the following week's business to be reordered, making time for Fitzgerald to give a 'full and frank statement'.

Harris accepted that such a statement would be welcome, but defended Zappone nonetheless. 'I'm telling you that the minister is satisfied that the terms of reference put forward by the judge encompassed the issues she was discussing.'

But Katie Hannon had been keeping an eye on the calendar. It was true that Fitzgerald had not drafted the terms of reference for the forthcoming inquiry – Iarfhlaith O'Neill had done that for her, but he would have written them at some stage before Christmas. His own scoping inquiry was based on protected disclosures sent to Fitzgerald in early October. But back then, McCabe had not known about the full extent of the Tusla file, nor of its wrongful provenance and winding bureaucratic journey. It had taken the results of his Freedom of Information request, received only in January, to discover that. Therefore, there was no way he could have known that detail when speaking to O'Neill.

Even before the show had ended, Louise O'Reilly's comments had already been superseded. Gerry Adams, spending the day in Belfast, issued a statement calling for a general election. 'The Fine Gael-led government is one without authority,' his statement read. 'It is stumbling from one crisis to another – in health, in housing, in homelessness … they are now playing the public for fools on the Garda/Tusla/McCabe controversy.

'Fine Gael is in power only by dint of patronage from Fianna Fáil, and Fianna Fáil is keeping the wreck afloat. Citizens are scandalised by the arrogance of Enda Kenny and his Cabinet colleagues. The Taoiseach should do the right thing. So should Micheál Martin. He should withdraw his support for the government.'

Though Sinn Féin had never expressed confidence in the government – and never would – the latest statement marked a pronounced escalation of an already delicate situation. Criticising the government was one thing; demanding its resignation was another.

But by the same token: what was Sinn Féin going to do about it? Calling for a government to resign, while a fierce gesture, was also an empty one unless some sort of Dáil vote was called to give effect to it.

Adams could hardly have known that, three minutes after his statement landed in journalists' inboxes, another email would add a spark to the very same fire.

* * *

Ireland may not be as obsessed with opinion polling as some other Western democracies. It does not live or die by Gallup polls or commission daily YouGov trackers to determine who its next prime minister will be. Nonetheless, its political classes pay very close attention to what pollsters tell them. Every politician will insist that the only poll that matters is the one held on election day – but opinion polls, both national and local, play a crucial role in determining how political parties use their resources, or where they field candidates.

The most regular polls are commissioned by the Sunday newspapers, and usually shared with national broadcasters on the preceding Saturday evening. This is a win-win: broadcasters get to help break the news, and Sunday newspapers get a few hours of free national advertising.

This was one such Saturday. The Irish edition of *The Sunday Times* had commissioned one of its regular surveys from pollsters Behaviour & Attitudes, whose staff had been conducting face-to-face interviews on doorsteps nationwide. Between 31 January (the day after Theresa May had visited Enda Kenny and made approving noises about avoiding a 'hard' border after Brexit) and 8 February (the day of Brendan Howlin's stunning Dáil proclamation and Nóirín O'Sullivan's rebuttal) 955 voters were polled. Their verdict, shared with broadcast journalists at 1.54 p.m., would be released to the public at 9 p.m.

Before then, however, the penny had dropped within Sinn Féin. Calling on a government to resign was a scream into the wind – but there was something tangible they could do to give effect to it. If Fianna Fáil's support for the government were to be truly tested, Sinn Féin did have one weapon in its arsenal.

At the previous Thursday's meeting of the Business Committee, Sinn Féin had been allocated two hours of time to use as it wished. It had opted to table a motion calling for special status for Northern Ireland during Brexit, so that the entire island might remain within the European Union even if the United Kingdom was leaving. That was a worthy and timely topic: on her visit to Dublin, Theresa May had insisted she wanted to avoid a hard border but couldn't explain how this would be achieved, and crucially had not yet triggered Article 50 to formally begin the Brexit process.

But as Saturday continued, it emerged that Sinn Féin still had the discretion to change plans and pursue an alternative agenda. The weekly schedule would not be set in stone until formally ratified by the Dáil on Tuesday afternoon – and opposition parties retained the power to rearrange their own business in the meantime. In short, the two-hour slot was Sinn Féin's to use however it wanted.

That evening the die was cast. At 7.30 p.m. Sinn Féin announced it would postpone its motion on Brexit and instead table a motion of no confidence in the government.

Confidence motions are the ultimate litmus test of governance. As with most parliamentary democracies, Ireland's constitution stipulates that the government as a whole (or individual members, as the case may be) can only continue to govern so long as they enjoy the confidence of the Dáil. A motion of no confidence is, in effect, an attempt to un-appoint those ministers, or the government itself. The motion, if passed, would be tantamount to sacking Enda Kenny and his administration, effectively guaranteeing a snap general election.

Fianna Fáil's willingness to keep Enda Kenny in power would now face the ultimate test. The confidence-and-supply arrangement required Fianna Fáil's forty-three TDs to abstain in the vote – and to keep Fine Gael in power until at least the tail end of 2018.

Given the present circumstances, this was far from certain. Enda Kenny had long made it clear that he did not want to lead Fine Gael into another general election, with the intention being an orderly transition to a new leader at some point during the government's lifetime. On a mischievous level, collapsing Kenny's government would not only prompt a snap election – it would also force Fine Gael to either retain Kenny as leader against his will or scramble to appoint a replacement. Sowing such disharmony in the ranks of its rival was a temptation many in Fianna Fáil would find hard to resist. On another level, with an enormous scandal now unfolding and Fine Gael on the ropes, choosing to support the government could leave Fianna Fáil equally contaminated in the eyes of the electorate. With so many reasons to leave and so few reasons to stay, could Fianna Fáil really sit on its hands?

Ninety minutes later, the results of the opinion poll added some extra weight to Fianna Fáil's burden. The stunning *Sunday Times* opinion poll claimed that if a general election were held on that day, Fine Gael would claim only twenty-one per cent of the vote – its lowest ever rating in that series of polls. Fianna Fáil would claim a mammoth thirty-two per cent, while Sinn Féin would creep up behind Fine Gael on nineteen.

'The finding marks an extraordinary 40-point swing in the relative fortunes of the two largest parties from August 2011,' noted the paper's political editor Stephen O'Brien, 'when Fine Gael was 29 points ahead of Fianna Fáil – 44 per cent versus 15 per cent – to today, where they lie eleven points behind.'

The satisfaction ratings also made for unhappy reading. Thirty per cent of the electorate endorsed Enda Kenny's performance as leader of Fine Gael and Taoiseach. That was nine points behind both Gerry Adams and Brendan Howlin – but all three trailed in the wake of Micheál Martin, whose job met with fifty-three per cent public approval.

Eleven points down was a bad place to be at any time. On the cusp of a national outrage, it was worse. With a motion of no confidence now on the table, it was almost catastrophic.

'This government's over,' a Fine Gael backbencher lamented.

A minister, neatly summarising the feelings of many party colleagues, simply texted: 'Fuck.'

The WhatsApp group populated by Fine Gael TDs and senators also burst into life as members pored over the details. Morale, it appeared, was shot. The straightforward presumption was that Fianna Fáil – having been given both an incentive and an opportunity to collapse the government – would grab it with both hands. Plenty of first-term TDs, only a year into their parliamentary careers, already feared a snap general election that might cost them their jobs: an election in which, under Kenny, Fine Gael would have an unwilling leader.

Already, the more febrile members were seeking a radical response. 'At 11 per cent behind,' said one, 'it's clear the time for action is now.' That call to arms went unanswered: it was late on a Saturday evening, the Sunday newspaper writers were in the market for gossip and plenty were wary of a leak. What's more, Enda Kenny himself was a member of the WhatsApp group (albeit never contributing) and there was little appetite for plotting a coup in plain sight.

One member of the Cabinet was so spooked that they allegedly began corresponding with sympathetic backbenchers, suggesting they should take issue with the party leadership in the coming days – helping Fine Gael to address the calamitous prospect of being plunged into a general election campaign under a man who had already ruled out leading them through it. That minister completely denied the claim when it was put to them, but the suggestion would set the tone for the party's days to follow.

* * *

Going to bed on Saturday night, Fine Gael TDs felt the very fabric of the government was being tested on several fronts. The most obvious source of peril was Fianna Fáil – and while publicly stating that it would not be influenced by opinion polling, some within Fianna Fáil felt the party was already reaching a crossroads. Fine Gael was the natural opponent, and it grated the soul of Fianna Fáil that the unusual Dáil arithmetic had forced the two parties into an uneasy détente. Moreover, if it turned out that ministers had conspired to stifle knowledge of a major smear campaign against a Garda who commanded huge public sympathy, wouldn't Fianna Fáil share the damage by refusing to pull the plug? There were also concerns about whether Micheál Martin's feet might get itchy. The confidence-and-supply deal was only nine months old, but everyone in Dublin 2 understood that Martin held a novel power for an opposition leader: the power to trigger an election at his own whim, and not that of the Taoiseach.

Fianna Fáil had always styled itself as the natural party of power. In its ninety-one-year history it had only ever been out of power when opposition parties could cobble together enough seats for a bare majority in the Dáil – and before 2011, Fianna Fáil had never *not* been the country's largest party. Every sinew, every pore, every fibre of Fianna Fáil craved power. Martin was only the party's ninth leader; every single one of his eight predecessors had been Taoiseach.

Martin wanted that title for himself too. The Cork South-

Central TD had already led Fianna Fáil into two elections, though nobody truly held him responsible for the meltdown first time out. Back in 2011, five weeks before the general election, Martin challenged Brian Cowen's leadership in the wake of the Troika's arrival; the challenge failed, leaving Martin to quit as Minister for Foreign Affairs, but Cowen walked four days later anyway and Martin won the resulting contest. The change of leader did not work: the trauma of the bailout was so deep-seated that Fianna Fáil was eviscerated.

The second election, in 2016, had gone much better. Martin had insisted throughout that Fianna Fáil was not just looking to prop up someone else's coalition: it was running to win. Most observers had scoffed, but the result had spoken for itself. Now, with fifty-three per cent of the public backing his performance, Micheál Martin's star had perhaps never been higher.

But the next election would likely be Martin's last as leader – if he had led Fianna Fáil into three elections, and ended up in opposition each time, he would likely not get a fourth opportunity. Bailout or no bailout, Fianna Fáil thought of itself as the Manchester United of Irish politics: every campaign was a failure unless it finished with the ultimate prize.

All of which must, to some degree, have factored into Martin's psychological calculus during this period. Most voters would have approved if Fianna Fáil had cited this new scandal as grounds to pull the plug. And if not now, then when? What other opportunities would come along where Fianna Fáil would be justified in collapsing the government and running straight to the country?

Some of his backbenchers would have been happy to take the plunge. Many felt constrained by the functionary nature of the Fine Gael partnership, a joyless marriage based solely on convenience. Sinn Féin had gained some traction by accusing Fianna Fáil of trying to control both government and opposition at the same time, but only a few Fianna Fáil TDs felt this was the case. Most, particularly on the backbenches, felt they controlled neither – and would embrace an election simply to conclude which side of the House they ought to sit on. The very fact that it was Sinn Féin initiating a possible collapse, and not themselves, was proof positive.

Fine Gael and Fianna Fáil were united not only in governance, but also in hating the experience. Both felt trapped under the responsibility of having to run the country, but neither felt like they were truly in power.

In truth, though, few would have much input into Fianna Fáil's response to Sinn Féin's new gambit. Decision-making in Fianna Fáil under Micheál Martin was a top-down exercise, with short- and long-term strategy mapped out with the input of Chief of Staff Deirdre Gillane and Communications Director Pat McParland. Within its Dáil ranks, only two TDs, Billy Kelleher and Timmy Dooley, could boast any meaningful contribution to Martin's centralised decision-making. The response of Fianna Fáil's forty-three TDs would be determined by just one of them.

This all meant that, while Fine Gael was having an anxiety attack over the *Sunday Times* poll, Fianna Fáil TDs were largely unmoved. Being eleven points ahead of the historical rival was nice in theory, but it would only ever be in theory. Public popularity might be used as a lever in talks with Fine Gael, but if the poll standings were to remain only hypothetical, the benefit was limited. Polls were an amusement, but little more. In any case, the election campaign of 2016 had taught Fianna Fáil to treat poll numbers with healthy scepticism.

Inside the government, the jitters did not end with the thought of Fianna Fáil. Some ministers feared a fatal schism from within. If circumstances led Zappone to leave the government, either voluntarily or by force, the government might collapse simply through the blunt force of Dáil arithmetic. The Independent Alliance had been curiously silent too. Was silence golden? Or was it the calm before the storm?

Some in Fine Gael privately reasoned that it was lucky Katherine Zappone was thousands of miles away and somewhat detached from the febrile atmosphere building at home. Having helped to instigate this political crisis, Zappone could easily have been caught up in hot-headed exchanges with colleagues, or fallen victim to a hostile comment that could send her packing and plunge Ireland into a general election. Maybe, they concluded, Zappone's long-distance relationship with Fine Gael had come at just the right time.

DAY 6

Sunday, 12 February 2017

In 1982 a young nurse had been attacked with a hammer while out sunbathing in the Phoenix Park. A few days later, in a similar unprovoked attack, a farmer was shot dead with his own gun in County Offaly. The attacker in both cases turned out to be the same man, a well-known and eccentric *bon viveur* – who, amazingly, was arrested for the two murders while staying at the home of his friend Patrick Connolly, the Attorney General in the government of Charles Haughey.

'It was a bizarre happening, an unprecedented situation, a grotesque situation, an almost unbelievable mischance,' Haughey called it later. Those four adjectives later became 'GUBU', a uniquely Irish catch-all term to refer to a political scenario that transcended all understanding and reached the realm of farcical lunacy.

At least two of the editors of Ireland's Sunday newspapers thought it fit the bill now.

'Grotesque, Bizarre, Unbelievable, Unprecedented' read the headline on the *Sunday Independent*. Underneath, Philip Ryan revealed he had spoken to Fianna Fáil's John McGuinness, the former chairman of the PAC who had previously revealed a hotel car park meeting with Martin Callinan in which the ex-Commissioner had made 'vile' allegations about McCabe. McGuinness had confirmed that those claims matched the ones now in the public domain. Callinan had declined to comment.

Ryan also had details of an internal Tusla review which criticised the decision to investigate the sex allegation against McCabe without first seeking the input of the alleged victim – or even seeking to vouch for her credibility.

The *Sunday Business Post* also carried a Haughey reference in its headline – simply referring to the case as 'Garda GUBU' – and added its own nugget of new information. Shane Ross, it said, was 'understood to have lost confidence in his Cabinet colleague Katherine Zappone for not briefing him at all about the existence of serious false allegations against McCabe'. Moreover, it had seen another internal Tusla email, this one drafted by the counsellor behind the copy-and-paste error. Two days after reporting her mistake to Tusla, the same counsellor emailed again. She had received a phone call from an unstated source. 'I was informed that the superintendent in the jurisdiction referred to in the report was not yet aware of the clerical error and has been asked to meet with the Garda Commissioner in relation to the case.'

How did this person know that local Gardaí had not been briefed? How did they know that Nóirín O'Sullivan was to be spoken to?

Elsewhere, *The Sunday Times* had more detail of Dave Taylor's protected disclosure – with seeming proof of Nóirín O'Sullivan's knowledge of his smear campaign. Taylor claimed he had been in contact with Paul Williams of the *Irish Independent* during a time when Williams was interviewing 'Ms D' – the girl behind the original McCabe allegation. The girl was calling for the handling of her own complaint to be included among a wider trawl of reviews prompted by the McCabe case. Taylor claimed he had texted news of Williams' interview to O'Sullivan, who had allegedly issued a one-word reply: 'Perfect'.

The *Irish Mail on Sunday*'s headline and subtitles offered a neat summary of the situation. 'Zappone flies into storm over McCabe crisis', 'Kenny faces vote of no confidence', 'FF insider calls Garda chief "lame duck"', 'Whistleblower wants a criminal inquiry', 'Warning of more revelations to come', all under the banner headline: 'A Coalition on the Rack'.

While Katherine Zappone was still abroad, the other two Cabinet protagonists hoped not to add to that milieu of headlines. Both, however, had pre-arranged media engagements to fulfil, just a few blocks apart from each other in Donnybrook.

* * *

Frances Fitzgerald was first, appearing on *The Week in Politics* on RTÉ One, left alone on the panel to sell the government line. Host Áine Lawlor got to business almost immediately, asking Fitzgerald to account for her own encounters with Zappone and her own handling of the whole affair.

'Katherine telephoned me – as it turned out, on the morning of the twenty-fifth, of the day that she was meeting with Maurice McCabe. 25 January. I remember distinctly taking a call. She said to me that she'd been asked to meet him, and she was going to go ahead and meet him. And I said to her, "Thanks for calling me, Katherine", and that was it,' the Tánaiste insisted.

'So she told me she was meeting him. And obviously, I wasn't going to say yes or no – it wasn't any of my business, in the sense of the meeting [to do so]. So she went ahead and met him. That was the only conversation I had with her about that meeting.'

Lawlor put it to her that when she was bringing significant McCabe-related issues to the Cabinet table, it was unthinkable that she not ask other ministers for relevant input. 'Why did you not ask her,' she said in urgent staccato tones, 'since the twenty-fifth, how that meeting went – or at Cabinet? ... You never look across the Cabinet table and say, "Katherine Zappone, is there anything in that meeting by the way that's of relevance to these terms of reference?"'

'Well, it's very simple for you to put the question like that,' Fitzgerald offered. 'But what I was doing was presenting a very detailed set of terms of reference. What I was doing, in terms of my interaction with Katherine and Maurice McCabe as a whistleblower ... I was respecting the integrity of her meeting with him. I was respecting it fully. Maurice McCabe has been subject to an awful lot of hassle. I did not know the facts as they emerged.'

Fitzgerald also sought to offer a first-hand account of her reactions when first faced with the Tusla revelations on TV three days earlier. 'Let me be absolutely clear. When I went home and watched *Prime Time*, I did not know the facts as they emerged. I did not have any of the information, in relation to the counsellor, the referral to the HSE [*sic*] – any of those details. That was all absolutely new to me.'

The format of the programme meant the Tánaiste was sharing a studio with three opposition TDs, each of whom expressed incredulity at this incuriosity. If Fitzgerald was telling the truth, her account was nonetheless odd: none of them could accept that she might have gone to Cabinet, briefed them on McCabe's sensational allegation that the Garda press office was directing a smear campaign against him and proposed a full State inquiry, without ever asking if Zappone had anything to add.

One of those three TDs was Fianna Fáil's Dara Calleary, who had been put forward by party headquarters in lieu of Jim

O'Callaghan – the justice spokesman was unavailable, having gone to Rome for the weekend to watch Ireland face Italy in the Six Nations rugby championship. Calleary set about scrutinising Fitzgerald's seemingly *laissez-faire* attitude to whatever information Zappone could offer. 'You honestly expect us to believe that you didn't even say to Minister Zappone, "How did that meeting go?"' he queried.

'Yes, because it's the truth,' Fitzgerald asserted.

'That's incompetence,' Calleary rebuked, immediately stoking further tensions between the two parties.

Also on the panel was Labour's Alan Kelly, who had been in contact with another Garda whistleblower who had alleged bullying and mistreatment within the force. Now, for the first time, Kelly revealed that this Garda had *also* alleged a vexatious role for Tusla – and, moreover, had included this claim in his letters to his Minister for Justice.

'Did alarm bells not go off in terms of another whistleblower making contact regarding Tusla?' he asked of his former Cabinet colleague. 'Did you not join up the dots?'

The Independents4Change deputy Clare Daly, the third opponent on the panel, declared herself 'struck dumb' by Fitzgerald's failure to show any kind of curiosity over a Cabinet colleague meeting a well-known Garda whistleblower who had brought about her predecessor's resignation. Neither could she believe that Fitzgerald, having knowledge of so many pieces of this scandalous jigsaw and with other parts of it clearly within reach, failed to piece together the bigger picture.

'The protected disclosure of Dave Taylor contained this information regarding the child sex allegation,' Daly claimed. 'The idea you hadn't heard of it, prior to *Prime Time*, is laughable.'

Fitzgerald's constant refrain was that she was legally prohibited from either discussing or investigating the contents of any protected disclosures. Digging in her heels, she insisted she had only learned of the Tusla role in the McCabe affair when it was revealed on TV three days earlier – meaning, for one, that she could not have identified the consistent thread as Kelly had argued.

'I didn't put Tusla in the terms of reference, because,' – and at this point it was becoming a mantra – 'as I have said to you, I had no knowledge of the facts that emerged on the *Prime Time* programme on Thursday evening. That's the reality of the situation.'

Kelly, for one, didn't buy it. 'It is quite obvious that cabinet has broken down and that Fine Gael are trying to throw Katherine Zappone under a bus,' he said.

* * *

While the credits were rolling on Fitzgerald's TV performance, the Taoiseach was only three buildings away, entering RTÉ's Radio Centre to be interviewed on the Sunday afternoon news programme, *This Week*. It was his first appearance before a microphone since the Tusla scandal broke three days earlier.

It was really by fluke that Enda Kenny was there at all: every year the programme conducts a series of interviews with the leaders of the major parties, usually at a rate of one per week, and Kenny was merely fulfilling a routine invite to appear in the Fine Gael slot. The interview was booked long before the Maurice McCabe story had exploded in everyone's faces.

But for a slot which was planned so far in advance, some journalists immediately noted the Taoiseach was displaying an unusual trait: he seemed out of breath.

'First of all, can I say that' – breathe – 'to have an allegation' – breathe – 'put against anybody of being' – breathe – 'a sexual abuser' – breathe – 'has to be absolutely soul-destroying. And I share the country's view of' – breathe – 'the resilience and the courage of Sergeant McCabe, his family and children.' Breathe. 'And' – breathe – 'the central issue that's going on here is to put in place' – breathe – 'a Commission to determine the truth' – breathe – 'as to whether there was a systematic, eh, scheme against' – breathe – 'Sergeant McCabe' – breathe – 'by senior members of the Gardaí ...'

This was not the calm and measured delivery of a fifteen-year party leader, or someone who had been Taoiseach for six. His visits to the batter's box for Leaders' Questions were never punctuated like this. While his Tuesday morning comments to reporters outside Cabinet might be a little breathy, this was easily explained: he lived around 500 metres away from the front gate of the office and he relished the exercise.

In this case, his breathlessness was harder to explain. There was no obvious reason for him to sound so winded – it wasn't as if the Taoiseach had been bundled out of his car and immediately sprinted down the stairs into the basement studio from which the show was broadcast. This was the only event in Enda Kenny's diary for the entire day. 'For such a fit man I could never understand that,' admitted one party colleague. 'It was an affectation to a certain extent. I don't know whether anyone's ever talked about it to the Communications Clinic or whatever, or whether they'd ever recommend it.'

Some hacks wondered if this was actually a deliberate tactic: if the Taoiseach sounded like he had been rushed, he might be forgiven for anything he said which later turned out to be imprecise.

This monologue had been offered in response to a question of when Kenny had first heard of the rumours, common in media and political circles, about Maurice McCabe's past. Having finished his prologue – and seeming to catch his breath a little – Kenny proceeded to a substantive response. 'I don't deal in rumours or in allegations or in hearsay. I have to deal in fact. So the picture here in respect of everybody around the country, which goes to the heart of our public people, is to determine the truth here. And I do hope the Supreme Court judge appointed will be able to deal with that.'

Be that as it may, presenter Colm Ó Mongáin suggested, it was the rumours and hearsay that made the treatment of McCabe so insidious – and so he asked again: when had Kenny first heard them?

'You work in Leinster House for many years,' the Taoiseach said, referring to himself in the second person. 'It is a place of inexhaustible rumours, hearsay and allegations. I'd point out to you that Justice O'Neill in his analysis of the two protected disclosures that he received, was not in a position to determine the truth here …'

That wasn't answering the question, Ó Mongáin noted.

'As Taoiseach – as any public representative will tell you – the extent of rumours, allegations and hearsay that you come across … you have to distinguish between that and what fact is. This is a really serious matter about probably the most high-profile whistleblower, certainly of the last fifty years, in the State … I just don't deal in endless rumours, allegations and hearsay. They're not relevant and they're not valid in my book.'

Kenny did have some new information to put on the record, though. While he was 'not ruling out' a criminal investigation into the treatment of McCabe, that might take some time. Peter

Charleton, on the other hand, had told the government he was ready to begin his inquiry that very week. What's more, while Frances Fitzgerald was happy to amend the terms of reference so that the Tusla issue could be investigated in full: 'I would also point out that Judge Charleton has already said that the terms of reference cover the issues that were aired in a *Prime Time* programme on Thursday, and that he's happy about that.'

This was new: the man running the inquiry had already decided that the Tusla file would fall safely within his net. Charleton had chosen not to take his terms of reference too literally, and would not be blinkered in considering all the germane information that might have landed before him.

This felt like a trump card, giving the government a vital dose of external vindication. Katherine Zappone's silence at the Cabinet table, or Frances Fitzgerald's incuriosity about what had transpired at her colleague's meeting, would not have any negative consequences. Whether the terms of reference were *designed* to include the Tusla file or not, Peter Charleton would consider it relevant and investigate it as required.

Under the circumstances, this assurance from the Supreme Court judge was akin to manna from heaven. The judge singled out for the job had unwittingly got the government out of a tricky predicament. It was an assurance on which the government would become increasingly reliant in the coming days.

That didn't, however, address the political questions still to be answered about those ministers' actions. Ó Mongáin had a couple of seemingly simple questions: what did Zappone tell you and what did her officials tell yours?

'Well, Minister Zappone – who is doing a very good job,' he began, almost determined to underline his support, 'did tell me that she intended to meet with Sergeant McCabe, in a private capacity. And that's all I knew. I said to her, "Well, if, if you do have a meeting, make sure that you have a thorough account of it." So when we had our meeting on, on Tuesday, I wouldn't have been aware of the details of her discussions.'

Did Kenny ask Zappone what the meeting was about? 'No, because she was meeting him in a private capacity, which she's entitled to do.'

It wasn't really a private matter though, Ó Mongáin pointed out. Part of the purpose was so that she could formulate an apology on the part of Tusla, an agency under her remit. This was surely going to become a matter of public controversy; surely, he reasoned, Zappone had a duty to tell others that this was coming. Wasn't it an omission on her part, or that of her officials, not to pass it on?

'I'm not sure how many meetings that the minister had, but she has a duty in respect of privacy of an individual, and not to have details of what might have been contained in any of those incidents made public, following her engagement with him.'

Kenny was pretty evidently not for turning. Whether or not Zappone really ought to have shared the information, the Taoiseach was standing by his minister. The threat of an internal fissure in the government suddenly seemed to be abating.

In other ways, however, Kenny's appearance had raised questions of its own. After all, a Taoiseach defending his ministers was hardly unusual. Ears had been pricked by something else Kenny had said: what exactly did he mean by 'private capacity'? Was he suggesting that the McCabes were only meeting with Mrs Katherine Zappone, and not with the Minister for Children and Youth Affairs?

Kenny's press team scrambled into action. Government Press Secretary Feargal Purcell, noting the confused reaction of political correspondents on Twitter, rang around to clarify that no – this was absolutely *not* the defence the Taoiseach was invoking. In fact, the Taoiseach had simply misspoken: when he said 'private capacity', what he really meant was that the content of the meeting was 'confidential', given the sensitive matters being discussed. (This perhaps raised other queries: how had Kenny arrived at this understanding? Had Zappone told him so? And if she had, why didn't Frances Fitzgerald offer the same defence?)

* * *

Though the threat of impending implosion seemed to now be staved off, the risks from outside were not entirely eliminated. Kenny was still facing a motion of no confidence in three days – and Fianna Fáil's position still wasn't secure.

As if to crystallise those doubts, Micheál Martin popped up in front of an RTÉ camera in Cork a couple of hours later: 'I need to put on the record that our spokesman for justice, Jim O'Callaghan, met with Frances Fitzgerald on Wednesday evening, specifically to broaden the terms of reference of the Charleton inquiry, to take on board the Tusla file, because we had been alerted to it. I had spoken to Maurice McCabe on the Wednesday, [and] I was anxious that the terms of reference would cover the Tusla file.

'Jim O'Callaghan met with Frances Fitzgerald, alerted her to the existence of the [Tusla] file, and that it needed to be covered.'

Boom.

The leader of the opposition – the man whose party was keeping Enda Kenny and Frances Fitzgerald in power – was accusing the Tánaiste of lying.

Fitzgerald had again told *The Week in Politics* that she knew nothing of the Tusla file before it was covered on *Prime Time*. She'd been asked in the Dáil on Thursday if she knew anything of any such file and said no. And now, three days before the Dáil voted on the future of the government, she was being accused of a blatant lie – which, if proven, would undoubtedly bring down the government.

The Tánaiste herself had not yet left RTÉ when she received news of Martin's intervention, and she told her press handlers she simply could not understand why he had done so. For starters, neither she nor her special advisor Marion Mannion could recall Fianna Fáil mentioning the agency in their contacts the previous Wednesday. Fitzgerald insisted that Jim O'Callaghan, in the meeting at the Dáil bar, simply hadn't discussed any role Tusla might have played in the Maurice McCabe affair. Mannion, likewise, was sure that Deirdre Gillane had made no mention of it either – and she could be confident that, if she had, she would remember it. Mannion was technically herself a staff member of Tusla, having joined Fitzgerald's team on secondment from the national agency governing school attendance among troubled children. Both women, simply, were mystified as to why Micheál Martin would now claim that the existence of a Tusla file had been mentioned to them the previous Wednesday evening.

But secondly, even if Fianna Fáil's claim were true, why would it choose to pick a fight about it in such a drastic manner? Fitzgerald's belief was that, scandalised though the public may be, little actually hung on the existence of the Tusla file. She saw at best a tenuous link between the file and Dave Taylor's alleged smear campaign – but if a link did exist, the forthcoming commission of investigation would no doubt find it, so why rush to judgement in between?

Perhaps, she and her aides suspected, O'Callaghan still harboured resentment over events a few months earlier, when the government had used little-known procedural devices to halt progress on Fianna Fáil's bill to overhaul judicial appointments. (A barrister of his standing, they reasoned, was probably embarrassed to show his face in the Law Library as a result.) Another possible motive was that Fianna Fáil didn't really want to collapse the government, and needed to focus its ire on someone other than Enda Kenny.

The Tánaiste's team dithered on whether to issue a reply. Fitzgerald herself saw little value in becoming embroiled in a he-said-she-said row of scant substance. But, assured by her aides that an accusation of lying could not be left uncontested, she eventually rushed out a denial: 'Deputy O'Callaghan spoke to me about the Terms of Reference the day before the Dáil debate (Wednesday). He suggested the Terms of Reference should be broadened to bring absolute clarity that the allegation of criminal misconduct against Sgt McCabe and the alleged smear campaign would be investigated ...

'Deputy O'Callaghan said to me that *Prime Time* would have a programme the following evening related [to] the establishment of the Commission. At no point did he mention Tusla or any of the details that emerged in the programme.'

It was about as assertive as a denial could get – and it wasn't finished.

'If Deputy O'Callaghan had information concerning the Tusla file, why did he not raise those issues during his statement on the Commission's Terms of Reference which took place the following day?'

Fair point. In his speech in the Dáil three days earlier, O'Callaghan had betrayed no knowledge of some kind of role for the child and family agency. If the Fianna Fáil justice spokesman knew there was a Tusla file on Maurice McCabe, he surely ought to have said so in the Dáil – and asked for a change in the terms of reference so that it would definitely be investigated. He had done no such thing.

A few hours later, Fianna Fáil retorted with a statement from a party spokesman: 'Our justice spokesperson Jim O'Callaghan met the Justice Minister on Wednesday evening to ensure that the Terms of Reference of the Commission of Investigation could be extended to incorporate anticipated revelations, which were due to be broadcast the following evening on *Prime Time*, including a Tusla report which wronged Sergeant Maurice McCabe.

'Our priority was to ensure that this Tusla report could be included in the Terms of Reference.'

Fianna Fáil was sticking by its man, and its man was sticking by his story. O'Callaghan claimed he explicitly told the Tánaiste about the forthcoming TV exposé – and specifically wanted it investigated. (Press officers cleared up any vagueness about the statement afterwards: yes, O'Callaghan *did* specifically bring up the Tusla file. They also explained why Micheál Martin had emerged so dramatically: O'Callaghan would not be back from Italy until late that night, and the party did not want to let Fitzgerald's account go unchallenged until the next day.)

O'Callaghan was now in direct contradiction with Frances Fitzgerald. Quite simply, they couldn't both be right.

***

By Sunday night, exhausted observers questioned whether Fianna Fáil could honestly be expected to sit on its hands and not vote, only days later, to remove Fine Gael from power – particularly given its sensational new assertion that Fitzgerald *had* been informed of the Tusla file a day before the TV broadcast.

In Fitzgerald's defence, even had she been informed about the existence of a Tusla file on Maurice McCabe, there was precious little she could do about it. She was not the minister responsible for the agency, and all she could do was try to ensure a full investigation to limit the damage to McCabe and his family.

Jim O'Callaghan's claim, however, seemed to cast a question over Fitzgerald's sheer competence. If he was correct in having told the Minister for Justice about such a sensitive file – and its need to be examined in the terms of reference for a forthcoming inquiry – she had apparently done little to appraise herself of its significance. What's more, if this were true, the Tánaiste – the justice minister from the 'law-and-order party' – had misled the public and the parliament.

There were few doubts over O'Callaghan's bona fides in making his claim. The Fianna Fáil justice spokesman had no reason to lie, in particular when his own reputation as a senior counsel had been so steadily forged over time. But while few had any doubts over O'Callaghan's position, some questioned whether the Tánaiste had firmly grasped the significance of what was being said. (Some uncharitable analysis drew superficial links to how the *Prime Time* programme was presented by Jim's older sister Miriam, and to how the encounter with Fitzgerald took place in the Dáil bar. The first link was purely coincidental and irrelevant in the current case, while the latter was purely a convenient location for Fitzgerald to meet O'Callaghan while the Fine Gael parliamentary party was still meeting upstairs.)

And to top it all off, when the government was accused of lying by the party keeping it in power, it was now replying in kind and accusing Micheál Martin and Jim O'Callaghan of peddling a malicious lie. At just the time when Fine Gael most needed it to hold firm, the nascent partnership with Fianna Fáil was turning sour.

DAY 7

Monday, 13 February 2017

The cold snap that had hit the country in the previous days seemed to finally be abating. Daytime temperatures, Met Éireann announced, would be shooting from a mere three or four degrees Celsius, up to a relatively balmy eleven or twelve degrees. It would be a welcome respite for journalists who had found themselves standing outside various ministerial visitations exposed to the chilly arctic winds. There was a poetic parallel, though, in how the political temperature was now rising as suddenly as the mercury in the thermometers – a febrile atmosphere in which every action, even a minister dutifully returning home for urgent Dáil business, now seemed to carry a deeper symbolism.

'Cabinet crisis over McCabe sex smear', roared the headline in the *Irish Independent*, over a collage of pictures of Zappone, Fitzgerald, Nóirín O'Sullivan and Leo Varadkar. The social protection minister had been absent from the present Cabinet crisis – he was acting as ministerial chaperone to President Higgins on his tour of Latin America – but was now being summoned home early from Bogotá to vote on Sinn Féin's motion of no confidence.

Kevin Doyle's piece was blunt. 'The chaotic handling of the Garda whistleblower scandal is destabilising the entire political system as Fianna Fáil and the Government clash over when the Tánaiste first learned of the Tusla file on Maurice McCabe … As the crisis deepens, the positions of Garda Commissioner Nóirín O'Sullivan and Ms Zappone are to come under renewed scrutiny.

Support within Fianna Fáil for Ms O'Sullivan has weakened over the weekend.'

Inside, the paper dove a little deeper on Leo Varadkar's return. While there was an obvious reason for him to fly home, it was also possible to surmise other motives. Varadkar had vocally expressed his interest in seeking the Fine Gael leadership whenever the job became vacant – and his intervention in the parliamentary party's WhatsApp group, quoted by the newspaper ('Worrying poll and trend. Important not to panic or be seen to panic. Everyone needs to stick together this week'), was being read several ways. Some within the group treated his return as a heroic intervention, though others were privately wary of painting Varadkar as some sort of superhero simply for easily securing Michael D. Higgins' permission to return to Dublin.

The paper also carried commentary from Fine Gael backbencher Noel Rock, the party's youngest TD, who had formally proposed Enda Kenny's nomination as Taoiseach and who offered a politely veiled criticism of his party leader. 'Opinion polls ask if there was an election tomorrow, "Who would you vote for?" This is obviously a problem for Fine Gael, as the Taoiseach has been adamant that he's not leading Fine Gael into the next election,' Rock reasoned. 'So, when people are polled they have no idea who they're being asked to vote for as Taoiseach.'

The Irish Times offered scant consolation for the government. 'Pressure is mounting on Tánaiste Frances Fitzgerald to clarify when she became aware of false allegations of child sexual assault against Garda whistleblower Maurice McCabe,' wrote Sarah Bardon, whose report carried an extra line of assertion from Jim O'Callaghan: 'I have no doubt in my mind that she is mistaken in her recollection.'

The *Irish Examiner*, too, sounded warning klaxons. 'McCabe meeting deepens crisis,' it said. Micheál Martin had arranged to visit Maurice McCabe, having asked to see the Tusla file for himself. That meeting 'could put more pressure on Garda Commissioner Nóirín O'Sullivan to step aside'. And given the 'shock development' of the sudden contradictions between Fine Gael and Fianna Fáil, the meeting even had the prospect of further undermining the confidence-and-supply arrangement that was keeping the government afloat.

The story had gone from zero to sixty in just a few frenetic days, at a scale and pace which conditioned the media to expect more fast and furious developments on the Monday. This frenzy meant that smaller local rows were given the status of national crises. One such scrap came from KFM, the local radio station in Kildare, where Martin Heydon – a local Fine Gael TD and chairman of its parliamentary party – was being interviewed about the new dispute with Fianna Fáil. 'It's difficult to see how both sides could be true,' he said. 'I believe that the Tánaiste is telling the truth, yes.' Did that mean Fianna Fáil was lying? 'If both sides can't be reconciled, that's what we're looking at, yeah.' That prompted a reply on Twitter from his constituency colleague, FF's Fiona O'Loughlin. '"Lying" is a very strong term,' she said. 'Where is the "confidence" in confidence and supply now? Clearly eroded, from my and [Fianna Fáil's] view.' Though merely a local row between backbenchers, the latter was the first suggestion that Fianna Fáil might be prepared to exercise its nuclear option.

* * *

Having returned from seeing Ireland run nine tries past Italy at the Stadio Olimpico, Jim O'Callaghan was back in the saddle.

Not long after 8 a.m. he popped up on Newstalk's *Breakfast* show, where he spoke publicly for the first time about his encounter with Frances Fitzgerald five days earlier, which came after Micheál Martin had summoned him to his parliamentary office.

Martin, knowing the Tusla file would be revealed on the following night's *Prime Time*, wanted his justice spokesman's advice on whether the existing terms of reference would cover it. O'Callaghan, deploying his legal experience, believed not: he felt the existing wording allowed Charleton only to investigate the specific allegations Dave Taylor had spread to the media, but not how or whether the Tusla allegation (should it be different) had been more widely circulated. There would be little point investigating Taylor's contact with journalists if, in fact, the real smoking gun was how such allegations had landed in his lap in the first place.

'We decided that I would go and talk to the Tánaiste about it. Micheál Martin, my party leader, instructed me to go to the Tánaiste and talk to her and tell her that we believed the terms of reference needed to be extended, because of this forthcoming allegation that was going to be broadcast on RTÉ the following night.'

McCabe had also told Martin that he had met Katherine Zappone, and that Zappone was fully aware of the issues concerning the Tusla file.

O'Callaghan followed his instructions, rang Fitzgerald and arranged to meet her in 'the members' section', just a few yards from the elevator that Fitzgerald would be taking from the Fine Gael party rooms to the ground floor. 'I told her that there was an issue about a Tusla file, that was going to be broadcast on RTÉ's *Prime Time* ...'

'You said "Tusla file"?' asked interviewer Shane Coleman, urging clarity.

'"Tusla file",' O'Callaghan confirmed, 'that was going to be broadcast on *Prime Time* on the Thursday evening.'

He then explained to Fitzgerald his concerns with the current terms of reference, before they then spent 'seven or eight minutes' specifically sounding out the clause that needed to be widened.

'I felt we were doing the government, and the Tánaiste, a favour. By dealing with it in this way we were forewarning her that there was this programme coming up – I didn't have the full details of the programme, [but] I knew it was coming up – and I said to her, "The terms of reference need to be extended".

'Initially she was sceptical about that. I said to her, "You know, the Government could end up with egg on its face if it agreed to a term of reference, and then on the Thursday night there's a programme that comes out … You know, it would look particularly bad for the government."'

O'Callaghan was setting out his stall quite clearly; his deliberate and lawyerly choice of words left little room for ambiguity. Coleman put it to him that his account simply could not be squared with that of Fitzgerald, who insisted that the existence of a Tusla file was *not* discussed, or even revealed at all.

'I'm 100 per cent certain I did. I also said to her – and I remember saying it distinctly – I said: "You need to speak to Katherine Zappone, as she met Sergeant McCabe and she has this information about the Tusla file, about which I don't have all the information."'

Coleman put it to O'Callaghan that, if his story were absolutely true, Frances Fitzgerald had misled the Dáil the previous Thursday. It was territory into which the Fianna Fáil spokesman seemed unwilling to venture. 'She may have been mistaken. I look for benign interpretations, I don't presume that there's malign reasons.'

But even if that were the case, Fitzgerald gave no indication on Thursday afternoon that she was aware of a Tusla file, or that the inquiry had to be structured to accommodate it. So why hadn't O'Callaghan repeated in the Dáil chamber, on Thursday, what he had told Fitzgerald the previous night in the bar? 'I didn't have sufficient information to stand up in the Dáil and say, "There's a programme coming on the television tonight, it's about a Tusla file, I think there needs to be an investigation in respect of that." I don't think I could have said that with credibility. I hadn't seen the programme, I didn't know what was going to be in it.' Given the sketchy details he had to hand, he felt a discreet conversation with Fitzgerald was the best way to act.

Coleman reminded O'Callaghan that a motion of no confidence would now be debated in the coming days. How, if its justice spokesman were being so flatly contradicted, could Fianna Fáil play ball? It was a point that the interviewee made a brief attempt to deflect, but Coleman granted him little leeway. 'There's an issue of competence though, here, isn't there?'

'Yes, there is an issue of competence there. But the most important issue here is not the matter of dispute between politicians, or the politics of this. The most important issue on this is that we have a full investigation into the allegation made against Sergeant McCabe.'

O'Callaghan seemed desperate not to bring the government to the brink – at least not over the he-said-she-said dispute, significant though it was. If he was to be taken at his word, there seemed to be no way Fitzgerald's story could be reconciled with his. But there was clearly, on Fianna Fáil's part, a determined effort to defend its side of the story: only a few hours later, O'Callaghan would show up in Seán O'Rourke's studio on Radio 1 to add one extra element: the meeting in the bar was curtailed because both he and Fitzgerald were required back in the Dáil chamber, where the Tánaiste was introducing some new legislation about bail. O'Callaghan claimed to have texted Fitzgerald with his proposed wording on how to amend the terms of reference. Midway through the debate, with other TDs making their contributions, O'Callaghan had physically crossed the floor and approached Fitzgerald in her seat to ask if his suggestion was followed up. Fitzgerald, this time, suggested O'Callaghan approach the Attorney General directly. It was an odd suggestion – Máire Whelan was the government's lawyer, not the opposition's – but O'Callaghan had got her number and passed on his concerns anyway.

O'Callaghan's story would carry so many precise details that it was implausible to think the story was anything other than watertight. Scrutiny of the Dáil footage just about proved his claim: while independent Mattie McGrath was speaking, the cameras caught a glimpse of O'Callaghan's shoulder passing him in the aisle on his way over.

But back on Newstalk, there was one further point on which to press Fianna Fáil's justice spokesman: what future for Nóirín O'Sullivan? The party's resolve was not weakening, he said. She should not be forced out only because an allegation was made against her (even though this was the same treatment meted out to Dave Taylor).

'If it gets to a stage where this story gets so out of control that the Garda Commissioner can no longer perform her functions,' he said, offering a hypothetical scenario under which the position may change.

'We must be getting pretty close to that point, aren't we?'

'I don't know if we're getting to that point,' O'Callaghan dismissed.

* * *

A little while later, O'Callaghan's boss also appeared on a constituency-based radio station. Micheál Martin took a fairly routine phone call from P. J. Coogan, appearing on his mid-morning talk show on Cork's 96FM. He remarked that Sinn Féin's motion of no confidence was opportunistic and ran the risk of delaying an inquiry to get the answers that Maurice McCabe needed – implicitly acknowledging, for the first time, that Sinn Féin's motion risked collapsing the government.

Coogan, meanwhile, pressed Martin on his position around Nóirín O'Sullivan. Fianna Fáil, it seemed, was unique among opposition parties in not demanding the Garda Commissioner's temporary recusal from office. Why was that?

Martin recited the party's consistent view that there were broader issues at play. 'This isn't about protecting individuals or supporting individuals. That is simply a basic principle that we adhere to, and one which we continue to adhere to, because it affects future events now in terms of new Commissions of Investigation into different things.'

But this time he went one step further – and invited Nóirín O'Sullivan to consider her own role. 'That said,' he added, 'I do think the Commissioner needs to examine it [her position] herself, now, and make an assessment as to whether, given all that has happened, she is in a position to lead the force with authority.'

Barely an hour after O'Callaghan had said Fianna Fáil's position would not be changing, the party leader had changed it. Fianna Fáil was not calling for Nóirín O'Sullivan to stand aside – but was calling on her to think about recusing herself anyway.

Word was not long reaching Garda headquarters at the Phoenix Park. Shortly after midday, O'Sullivan issued an assertive defence of her position. 'My position remains unchanged,' she said in a press statement. 'Nothing has emerged in the last three weeks which in any way changes that situation. A campaign of false accusations, repeated and multiplied, do not make me guilty of anything.

'I have made it clear that I was not part of any campaign to spread rumours about Sergeant McCabe and didn't know it was happening at the time it was happening. I have repeatedly refuted that claim and do so again.

'The easiest option for me would be to step aside until the Commission finishes its work. I'm not taking that option because I am innocent and because An Garda Síochána, under my leadership, has been making significant progress, with the help of our people, the Government, the Policing Authority and Garda Inspectorate, in becoming a beacon of twenty-first-century policing.'

O'Sullivan may have been digging in her heels, but the fact she had been compelled to issue a second statement within forty-eight hours was a telling indication of the political pressure being exerted on her office. Moreover, the second statement had an even rarer trait: it was issued in the first person. The Garda Commissioner, it seemed, was taking this flak personally.

A few hours later, however, news broke of another possible headache for the Commissioner. The DPP had decided to drop its investigation into Dave Taylor, who had been out of work for almost eighteen months amid accusations of wrongful leaking of sensitive Garda information. The former press officer – whose protected disclosure was now paving the way for a public inquiry into his boss – was free to return to work.

'I have waited a long time for this decision to be made,' he said in a statement through his solicitors. 'It has been an incredibly stressful and difficult time for my family and friends. I would like to thank my friends and colleagues who supported me through this time.

'I have now been vindicated and I will shortly be resuming that part of my life which has been on hold since the start of this process.'

Officially speaking, this decision ought to have had no impact on Nóirín O'Sullivan: it was simply a case of a criminal investigation being dropped. But given the circumstances of Taylor's suspension – in an investigation led by her husband, where Taylor's now allegedly incriminating mobile phones were seized – his acquittal carried a far deeper symbolism.

Elsewhere, journalists were desperate to nail down Frances Fitzgerald over the war of words brewing with Fianna Fáil. The latter's statement had been the last word the previous evening, and now Jim O'Callaghan had appeared on both Newstalk and Radio 1, so it was the Tánaiste's turn to reply to the claim that she knew about the Tusla file earlier than she cared to admit.

Thankfully for those journalists, an opportunity appeared to have come. The Department of Justice had announced a few days earlier that Fitzgerald was due to attend an event at her department's headquarters on St Stephen's Green, launching a report on a novel programme called 'Family Links', where prison inmates were offered parenting training in the hope it would lower their risk of re-offending.

From early morning, hacks waited dutifully on the steps outside the department's offices – rejoicing at the much milder weather – hoping to catch Fitzgerald on her way in. Departmental press officers even loitered at the entrance, hoping perhaps to shield their minister as she arrived. Both of Fitzgerald's titles, Tánaiste and Minister for Justice, entitled her to the provision of a Garda driver, so surely her arrival could not be inconspicuous.

Eventually, though, another civil servant wandered out: *Too late, lads, she's already inside.* The Tánaiste had arrived through a back-door entrance and was already in the main atrium of the building preparing for her speech.

The fourth estate trooped inside to watch the speech, wondering whether there would be a formal Q&A session through which the conversation could be steered towards the Tusla issue. As it turned out, there was – but Fitzgerald was not there to hear it. As soon as she had delivered her set-piece speech, she apologised for having to be elsewhere and disappeared through a back door. A few journalists broke decorum trying to yell some questions as she left, but it was of little use: she was gone.

A hardy few spent the following hours at the department's rear entrance, where Fitzgerald's ministerial car had been parked, hoping to catch her on her way out. The stakeout only ended when her Garda driver was seen leaving the building – which those journalists interpreted as a coded hint that the Tánaiste was planning a long day in the office. In fact, the driver's services simply weren't needed: Fitzgerald had a lunch appointment at the Cliff Townhouse on St Stephen's Green, three minutes' walk from the department's front door. The journalists, abandoning the stakeout, gave her a clear path.

* * *

In Cork, Enda Kenny was also keeping his counsel. The Taoiseach was due at a jobs announcement by a software company, bypassing journalists who asked for comment as he entered. 'I'm going in here now ... What we want is a working and effective commission as soon as possible,' he said, flatly ignoring questions about the contradiction between his party and Fianna Fáil. 'Nobody is objecting to a commission of investigation, I hope. And it can start this week.'

Simon Coveney, at the same event, did accept questions from journalists. 'There are a lot of things about this case that people find hard to accept,' he said, including 'that there could be a clerical error that could result in the most high-profile whistleblower in the State's history being the victim of a smear campaign ... It seems impossible to me that this could be a coincidence.'

By this point Kenny had been Fine Gael leader for almost fifteen years and was, objectively, the most successful leader the party had ever had. Precious few members of the Fine Gael parliamentary party had been around long enough to remember a time in Leinster House when Kenny had *not* been the party head. He had led the party to its greatest ever election triumph, become its first leader to serve two consecutive terms as Taoiseach, and was regularly touted as a popular nominee for any senior European Union job he cared to pursue. But uneasy lay the head that wore the crown. Even before the present scandal had emerged, Kenny was facing into the twilight of his career. While he would probably take huge personal satisfaction from being the first Fine Gael Taoiseach to serve two consecutive terms, his public declaration of not seeking a third term had already set the tone for his eventual departure.

The prospect of an orderly leadership change was greatly hampered by the set-up of Kenny's second government. In a traditional majority government, a premier could happily stand down and give way to a successor at a time of their choosing. But with Micheál Martin sharing the power to collapse the government, Enda Kenny did not have the discretion to choose his own exit date.

This had never appeared to bother Kenny all that much, however. His deal with Fianna Fáil was scheduled to last for at least three budgets, which would take until Christmas 2018. Vocally, at least, Kenny had always insisted this deal would be honoured – and that it would be Fianna Fáil's fault if the government fell apart before that. There was plenty of time to think about leadership changes, he felt, and no need to rush the process.

Suddenly, however, the Taoiseach was facing a perfect storm. A motion of no confidence had been tabled in himself and in his government, which, if passed, would constitutionally compel him to resign. The opposition party on which he depended was suddenly racing ahead in the opinion polls. Now, incredibly, with WhatsApp groups demanding a regime change and Coveney accepting that the government's story was tough to believe, even his own ministers were undermining his authority. Fine Gael was suddenly facing a grim vista, with a realistic prospect of being bounced into a general election, under a leader who had explicitly stated he did not want to fight another election campaign.

Noel Rock, who had commented on the subject in the *Irish Independent*, was invited onto the *News at One* to discuss his comments further. He repeated his explanation that opinion polls were always predicated on the idea that the voter knew who they'd be electing if they voted for a certain party. Given Enda Kenny had disqualified himself from leading a future government, the party's poll performance would always be affected.

In that case, was it time for Kenny to set out a timeline for leaving? 'Realistically, yes,' Rock replied, offering a more direct analysis than his earlier newspaper comment. 'I don't think it's anything personal, and I would leave personalities aside. Realistically, it is now the appropriate time to begin setting out timelines for the future – not only for himself, but also for the sake of the Fine Gael party as well – so we have clarity in our own minds that if there is a general election in the next six or nine months, we know who will be leading us.'

A few hours later, discussing the same topic with this author for Today FM, Rock suggested an even shorter timetable was needed. 'Once we are over the hurdle of the motion of no confidence,' he said, 'we do need to have a serious and frank discussion about the future of the party, and the future of its leadership under Enda Kenny ... We need to accept that there's always the possibility of a snap general election being called. Logic would lead us to deduce we need to have a discussion about the future leadership of the party.'

Albeit only from a junior backbencher, suddenly a deadline was being set for Kenny's departure. The Dáil would have disposed of the motion of no confidence, one way or another, by Wednesday night. Rock now wanted the conversation around Enda Kenny's future to begin almost immediately afterwards.

Such an explicit call, however, sounded politically loaded. Rock was known to be close to Leo Varadkar, one of the presumptive frontrunners to succeed Kenny. Indeed, in the latter days of the 2016 campaign, Varadkar had been assigned by party headquarters to cross the constituency boundary and canvass for Rock instead of staying within his own patch of Dublin West in support of his own running mate, Senator Catherine Noone. (This was especially noteworthy because Rock's day job was as Noone's parliamentary assistant and so he was still technically a member of her staff at the time.) Rock had also gone on record as supporting the premise of a Leo Varadkar premiership whenever the Taoiseach's job eventually came vacant.

Varadkar himself was wary of Rock being seen as a stalking horse, and scurried to divorce himself from Rock's comments as he returned from Bogotá. Junior finance minister Eoghan Murphy was tasked with messaging journalists, as a 'source close to Leo', distancing Varadkar from any explicit threat to Kenny and effectively casting Rock as a rogue operative. Later, stumbling across Rock in Leinster House that afternoon, Murphy beckoned him – in a tone that equally suggested playfulness and frustration – by bellowing, 'Hi, you little shit.' The two then went for a more sedate coffee, simply so Murphy could scope out whether Rock had lined up any further media appearances and offer himself as a counterbalance if needed. The only such instance was the *Six One* news, where Rock had agreed to repeat his radio comments to a TV camera, while Murphy waited just out of shot for his own chance to rebut them.

Nobody wanted to fire the first salvo in the inevitable war, and while some privately scolded Rock for daring to question Kenny, others were glad he had begun a conversation the party needed to have. After all, the clock was ticking.

For good measure, Jim O'Callaghan had also returned to the plinth to film some comments for TV, as well as offering other interviews yielding sound bites for radio bulletins, and was asked what consequences there would be if his disagreement with Frances Fitzgerald could not be remedied.

'Look, if we don't get this sorted out, the government will collapse, okay? I think that would be crazy, for the government to collapse.'

* * *

It was into this storm that Katherine Zappone arrived home from Washington State on Monday lunchtime, and announced an appearance before journalists at 4.30 p.m. that afternoon. Enda Kenny had already departed for Cork by the time of Zappone's return, politely overruling the advice of other ministers who wanted him to stay in Dublin and speak with Zappone directly. The Taoiseach's diary for the day had five different appointments, including the jobs announcement that lunchtime and a public meeting on Brexit that night, and Kenny felt it would create a needless air of crisis to abandon a public schedule and retreat to his office. Besides, the Taoiseach's diary was carefully curated, and Kenny hated accepting invitations only to let down his prospective hosts.

Other ministers also wanted to speak to Zappone directly before she had a chance to make any further public pronouncements. Frances Fitzgerald, still hurt by the rushed statement the previous Friday, knew Zappone was due back in Ireland at around lunchtime and eagerly reached out to the Department of Children, asking the ministerial handlers to arrange a face-to-face meeting between the pair. Her overtures were unsuccessful: just ten minutes before her appointment with the media, Zappone texted her Cabinet colleague saying a meeting would not be possible. Those in Fitzgerald's circle were not impressed at what they saw as Zappone's own self-interest, prioritising her own reputation above the harmony of the Cabinet. One colleague recalled the Tánaiste being 'livid' that a request for a one-on-one meeting on such a sensitive topic would be so simply dismissed. 'If she had been a Fine Gael minister,' another lamented, 'there's no way she would have just stonewalled a request like that.'

The press gaggle on the fabled plinth of Leinster House can often be an unruly beast, and politicians with varying experience in public address have different ways of handling the crowd. A regular complaint at so-called 'doorsteps' is that, with TV cameras occupying the places directly in front of the politician, other reporters are pushed out to the sides – prompting the politician, in turn, to face those reporters as they answer their questions, and to look away from the camera as a result. Some seasoned politicians know that this lessens their chance of appearing on the TV news, and pointedly fix their gazes forward, even if it means facing away from the reporter to whom they are speaking. Others, whose nature is more personable, cannot resist looking directly towards their inquisitor.

It was a sign of both Zappone's personality and her relative political youth – sixty-three years old, but less than a year in the Dáil, and a rookie in the pressured environment of a hot-topic press conference – that her Monday afternoon doorstep was very much of the latter variety. Crowded by journalists gathered around her in a U-shape, the Minister for Children sought to look each of them in the eye as she made some opening remarks, which sent her in an almost theatrical pivot as she sought to make eye contact with the reporters who were effectively formed into an arc around her. Those in the broadcast trade, with microphones fixed on a small podium, regularly had to ask her to face the cameras simply so that her comments could be clearly picked up.

Zappone's unusual speaking manner had two results. The primary one was that much of what she said was useless for broadcast, especially for TV. While radio could salvage some of the audio by increasing the volume level wherever needed, TV simply could not carry clips where you could only see the back of her head.

Secondly, however, it led reporters present to conclude that Zappone was nothing but earnest. Frustrating though it was at times, the minister's wish to look her questioner in the eye had a charming effect. Other ministers attached to a scandal of such severity might simply have gone out and stuck to the script, prepared to perform moral gymnastics if circumstances demanded it. If they knew their comments were not entirely truthful, they might not be inclined to look their inquisitor in the eye. Zappone, who either had not been briefed on the positions of her colleagues or simply did not feel obliged to adhere to their stories, came across to eyewitnesses as earnest and trustworthy. From afar the effect was less pronounced: one Cabinet colleague, watching later footage on TV, believed their colleague was guilty of hamming it up. 'The arms were flapping and gesticulating,' they recalled. 'I thought it was the most theatrical performance.'

Whether natural or not, the disarming effect of Zappone's animated performance was crucial, as the content of her remarks was to add another dollop of drama to the affair – and to suddenly escalate the dangers to the Taoiseach.

Zappone's press conference was not organised simply so that she could wade into a political scandal and start pointing the finger. As the minister responsible for Tusla, she had to find out whether lessons could be learned from this catastrophic error – or, indeed, if any similar mistakes had been made in the past.

Zappone was therefore announcing that she had asked HIQA, the health services watchdog, to undertake its own independent statutory investigation into how Tusla manages allegations of child abuse. HIQA's chief executive would be asked to help draw up the terms of reference, and Zappone would seek input from Máire Whelan to make sure it didn't overlap or conflict with the Charleton inquiry.

That, of course, was not really what journalists wanted to ask about. After some cursory questions about this new inquiry and how long it might take to report, reporters moved on to the bigger question of why Zappone hadn't spoken up at Cabinet or shared the outcome of her McCabe meeting with any of her colleagues.

'I spoke with the Taoiseach prior to the Cabinet meeting last week, to let him know that I had met with the McCabes, [and] that we had discussed Tusla,' Zappone said. 'I didn't go into the detail of any of the allegations that I was aware of, but I did indicate to him that that was the nature of the conversation.'

Boom.

Immediately, journalistic eyelids were twitching. Amid all the rancour between Fine Gael and Fianna Fáil, and the allegation that Frances Fitzgerald was informed of the Tusla file a day before the rest of the nation, had Enda Kenny himself also known more than he had let on?

There was more. 'My advisors were also in touch with the Taoiseach's office to let them know that I was going to meet with the McCabes prior to that.'

There was plenty of new information here. Zappone was asked: what exactly did you tell the Taoiseach before Cabinet? 'I said to the Taoiseach that I had met with the McCabes. He already knew that, because he had been informed of that; [and]

that I had discussed Tusla, as part of that discussion … I gave no more details than that.' Did he ask any further questions about it? 'No, he did not.'

The present author was one of those in attendance who understood how the Taoiseach's story was now being dramatically undermined. 'Can I just ask, for clarity, Minister: is that the first time you directly told the Taoiseach about your meeting? That it had been at official level before that, and *that* was the first time you had spoken to him?'

'… that I had spoken to An Taoiseach,' Zappone nodded, completing the question almost before it was finished. 'Yes. That is correct.'

Danger here. Kenny had been on live national radio the previous day, and recalled – with some specific detail – his conversation with Zappone, where his minister had told him of plans to meet with Maurice and Lorraine McCabe. 'I said to her, "Well, if, if you do have a meeting, make sure that you have a thorough account of it …"' Yet here, a mere twenty-seven hours later, Zappone was not only disputing the Taoiseach's account: she was now claiming this conversation had never happened at all.

What's more, Zappone had now unwittingly cast further doubt on the Taoiseach, by revealing he knew of *some* Tusla connection to the McCabe scandal before Tuesday's Cabinet meeting. Kenny and his press team had insisted he knew nothing of this dramatic and damaging Tusla file until the Thursday evening's *Prime Time* programme. Now, here was a minister in his own government saying she had mentioned a Tusla involvement in the Maurice McCabe affair two days earlier, before a full meeting of the government.

Suddenly Frances Fitzgerald being questioned by Fianna Fáil was not the biggest problem facing the administration. The fissures from within, which had seemed to momentarily close up twenty-four hours earlier, were now gaping large once more. Enda Kenny had been so fulsome in his defence of Katherine Zappone ... and now Zappone, ever so casually, was completely undermining him. Whether she knew it or not – and Fine Gael ministers could not settle on a common position about whether she did – the Minister for Children had just, dramatically, thrown her own Taoiseach under a bus.

That's it, the reporters remarked, as they scurried back inside to file this dramatic new information. *There's no way Fianna Fáil can back this.* Sinn Féin's motion of no confidence would be heard in the Dáil in little more than forty-eight hours. Surely – *surely!* – there was no way Fianna Fáil could declare confidence in Enda Kenny if his account of a national scandal was being openly contradicted by one of his own ministers.

* * *

While Zappone was speaking, an email landed in the inboxes of national newsrooms from Seán Costello & Company solicitors. It carried a statement from 'our clients Maurice McCabe & family':

> We have endured eight years of great suffering, private nightmare, public defamation, and state vilification arising solely out of the determination of Maurice to ensure that the Garda Síochána adheres to decent and appropriate standards of policing in its dealings with the Irish people.
>
> Our personal lives and our family life, and the lives of our five children, have been systematically attacked in a number of ways by agencies of the Irish state and by people working for those agencies.

These events have, one way or another, given rise to a long series of state investigations [...] All of these have taken place in private.

We have also been the subject of a long and sustained campaign to destroy our characters in the eyes of the public, and public representatives and in the eyes of the media.

Today we have heard one Minister, Simon Harris, state that we are entitled to 'truth and justice'.

Then came the punchline:

We wish to make it clear that we are definitely not agreeable to that entitlement being wholly postponed so that another Commission of Inquiry can conduct a secret investigation behind closed doors and make a report, into which we have no input as of right, in nine or eighteen months' time.

We are entitled to the truth today – justice can follow in its wake.

Maurice and Lorraine McCabe had been through the wringer. They had been at the centre of countless different State inquiries at various levels – but none of them had been conducted in public. As the statement continued, it became clear this had come at a cost:

Our experience of the O'Higgins Commission is too fresh in our minds to allow for a repetition. Although that Commission investigated a number of serious instances of malpractice in the policing function in Bailieborough and upheld Maurice's complaints in respect of all of them, the public has never been made aware that, throughout the proceedings before that Commission, Maurice, at the hands of the legal team representing the current Commissioner, was cast in the role of culprit and/or defendant, and as a person making those complaints in bad faith and without cause.

When challenged in that respect, that legal team sought and obtained confirmation from the present Commissioner that they did so on her personal instructions.

Because the 2004 Act prohibits under pain of criminal law the publication of the actual evidence tendered to such Commission, the public has little or no appreciation of what was done, and attempted to be done, to Maurice in the course of its hearings.

For example, against the backdrop of the current Tusla controversy, the entirely false allegation made of sexual abuse in 2006 against Maurice was repeatedly the subject of attempts at introduction in the proceedings for the purposes of discrediting his motives and testimony.

The statement also pointed out that the full transcripts of the O'Higgins Commission had been lodged with the Department of Justice. In that light, the McCabes noted, this claim should be easy to prove.

For these reasons, we have consistently submitted that any further inquiry into these matters be a public inquiry.

The truth now.

The statement concluded with six questions querying how the allegation was handled by Tusla and the Gardaí, which the McCabes believed were already in the government's gift to answer. Those answers could be offered quite quickly, they felt, but the bigger issues deserved a public inquiry – one that operated in full view, with no cloak of confidentiality.

A commission of investigation would no longer cut it. If there were to be a State inquiry, it would have to be done in public, with open doors and real-time reporting of the contributions being made.

That, in effect, meant one word: tribunal.

Tribunals had become something of a dirty word in Irish political discourse. On paper, the concept of a tribunal was straightforward: a judge hears evidence in public, with the power to compel oral and written evidence, and investigates the issues they are specifically asked to investigate. In practice, they had become long and expensive trawls of information, complicated by legal challenges and absent witnesses, enormous sinkholes of resources, producing findings that carried no prosecutorial standing and which could still be challenged in court. Two different tribunals into political corruption set up in 1997 had taken until 2011 and 2012 to conclude. Nobody had any appetite for similar lengthy inquiries: in fact the idea of a 'commission of investigation', with a similar format but with hearings in private, was created simply so that further inquiries did not require such expensive and time-consuming litigation.

What a commission of investigation gained in privacy, it lost in transparency. As the McCabes had pointed out, it was illegal for anyone to reveal whatever evidence was given behind closed doors (save for any occasion where a commission agreed to conduct its business in public, which none had ever done). Maurice McCabe felt his fingers had been burned too many times with private inquiries – and with claims that the false allegation of sexual assault had been broached at the O'Higgins Commission, few could blame him.

Though the recent memory of tribunals still lingered fresh,

the near-immediate reaction of the government was to accept it. Kenny, still in Cork, was scheduled to attend a Fine Gael-organised Brexit meeting at the Clayton Silver Springs hotel and was duly doorstepped by local reporters on the way in.

'Will you have a public inquiry, Taoiseach?'

'Yeah, well,' replied Kenny, acknowledging the question rather than answering it. 'Well, I'm going to talk to Micheál Martin in the morning, actually.'

'Are you?'

'Yes.' He was still walking at full speed.

'And will you grant a full public inquiry? They [the McCabes] say they won't cooperate with a private inquiry.'

'The most effective way of finding out the truth, here,' Kenny semi-answered, pacing out of reach of the reporters and cameras.

This, in a curious way, bought some vital time for the government and immediately changed the political dynamic in two ways. Firstly, if the premise of a commission of investigation was to be abandoned and a tribunal pursued instead, the clock was effectively reset back to zero. Pretty much everything which had already been done for the commission had to be redone for a tribunal: the Cabinet would have to agree to hold one, terms of reference would have to be produced (though Iarfhlaith O'Neill's recommendations would still be used as the foundation), and the Dáil and Seanad would have to be given a chance to debate and approve them.

That timeline could not be met inside forty-eight hours. If all sides were determined to make sure McCabe was given a fair public hearing and a chance to vindicate his name – as they all said they were – then they would have to hold fire. Journalists, scuttling back inside Leinster House after hearing Katherine

Zappone undermining her Taoiseach, now realised that the political anger built up over the McCabe/Tusla story would have to be parked. Opposition TDs knew, too, that the McCabes' intervention might have to take precedence: after all, if the government collapsed on Wednesday night, it could take months to set up the inquiry that everyone felt the McCabes deserved.

The Taoiseach was being contradicted by one of his own ministers, while the Tánaiste was being contradicted by the party keeping her in power. Yet Maurice McCabe – having accidentally brought the government to the precipice of disaster – now seemed to have accidentally saved it.

Or had he? Nobody had heard from the Independent Alliance, whose members were normally quite talkative. One TD would later admit that, while the contradiction posed clear political problems, they were not all too surprised that Enda Kenny could not be taken at his word. 'Enda was prone to porkies,' they said. 'He had the whole hail-fellow-well-met routine, he'd *plamás* you and slap you on the back – "Don't worry, we'll get that sorted for you, no problem." But then when you'd look at the next Budget there'd be no funding for it.'

What's more, few had known – until Kenny revealed it to reporters in Cork – that Micheál Martin had asked for a meeting with the Taoiseach, and that the two leaders would meet the following morning.

That was the second way in which the political wind had now shifted. Fine Gael TDs, already unhappy at how Kenny was allowing himself to be contradicted by a subordinate, were almost furious to hear the Taoiseach explicitly name-check his Fianna Fáil counterpart in such a way. Confidence and supply was only nine months old, and nobody was entirely sure that Fine

Gael and Fianna Fáil had permanently buried their historical hatchet. Seeing Kenny on TV, clearly uncomfortable with any press scrutiny – and implying an inability to make any concrete decisions without first consulting Micheál Martin – now elicited serious anxiety elsewhere in the party. For many, it was the most naked admission yet of how Fine Gael had been lumbered with responsibility but not blessed with power.

'He's Micheál's lapdog now,' one TD said. 'The Taoiseach has served the party well for over a decade but his time is over.' Across the country, many Fine Gael TDs watching the evening news reached a similar conclusion: the present situation could not be tolerated any longer, and some drastic change was required. Just hours after Noel Rock had been scolded for daring to question Enda Kenny, a growing mass of party colleagues was now sharing his point of view.

Others were becoming concerned that Kenny had simply given himself too much work to do. 'The whole thing was so fraught,' one felt, 'with deep-running seismic cracks at that stage, that Enda found it tremendously hard to hold all the disparate elements together, while also simultaneously tanking in the polls.'

The motion of no confidence was now two days away, and Micheál Martin held the government's fate in his hands. 'We were very, very concerned that Fianna Fáil would end it all,' another TD conceded, fearing that the historical antagonism between the Civil War parties could no longer be buried. 'It was the perfect time for Micheál Martin to do the job.'

DAY 8

Tuesday, 14 February 2017

The complex interlocking of shifting political landscapes had now completely consumed life in Leinster House. Every chance corridor conversation, every water-cooler whisper now centred on the same series of questions. *Did Zappone realise she was throwing Enda under a bus?* some inquired. *Did she care?* would come some replies. *Did McCabe deliberately try to buy time for the government?* wondered others. *Has he actually done that?* some would counter. *Are we heading for an election?* most simply wondered, with a universal reply: *Who knows?*

The previous evening's intervention from Maurice and Lorraine McCabe – and the likelihood of Cabinet approval for their requested tribunal – featured strongly in the morning newspapers. 'Nothing but a public inquiry will do', led the *Irish Examiner*, over a giant picture of the couple, whose statement was published in full inside. 'There is growing pressure for a public inquiry into an alleged orchestrated smear campaign and attacks by agencies of the State against Sgt Maurice McCabe,' wrote Juno McEnroe, who said the Cabinet was set 'to scramble to set up the inquiry in a bid to quell public anger and mounting criticism'.

The Irish Times' more sedate headline, 'McCabe tribunal expected to be set up', belied the more dramatic text underneath. 'A full tribunal of inquiry into the alleged smear campaign against Garda whistleblower Sergeant Maurice McCabe is now likely after a day of division and contradiction in Government,' it said.

'Taoiseach Enda Kenny and Fianna Fáil leader Micheál Martin will meet this morning in an attempt to agree a way forward through a controversy that has brought the nine-month-old minority Government to the brink of collapse.'

The *Irish Daily Mail* also led with the story, under the booming all-capitals headline, 'We need a public inquiry' ('A full public inquiry into the McCabe smear scandal seemed likely last night after Enda Kenny prepared to bow to pressure for one'). Even the Irish edition of *The Sun*, which didn't often lead with political stories, carried the story as its lead, summarising the McCabes' statement under the heading, 'Our 8-year private nightmare'.

Other papers focused on the internal rift at Cabinet, and the contradictions between Enda Kenny and Katherine Zappone. 'Day of days as Kenny's grip on power loosens', ran the dramatic headline on the *Irish Independent*. 'A day that was made up of a series of seismic political shocks has spelled the dusk of Enda Kenny's term as Taoiseach,' wrote Kevin Doyle and Niall O'Connor. 'As Fine Gael ministers and TDs openly spoke of replacing Mr Kenny, Fianna Fáil fell short of toppling the Government – for now.'

The *Irish Examiner* carried a separate off-lead story to outline the inconsistencies, pointing out that Zappone's contradiction of her boss 'raises further questions about what the Government knew about the scandal and is set to put additional pressure on what is already a weak minority government'.

The Irish edition of *The Times* put it plainly: 'The government was under severe pressure last night as the Taoiseach became embroiled in the Garda whistleblower scandal.' The simple statement was true: Katherine Zappone's contribution had led the scandal to the door of the country's most powerful office.

* * *

It was set to be a testy day. It being Tuesday, the Cabinet was due to meet in full session – its first meeting since the Maurice McCabe Tusla file came to light. *The Irish Times* predicted that 'a stormy Cabinet meeting is expected today, with Minister for Transport Shane Ross seeking answers as to why Ministers were kept in the dark at last week's meeting about the false abuse allegations about Sgt McCabe being made to Tusla'.

Indeed, the position of the Independent Alliance was still somewhat unknown. The gang of five had regularly complained of being sidelined or left out of the loop on major issues in the past – one refrain was that Fine Gael gave better information to its outside supporters in Fianna Fáil than it offered to its own coalition partners. Shane Ross's group had styled itself as an internal guardian against reckless use of power; part of its practice was to involve itself in other ministers' roles under the guise of collective responsibility. If the group were to remain consistent, it would almost certainly voice concern about Katherine Zappone not sharing pertinent information about a role for Tusla in a public inquiry. The few signals emerging from the Independent Alliance were, indeed, that this was the case. But the Alliance had descended into radio silence before Zappone had cast questions over the Taoiseach. Any grievance it had against Zappone, by extension, was now held against Enda Kenny too.

The notion of collective responsibility may have seemed abstract, but the weekly Cabinet agenda included a conscious and explicit reminder that each and every minister was responsible for each and every department. Every week, ministers are presented with the Dáil and Seanad agendas, including the motions or bills tabled by opposition parties in their allotted time slots. Ministers are required to decide a common response – whether the motion should be accepted or not, and if not, whether to table a counter-motion instead.

Motions of confidence usually met with a predictable response. If an opposition party wanted to use the Dáil's time to discuss sacking the government, the government would traditionally table a counter-motion. Sinn Féin's motion ('that Dáil Éireann has no confidence in the Government and calls on the Taoiseach and his entire Cabinet to resign forthwith to allow fresh elections') would therefore be countered with a simple motion, from the Government, declaring confidence in itself.

But before facing any internal dissent at a Cabinet meeting, Kenny had to deal with other issues: a crisis meeting with the leader of the opposition, the man with the power to bring him down.

Bilateral meetings between the leaders of Fine Gael and Fianna Fáil were still fairly rare events. Under the confidence and supply arrangement, meetings between the party leaders were intended to act as a 'clearing house' – a forum through which unresolved disputes could be thrashed out. Only a handful of those meetings had been held in the nine-month lifetime of the confidence and supply deal. Martin had sought the meeting on this premise: Jim O'Callaghan and Frances Fitzgerald had been unable to square their differences on the conversation in the Dáil bar, and so the dispute was escalated up the food chain for the two leaders to consider.

Early into the 9.30 a.m. meeting it became clear that Micheál Martin had not sought the meeting simply to inform Kenny that the government deal was being torn up. Instead, Martin wanted to be debriefed on exactly what had transpired over the previous week and what ought to be done about it. Kenny assured Martin that a public inquiry *would* be set up into the whole treatment of McCabe, in line with the whistleblower's (and Fianna Fáil's) own wishes. Martin handed over some proposals for the terms of reference, on which O'Callaghan had worked overnight, and Kenny agreed to give them some thought.

As Martin saw it, the McCabes' demand for a tribunal was now the supreme concern: a snap election would only serve to delay the inquiry that Maurice and Lorraine McCabe rightly sought. The two leaders now had a point to rally around: kick out Enda Kenny and there would be no inquiry.

Privately, Fianna Fáil had other, more strategic reasons to keep Kenny in situ. Micheál Martin had long made up his mind: while Fine Gael panicked about Fianna Fáil's position, there had actually been little to fear. Martin knew the stakes for his own leadership if a snap election did not go to plan, and had opted for caution. The party's public justification for propping up a Fine Gael government was that it was the only government the present Dáil could offer. Terminating that government after nine months, sending the country back into electoral flux simply to harvest a few more seats, would swiftly be labelled as naked opportunism – with political damage to follow.

That was a risk Martin could not take. Fianna Fáil was still in the midst of a long-term project to rehabilitate itself with Irish voters after the deep national trauma of losing fiscal sovereignty at the end of 2010. Convincing the electorate that Fianna Fáil was worthy of being returned to power would not be easy, but central to the task was demonstrating that the party could keep its word and that when agreements were reached, they were honoured. The confidence and supply deal was intended to last for three budgets, and Martin would fervently guard the party's reputation in making sure that deal was honoured.

On another level, the internal harmony of the government was far from secure and an election might still happen without Fianna Fáil having to prompt it. If it did, Martin's unsettled backbenchers would take comfort (and immense *schadenfreude*) in Fine Gael's turmoil. In a snap election, with its main opponent in total disarray, Enda Kenny's continued leadership would be Fianna Fáil's greatest weapon.

Frances Fitzgerald, who had been so baffled three days earlier when Martin took issue with her account of discovering the Tusla file, was now beginning to theorise why Fianna Fáil had so dramatically upped the ante on her. Martin could not unload his arsenal on Enda Kenny in case he caused a fatal injury. If the Taoiseach had to be reluctantly protected, the unfriendly fire would be aimed at the Tánaiste instead.

***

Martin and Kenny's meeting had been expected to take little more than half an hour, but the bilateral encounter went on for almost three times the scheduled duration. The Cabinet meeting, pencilled in for 10 a.m., did not get underway until 11.30 a.m.

With Fianna Fáil's support in the bank, the Cabinet meeting itself should have been relatively routine. But, just as Kenny had repelled the immediate threats from outside, the internal tensions simmered and came to the boil. Shane Ross and Finian McGrath, already aggrieved at being left out of the loop on the Tusla problem, took umbrage at the problems simply being played down and ostensibly buried, with no proactive attempt on the government's part to root out what seemed like major cultural issues within the Gardaí. Not only that, but their concern about the overlapping and contradictory statements of Kenny and Zappone, Fitzgerald and O'Callaghan ran deep. Ross informed the room that he had spoken to Maurice McCabe and was effectively anointing himself as McCabe's spokesman within the Cabinet ranks.

With so much focus on the uneasy alliance of Fine Gael and Fianna Fáil, the Independent Alliance might legitimately have felt overlooked as a vital ingredient of government. It was understandable that the gang of five might want to flex their muscles and make it clear that Micheál Martin was not the only one who needed to be kept happy. Shane Ross, in particular, was reported to be apoplectic over Zappone's failure to reveal her meeting with McCabe, or to relay the hugely sensitive details that the whistleblower had brought to her attention. It was clear to all present, witnesses later recounted, that the Alliance's *de facto* leader was practically seething at being kept out of the loop.

One Independent Alliance source reflected on the group's competing interests. The government was barely nine months old and each of its members had their own pet projects that needed more time to bring to fruition. 'We all had our own issues to achieve,' the member said. 'We never wanted to pull the plug. Even through every issue that came up … We all had our own issues that we wanted to achieve. So every time an issue was raised, there was never a wish to pull the plug. It was a case of, "we'll take a hit, and refocus".'

This 'shopping list' had never been a secret. Shane Ross was thrust back into the Dáil by the people of Dublin Rathdown partly on the premise of reopening the shuttered Garda station in the constituency village of Stepaside. Finian McGrath wanted an upgrade to hospital facilities in Beaumont, and to ratify the United Nations Convention on the Rights of Persons with Disabilities. John Halligan had promised his Waterford constituents he would provide a twenty-four-hour catheterisation laboratory, a vital component in providing effective cardiac services and averting the need for heart attack patients to be sped to Dublin or Cork. Kevin 'Boxer' Moran was elected in the wake of devastating floods and wanted investment in flood defences, in particular along the Shannon that bisected his hometown, Athlone. Seán Canney had similar concerns, as well as looking to address imbalances in how the west was funded by comparison to the more urban east, especially when it came to rail services.

But, at the same time, the Alliance could not simply be seen to roll over. 'We were putting it up to him … making it very clear to him that we weren't kidding around, that we were near [to] going over the cliff. There was genuine anger and upset over how the whole thing had been handled … It was about our role in government and the stupidity of how the last week had been handled.'

The Alliance ministers were not the only ones with grievances. The Fine Gael contingent, too, wanted to vent at Katherine Zappone's failure to share materially important information in the confines of a confidential Cabinet discussion. Her belated volunteering of salient details had proved monumentally damaging to the collective government. Moreover, though Zappone was acting within the boundaries of her own ministerial prerogative, Fine Gael remained aggrieved at Friday's press release shambles – where the original problematic statement was released without the approval of the Merrion Street mandarins – and Monday's PR catastrophe, when Zappone had thrown the Taoiseach under a bus after turning down the chance to confer with the Tánaiste first.

This was serious business and nobody wanted to cut the Cabinet meeting short. One minister present observed that it was better to allow the Alliance to vent inside the walls of the Cabinet room, rather than sending them out into the embrace of journalists who would be only too happy to give them a forum to complain. If Shane Ross wanted to vent his grievances, and receive assurance that there was not some grand conspiracy being pursued against Maurice McCabe, it was better to do so in a calm environment behind closed doors.

The downside was that with an already lengthy agenda, including the draft of a new law on drink-driving and the annual reports of a few State agencies to be approved, the belated Cabinet meeting dragged on much longer than anyone had anticipated. An ordinary Cabinet meeting would end by 1 p.m., giving ministers a chance to grab lunch (and the Taoiseach a few minutes to prepare) before Leaders' Questions kicked off the Dáil's working week at 2 p.m. The result of the Independent Alliance's accidental filibuster was that the meeting wasn't finished – or anywhere close to it – by 2 p.m. The remaining items on the agenda would have to be addressed when the meeting resumed, presumably at around teatime, when Enda Kenny would be released from Dáil business.

Detail on the remaining items on the agenda was scant – and it was not clear whether the government had been able to perform the one task that should have been routine. One of the routine items on a Cabinet agenda is to consider the motions or bills being tabled by opposition parties, and to affirm the government's collective response. Sinn Féin's motion of no confidence, then, ought to have been quickly dealt with: the easy response would be for the government to table a simple counter-motion, asking the Dáil not to withdraw its confidence, but instead to restate it. Further, under Dáil rules, a motion of confidence would take precedence over all other business – and ought to have been scheduled accordingly.

But as 2 p.m. rolled around, with Enda Kenny due in the chamber to face the fire of the opposition, there was no sign of the motion of confidence. The Dáil schedule hadn't been changed to accommodate it, and it hadn't yet appeared on the Oireachtas's online document management system.

It seemed, for all the world, as if the Government of Ireland was unwilling or unable to declare confidence in itself – with the suspicion being that the Independent Alliance provided the hold-up. That fear was bolstered by the fact that, as TDs gathered in the Dáil chamber for Leaders' Questions at 2 p.m. – and other ministers were filing into the chamber to sit alongside Kenny, in unspoken solidarity with their party leader – the five members of the Alliance were nowhere to be seen.

* * *

'Happy Saint Valentine's Day,' remarked the Ceann Comhairle, Seán Ó Fearghaíl, with a wry smile as business got underway.

'We will try to avoid a massacre,' replied Micheál Martin.

For all the focus on Kenny's travails, Martin was not in an easy position either. The country was demanding political heads on a plate – including that of the Garda Commissioner – but Martin, having merely demanded a public inquiry and already secured it, could not immediately launch a new offensive. He also faced the tricky situation of needing to lead the attack on Kenny, but not going so far that he couldn't still help the government survive the motion from Sinn Féin the next night.

Instead, Martin told the Dáil of going to meet the McCabes in their home in Mountnugent, Co. Cavan, just inside the border with Co. Meath. He told of seeing the 'truly shocking' Tusla file for himself, and how he had concluded that there had been 'a campaign to undermine the integrity of Maurice McCabe because he was proving to be a major thorn in the side of senior people within An Garda Síochána.' He concluded, for the benefit of the public record, with a call for the public inquiry he had already secured.

Kenny, in turn, was happy to confirm that the Cabinet – which seemed not to have time to state confidence in itself – did at least have the time to formally agree that the (private) commission of investigation would be dumped, and a (public) tribunal of inquiry pursued in its place. 'Sergeant McCabe has pointed out the litany – the appalling litany – of his treatment. There is nothing worse in this country than being called a sexual abuser, and it has to be soul-destroying for any individual or their family to have to put up with that.'

Martin, now treading the line between needing to land punches and needing to keep his opponent alive, offered a guarded response. A tribunal was welcome, he said, but if the inquiry were being set up on foot of the complaints of Maurice McCabe and Dave Taylor, the Tusla file would not fall within it. 'I also want to put it to you that the establishment of a tribunal of inquiry – and it hasn't been established yet – is no basis for ministers not coming in here to this House, to answer questions to the House, and to be accountable to the House in relation to the Tusla file.'

He went on. 'I do think there is an onus – because this is an important chamber in terms of accountability – that ministers, this week, should come before the House to answer in relation to their responsibilities pertaining to it. And to give straight clear answers, which may clear up a lot. Because there has been incoherence at the heart of the Government's response to the Tusla file. That is to put it mildly.' Bringing ministers in to account for themselves is 'what parliaments normally do', he added.

Kenny would have known before stepping into the room that the calamitous contradictions between himself and Katherine Zappone, and between Frances Fitzgerald and Jim O'Callaghan, would need to be addressed. Martin's reference to the 'incoherence' of some ministers was the invitation he needed to try and do so on his own terms.

Having rebuffed Martin's demand for extra questioning by simply remarking that he was, at that moment, answering questions in the Dáil anyway, Kenny took his chance – seeking to vindicate Zappone in as self-preserving a manner as possible. 'When she informed me that she had spoken to the McCabes, that the discussion that she had with them was about allegations – false allegations – made to Tusla, she did not indicate to me any issue of the detail of the discussions she had had with the McCabe family, or indeed the existence of any content of any file that you mention. Obviously this became very public knowledge on the relevant *Prime Time* programme.'

Martin cocked his head and furrowed his brow as the Taoiseach continued. 'Minister Zappone is very clear that the discussions she had with Sergeant McCabe were of a confidential nature, had to respect his privacy; that these things were not in the public domain at the time that she met with him.'

At this, Kenny raised his right hand and put it across his breast. 'And I might say "mea culpa" here, because I did say – and I'm guilty here of not giving accurate information … I understood, from thinking myself that I had,' – he raised his hand to touch his forehead in frustrated illustration – 'that she had asked me about meeting Sergeant McCabe in the first place. It actually was her office that consulted with my officials, who told me … so I regret that. I regret that.'

The opposition benches broke into a predictable din of disbelieving and disapproving jeers. Kenny may have hoped this act of self-admonition would have been enough to ward off the hounds. Amid the wall of heckles, Kenny's final sentence was barely heard: 'She did tell me, before the Cabinet meeting last Tuesday, that she had met with him and they had discussed allegations that were false in respect of those given to Tusla.'

Not only did this appear to be at odds with what he had said barely a minute earlier – had Zappone told him about the nature of the false allegations, or hadn't she? – but the Taoiseach was now confirming, on the record of the Dáil, that in fact he had known about Tusla holding false claims against Maurice McCabe a full two days before the *Prime Time* programme – and about twenty-seven hours before Brendan Howlin rose to his feet in the Dáil and informed the nation that McCabe was being smeared as a sex offender.

This was not only a new admission, but also a total contradiction of what his spokesman had repeatedly told reporters in the previous days.

The immediate significance of this did not seem to occur to Sinn Féin's Gerry Adams, the next speaker, who told the Taoiseach that if he wanted to know why Sinn Féin was tabling a motion of no confidence in his government, he need look no further than his 'mea culpa moment' just a moment earlier. 'The tipping point for Sinn Féin,' he said, 'was the way your government dealt with the campaign of vilification, smear, and false allegations against Garda Sergeant McCabe.' In Adams' eyes, not only had Kenny and Fitzgerald failed to fix the problem, they had 'enabled' it.

Martin's gentler tone of questioning had caught Kenny in sombre form. Adams' accusatory timbre was more akin to a red rag to a bull. 'Well, you're an absolute hypocrite,' he opened, 'after what you did, and what you said, to former Senator Máiría Cahill, and what you did and didn't do in respect of "safe houses", and "safe houses" this side of the border, where sexual abuse was conducted by members of your organisation on young men. You are an absolute hypocrite.' The mere mention of Máiría Cahill's name was enough to raise partisan tensions: hailing from a family of well-known Belfast republicans, Cahill was the subject of a 2014 BBC documentary where she accused Adams and Sinn Féin of helping to shield a former IRA member who raped her in 1997. Becoming a public ambassador for other assault victims, Cahill was eventually co-opted into the Seanad by Labour.

With his troops now more exercised behind him, firing verbal barbs to beat the band, Kenny continued his attack. 'If you want to play politics with an issue that is so sensitive and so personal that it goes to the very heart of the public soul of Ireland, then do so. But I don't agree with you ... it's not about running away, but about facing the issue here, which is to determine the truth.'

'Well, Taoiseach, I'm not going to rise to your bluster,' Adams retorted, to even more sneers from the government seats.

Sinn Féin's tabling of a motion of no confidence in the government was, self-evidently, intended to collapse the administration and cause a general election. Doing this, Kenny said, would render his administration unable to launch a public inquiry. 'What you want to do is bring down this government, so that this thing cannot happen.'

Next in the queue of speakers was Paul Murphy of the Anti-Austerity Alliance (AAA), whose presence posed a different challenge for the Taoiseach. Having already faced questioning from men of his own vintage, Murphy symbolised an obvious divide. On one side, Kenny, sixty-five, the calm operator of Castlebar, an earthy man of the west retaining a fine head of hair, a schoolteacher by training, never seen at work without a necktie, a master of folksy canvassing and the everyman handshake. On the other, Murphy, thirty-three, whose own father also came from Castlebar, but who had been raised in south Dublin, studied law in UCD, and who now represented some of Ireland's most disadvantaged areas; balding and shaven-headed; whose politics provoked struggle over consensus, who was more comfortable with a loudhailer than a handshake and whose only nod to the Dáil dress code was to pair a blazer with his jeans.

Murphy had become a *cause célèbre* for his role in opposing water charges, a cause which catapulted him not only into Dáil Éireann but also into Dublin Circuit Criminal Court. At the height of the campaign, he had been involved in an infamous protest at Jobstown in his Dublin South-West constituency, where the then Tánaiste Joan Burton had attended a graduation ceremony at a community college (which, by pure coincidence, had been founded by Katherine Zappone and Ann Louise Gilligan). The protest saw Murphy sitting in front of Burton's car, refusing to allow it – or the Tánaiste and her special advisor – to leave the site. This later led to Murphy and five others being charged with false imprisonment, for which trial was still awaited. The pending charges meant Kenny could not risk partisan bickering for fear of collapsing the trial.

Moreover, Murphy – deploying his legal training with an eye for fine detail – had understood the precarious nature of Kenny's narrative and went straight for the jugular. 'Taoiseach, you mentioned the truth quite a few times there. You're well known for having, let's say, a casual relationship with the truth.' ('That's outrageous,' piped up Frances Fitzgerald, seated alongside the under-fire Taoiseach, eliciting a few murmurs of agreement from their party colleagues.)

Those on the Fine Gael benches might have been aggrieved, but Murphy himself had the truth on his side. Kenny had developed a much-documented tendency to venture off script and to stretch the parameters of the truth, in largely harmless attempts to underline his point of argument. Four times in 2015 – most notably at a European People's Party conference in Madrid – he recounted a conversation with the Central Bank governor Patrick Honohan, purportedly at the height of the State's financial crisis, when Honohan warned of such crazed public panic that the Defence Forces might have been needed to guard the country's cash machines. (Why this would have been said to Kenny wasn't clear; the public's financial concern had peaked four months before he would ever take over as Taoiseach.)

Those comments had sparked a measure of anger from the opposition benches – especially when Kenny had failed to make this otherwise unsubstantiated claim when giving evidence at the Oireachtas Banking Inquiry – but they were not Kenny's only flirtations with the realms of fantasy. In January 2015 he claimed people had been calling his office, inquiring as to whether a modest increase in their net pay was a mistake; no, he could happily advise them, we've merely delivered modest cuts to payroll taxes. The incredulous reaction to this anecdote was matched only by the response to a later explanation from Kenny's spokesman that there had been no such phone calls and that Kenny was simply using 'a turn of phrase' which was not supposed to be taken literally. (This explanation would turn out to be especially prescient, given the storm Kenny was now facing.)

A month later Kenny introduced the public to a supposed acquaintance of his, the 'Man with Two Pints in His Hand'. This fabled character had supposedly complained to Kenny about the extent of the new water charge regime, which would see a lone householder hit with a net charge of €1.15 per week. 'I reminded him that one pint would pay for his water charge as a single person for a couple of weeks,' the Taoiseach told the Dáil on 17 February. The credibility of this watery story was diluted when, six weeks later, Kenny recounted a near-identical exchange with another 'Man with Two Pints', who he also knew to be single, the previous week. The watching media were most amused. Had Kenny met the same man, and conducted the same exchange, twice in a few weeks? Had he happened to meet two different men, both of whom were single, known to the Taoiseach and carrying two pints in their hand? Or had he, perhaps, invented a convenient everyman to downplay the financial cost of these hated new water charges? The media, in reaching its verdict, had an obvious clue: Kenny's second encounter with his sociable acquaintance was reported to the Dáil on 1 April.

The crisis unfolding now, however, could not be laughed off as an innocuous April Fool. 'The admission, the "mea culpa", made by the Taoiseach a moment ago goes well beyond the man with two pints in his hand, or the army protecting the ATM machines, or the people ringing up your department to tell you how great the Budget was,' Murphy said.

Partly for posterity, and partly as evidence, Murphy read into the record the words Kenny had used on Radio 1 two days earlier – accounting for a conversation with Katherine Zappone that had clearly never taken place. The eerie silence continued as the shaven-headed deputy, thirty-two years Kenny's junior, neatly articulated the question that was now on the mind of almost everyone in the room – including many seated behind the Taoiseach on the government's own benches: 'How could you remember it in such detail, if it didn't take place?'

Acting almost as a prosecuting barrister, with the rest of the Dáil in an attentive hush, Murphy cast Kenny's omission as a grave constitutional sin, intimating that the Cabinet could not collectively carry out its functions if information was being withheld from some of its members. Kenny's belated admission of knowledge about Tusla's role meant, for example, 'that at the Cabinet meeting on Tuesday, you knew about Tusla and you didn't brief the Cabinet; it means you consciously didn't include [the Tusla file] in the terms of reference [for the proposed commission of investigation], and that you misled the public on RTÉ.

'Having admitted that moments ago,' Murphy inquired, 'how can you now continue as Taoiseach?'

Kenny had been able to shake off Gerry Adams' complaints by reverting to simple party political mode. With this off the table for Murphy, the Taoiseach sufficed himself with a slightly self-comforting comment on the topic at hand. 'It is a funny thing,' he opened, 'that when you come to the House and the people, in this position, and you actually tell the truth, that you get pilloried also. There are many people who were here before me for many years who've made mistakes.'

Before moving to the substantive part of his answer – that questions had arisen, an inquiry was needed and that such an inquiry must be given time to inquire – Kenny again sought to clear up the confusion regarding his own story, and that of Katherine Zappone, who he said 'did not refer to any of the details of the discussion with the McCabes, the existence of a file in Tusla, or the information contained in that file'.

He added: 'It is not true to say that I had any information about the existence of that, prior to the Cabinet meeting in Government Buildings here.'

Had the final sentence just been clumsily worded, or was Kenny now suggesting he had *no* knowledge of the Tusla issue before the Cabinet meeting of the previous week – despite having earlier admitted he had met Zappone beforehand to debrief? The former was the more likely explanation, but more seeds of doubt were being sown.

Murphy allowed this point to slide, continuing: 'Taoiseach, I would suggest that the reason you have made the "mea culpa" here isn't because you re-remembered what happened – but because you were caught out.' (The silence, at this point, was punctuated by a smattering of sympathetic 'hear hear' remarks from the left-leaning deputies sitting immediately behind Murphy, and on the Sinn Féin benches to his right.) 'You got caught out by the contradiction between what you said and Minister Zappone said. Just as either Minister Fitzgerald or Jim O'Callaghan were caught out.'

Kenny, looking to avoid another embarrassing restatement of his earlier error, offered what would become a regularly rehearsed line of counter-attack: suggesting that those calling for a full State inquiry were already positing its outcome and undermining the very investigation they were clamouring to support. 'You are supporting, in principle, the setting up of a tribunal of inquiry,' the Taoiseach commented, 'and then you prejudge its outcome before it ever starts ... A tribunal of inquiry has to be balanced, has to be fair to everybody, has to have terms of reference that include that, and then allow it to do its job.'

Kenny's reply was not without merit, but it did not address Murphy's substantial charge: that the Taoiseach had known more about the Tusla issue than he had ever let on, even to his own Cabinet, and that ministers had therefore agreed a course of action without the full facts before them.

The final inquisitor scheduled for Leaders' Questions was the independent TD Mick Wallace, who symbolised more than most the transformation in Irish political culture since the fiscal crash of 2010. Wallace had made his career as a property developer – best known for building the so-called 'Italian Quarter' of taverns and restaurants on Dublin's north quays – but was also an avowed socialist, sinking much of his property profits back into Wexford Youths Football Club, which he had founded, funded and even coached.

Despite being for all intents and purposes an independent TD, Wallace had set up a political party – 'Independents4Change' – as a common banner for independent candidates running under a common set of policy principles. Four such candidates were elected, and with three others joining its Dáil grouping for administrative purposes, Wallace now found himself at the helm of the Dáil's fourth-largest grouping and thus with the right to question the Taoiseach at Leaders' Questions.

But rather than challenge Kenny over his contradictory accounts of who-knew-what-and-when, Wallace turned his attention to Nóirín O'Sullivan, the Garda Commissioner whose own future remained a matter of open debate and was in the hands of the Taoiseach. Invoking parliamentary privilege, Wallace claimed a well-known journalist had contacted Dave Taylor in 2014, while he was still serving as Garda press officer, and informed him of plans to pursue 'a great story, which would be really damaging for McCabe'. Taylor, he claimed, had then passed on this good news to both Martin Callinan and Nóirín O'Sullivan, prompting a lengthy phone call with the latter.

If it were true, Wallace outlined, this tale would be impossible to reconcile with O'Sullivan's public claims of total innocence, disconnect from and ignorance of any smear campaign being pursued against members of the force. Conveniently for some, however, Taylor no longer had access to the mobile phones he used at the time, as they had been taken from him during an internal disciplinary inquiry. Wallace reminded his colleagues that it just so happened the officer leading this inquiry was Nóirín O'Sullivan's husband.

Diverting momentarily to Frances Fitzgerald, still sitting directly beside Kenny, Wallace insisted that the government could not be blind to the human effects felt by whistleblowers under O'Sullivan's regime. The Commissioner had 'hounded and harassed' other whistleblowers too – some of whom, Wallace knew, had written directly to Fitzgerald in complaint. 'Ye've got the information, Tánaiste. It's not like ye weren't told about it. Ye know this is going on. But ye've decided to turn a blind eye. Ye don't want to know what was happening. It just didn't suit.'

Wallace wrapped up by returning his attention to Kenny. 'If you've any interest in how we do policing in Ireland, let's change it now. Get rid of the Commissioner. Get rid of all that hierarchy – there's several assistant commissioners due for retirement anyway. Let's make a fresh start, Taoiseach, before you retire. And be seen to be doing something for policing.'

Kenny began to take some handwritten notes as Wallace concluded, trying to inject one final modicum of shame. 'There was a time when Fine Gael were seen as the party of law and order. Well, you know what? You've rubbished that.'

This claim may have been true in the eyes of many voters, but it gave Kenny an easy point on which to quibble as he removed his earpiece (which he had begun using as a hearing aid to follow contributions from the other side of the chamber) and rose to his feet. 'I disagree fundamentally with the view from Wexford, from you, on this case,' he said, launching into a summary of policing reforms already carried out under Fine Gael's watch. If Wallace wanted a worldwide trawl for the best possible candidate to lead a reformed force, he already had one: O'Sullivan may have been second-in-command under the previous Garda regime, but she had only got the top job after a global contest to scout out the best-placed talent.

There was more. This government had only recently set up a Policing Authority to take over the appointment and scrutiny of senior Gardaí, and reformed the role of the Garda Ombudsman, including giving it the power to hear complaints directly from members of the force. This amounted, in its own way, to extra encouragement and protection for whistleblowers.

It was a long-winded but somewhat triumphant note on which Kenny concluded Leaders' Questions. It had been a longer session than usual; the slot routinely ran over its allotted thirty-two minutes, but this had been an especially long bout (forty-four minutes) of hostile interrogation for Kenny, who resumed his seat with his back rigid and arched, his lips pursed, and his eyes wearily turned to the Tánaiste beside him.

Virtually all political scandals can be attributed either to corruption or incompetence. Whenever any wrongdoing is found, or failure uncovered, the dilemma of political spinners is which of the two explanations to choose and how best to obscure that choice. Kenny knew, upon entering the room, that he would have to choose the latter explanation – that he had gone on the national airwaves and got the story wrong – and seek shelter in an innocent explanation of a momentary lapse in memory. If his mission objective was to enter the chamber, confess to his error and get out alive, he had made a fair attempt at success. The very wording of his admission – delivered through Latin with an assertive cadence – amounted to a sincere acknowledgement of his error, while also depriving his opposition of a self-flagellating 'gotcha' sound bite.

By now, however, the Fine Gael parliamentary party was fragmenting into two camps. The suspicion among Kenny's more supportive colleagues was that the ever-busy Taoiseach – so laden with meetings, briefings and encounters of all sorts – simply couldn't remember exactly how, or when, he was told of Zappone's planned meeting with the McCabes. When asked about it on radio, therefore, he simply recounted the most *probable* chain of events: that Zappone had called him up, he had given his blessing, reminded her to be diligent in taking notes and that was that. This was a painless white lie, they would argue, and too much was being made of its discovery.

But not all in Fine Gael were so forgiving or optimistic. Other TDs, though agreeing that Kenny was free of deliberate wrongdoing, were less inclined to write off the matter as a simple lapse in memory. As they saw it, Kenny was now beginning to show the physical strain of six tumultuous years in the country's highest office and the toll of spreading himself across so many subjects. They could forgive a well-intended try to cover up this momentary lapse in memory, but worried that this might not be an isolated incident. The political damage being incurred from this error was significant enough; neither Fine Gael, nor the country as a whole, could afford much more. Moreover, with Kenny already having foreseen his own eventual departure as Fine

Gael leader, and without absolute control over when the next general election would arrive, perhaps it was now time to consider alternative options.

These two rival camps, however, would have little time to confer and thrash out their position. Just as they had done for the previous week, events would soon take over.

***

The next item on the Dáil agenda, following Leaders' Questions, required TDs to sign off on the schedule for the rest of the week. In the consensus-driven era of 'New Politics' this schedule was no longer dictated by the government, but instead drawn up by the Dáil's new Business Committee, with one TD from each of the chamber's nine distinct factions.

This new consensus-driven model had worked fairly well for its eight months of existence, but one major flaw was now becoming apparent: a timetable agreed on a Thursday morning could be completely redundant if major events had unfolded before the Dáil ratified it in plenary the next Tuesday. This period was one such example. The agenda agreed five days earlier – dutifully read now into the record – was hopelessly out of date, including a proposed debate on the terms of reference for the private commission of investigation that was no longer taking place. A new meeting of the Business Committee had been set for 1 p.m. that afternoon, but abandoned because the government chief whip, Regina Doherty, was still tied up at the long-running Cabinet meeting. It was refixed for 4 p.m., but that was still over an hour away.

There were other factors in play too. Opposition TDs knew that as soon as the Tribunal was set up, the government would try to pull down the shutters, deflecting any further questioning about the Maurice McCabe affair on the basis that the Tribunal's independent work might be compromised by separate public commentary. This posed a delicate predicament for Fianna Fáil, which had already ceded some opposition momentum to Sinn Féin following the motion of no confidence and had to find some other means of flexing its muscles.

'The entire nation has been convulsed by an issue of major public concern,' Martin announced, 'and I asked the Taoiseach during Leaders' Questions if he would confirm that ministers would come before the house to answer questions in relation to their stewardship on this issue, and be accountable to the House … I would put it to you that given the enormity of this issue, that Ministers should come before the House on this issue.' Martin was effectively asking for the Dáil agenda to be suspended and for the relevant ministers to be hauled into the chamber while TDs had free rein to question them.

This was *not* the done thing in Dáil Éireann. Scheduled questions to ministers on predetermined subjects were a daily norm. A freeform session, where ministers could not rely on scripted replies, was a novel departure; putting multiple ministers in the dock at once, even more so. 'There's nothing to be worried about in coming before the Dáil,' he concluded. 'Actually, one could enlighten debate, give more coherence to the arguments, and take away a lot of the hype that surrounds this.' Other party leaders quickly lined up to endorse the proposal of dragging Kenny back in for further questioning – there was, evidently, plenty of enthusiasm to give the government another kicking.

This idea, coming almost completely out of the blue, forced the government to improvise. Schedules weren't supposed to be set like this anymore; the Dáil's relatively new Business Committee had been set up so that public squabbles on the fixing of business like this could be avoided. Micheál Martin's gambit was now asking the government to agree to a public flogging by appointment.

Kenny and Regina Doherty did their best to buy some time, proposing that an interim three-hour schedule be approved to avoid the chamber 'going dark' with no agreed agenda. The Business Committee could use that time to thrash out the request further.

But Micheál Martin, needing an opportunity to vent grievances in advance of the motion of no confidence, was having none of it. 'The ministers should come into the house and answer questions about this issue … we want answers, I think we need questions … They have to happen.'

Martin was not toiling alone: Labour's Brendan Howlin, formerly of Kenny's Cabinet, agreed. 'Nobody's going to object to the Business Committee meeting at four [p.m.], but I think because the Taoiseach is present now' – turning briefly to Kenny – 'if you just indicate, and it's a very simple matter, that he and the other two ministers will make themselves available to make statements, to take questions later in the day. I think that would satisfy the house.'

Knowing it was now inescapable, Kenny leapt to his feet before his microphone had even been turned on. 'I think we can agree to that,' he chirped, matter-of-factly. 'Short statements and a number of questions. If the Business Committee make that recommendation, Deputy Howlin, I'm happy to go along with it.'

Howlin nodded his thanks, causing Kenny to break out in a

Cheshire Cat grin. It seemed to be the only time all day that the Taoiseach had smiled.

With Kenny being cajoled into accepting the idea of a special Q&A session, the rest of the day was a *fait accompli*. The Business Committee dutifully met at 4 p.m., arranging for Kenny, Fitzgerald, Zappone and Harris to return to the chamber at 6 p.m. and give a ten-minute speech each. Each of the seven opposition groups would then get a chance to ask further questions, before the floor would be opened for an hour of further inquiries. The whole session – two and a half hours in duration – would take place under the challenging title, 'Statements of Clarification on Statements made by the Taoiseach and Ministers'.

The marathon session, if managed properly, would allow the government to lay all its cards on the table and convince the world that the grand scandal was actually no scandal at all. All it would take was for the four ministers to offer a coherent story and not to contradict each other.

Kenny was detained in the Dáil chamber for almost another hour, entertaining more sedate pre-submitted questions about his departmental duties, such as the work of his special taskforce to tackle urban disadvantage in north inner-city Dublin. As soon as he was finished, Zappone herself was due for ninety minutes of questioning on her own brief, again on less contentious issues such as the cost of childcare.

There was only one point of note about Zappone's hour-and-a-half on the government benches. A bout of Minister's Questions is a fairly standard part of ministerial duty, and every minister is rostered to attend for questions once every five weeks. This is such a routine part of ministerial life that ministers would often carry out their business alone and might only have their own junior ministers (or, at best, a lone supportive backbencher) for company. On this instance, Zappone also enjoyed the company of Leo Varadkar, who was seated alongside her.

This was unusual; there was no function Varadkar could dispose of. As Minister for Social Protection, there was nothing he could contribute during questions to the Minister for Children. Not only that, but being trapped in the chamber for ninety minutes, with only a mobile phone for company, also prevented him from doing much work anywhere else. If Varadkar was simply at a loose end, he could have passed the time sitting in his Leinster House ministerial office which was barely two minutes' walk away, where he could deal with any correspondence that might have built up while he was away.

There were three possible explanations. One was that Varadkar might have appreciated the difficulty Zappone was facing – with the government suddenly imperilled and her partly to blame – and wanted to offer moral support. A second was that, having been away for the weekend, he simply wanted to hear Zappone's account of events first-hand. A third was that, with murmurs about Enda Kenny's tenability, Varadkar pointedly wanted to be out of reach – one of Kenny's aspiring successors effectively hiding in plain sight.

Also in hiding was the Independent Alliance. Opposition TDs had keenly pointed out the group's absence from the chamber, and some of its more talkative members were not picking up the phone. That would soon change: not long before the Q&A session was due to begin, word went around from the Alliance's press handler – Catherine Halloran, the deputy government press secretary – that the group would give a press conference on the Dáil plinth at 6.15 p.m. The press corps would have to bilocate:

while Kenny was accounting for his government's actions inside, his coalition partners were outside announcing whether it would survive at all.

Many of Leinster House's journalists, meanwhile, were otherwise occupied at their weekly briefing with the government press secretary, Kenny's spokesman Feargal Purcell, where reporters would be apprised of the business disposed of at the Cabinet meeting. The briefing doubles as an opportunity for correspondents to raise other issues of the day and tease out the government's position on pertinent issues. The lion's share, predictably, was taken up by Kenny's imprecise account of his knowledge of the Tusla file on Maurice McCabe.

Purcell insisted to journalists that it 'wasn't intentional for a second' that Kenny would mislead the country as to his knowledge, or wrongly account for his interactions with one of his own ministers. So why had he then given a wrongful account? Was he becoming overwhelmed by the scale of his duties? 'No,' came the assertive answer. 'Not a bit.'

Kenny's spokesman had been dealt a tough hand, having to give an upbeat and positive 'nothing to see here' account of what was clearly becoming a major mishap. But he, as Kenny's conduit to the media, had found himself in the firing line too. Purcell had been on the front line defending the Taoiseach on Friday to insist that, despite what Zappone's department had claimed, Kenny knew nothing of Tusla's allegations against McCabe until they were documented on TV. He had stuck to that line, in good faith, when ringing around on Sunday to clarify the Taoiseach's misuse of the phrase 'private capacity'. It was now clear that Purcell – much like the journalists – was being asked to communicate a story which was quickly unravelling.

All of which led to some difficult exchanges with the media now before him. It was nothing personal, they said, but if the Taoiseach's own accounts of events could not be taken as gospel – and if the spokesman was using Kenny as his primary source of information – it followed that Kenny's spokesman could not always be believed either.

It was a fair conclusion, and one to which Purcell made no reply, other than to reassert that nobody had set out to mislead.

***

Kenny, who was notorious among journalists for being late to public events, was back in situ in the chamber a few minutes early – so much so that he asked the foreign affairs minister, Charlie Flanagan, at the opposite end of the bench, to sidle into the seat beside him and keep him company until others arrived. Flanagan lasted in the second seat for barely thirty seconds before Frances Fitzgerald and Simon Harris arrived to remove him again; it was another ninety seconds before Zappone arrived to complete the line-up.

Kenny went first and stuck to his script, channelling a certain amount of anger on McCabe's behalf ('Sexual abuse is probably the worst crime a person could be wrongly accused of … so we owe it to Sergeant McCabe and his family, and to all others about whom allegations have been made, to ensure that the truth of all of these matters is definitively established'), while also defending the government's response. He spent only a brief moment addressing his flawed account of the government's original knowledge – this time not only defending Zappone and her involvement, but actively praising her 'important work'. As the minister responsible for Tusla she had engaged with McCabe while rightly upholding his privacy in a very sensitive matter. 'I was aware of the meeting between Minister Zappone and Sergeant McCabe,' he said, 'but I was not aware of the details, or of the very serious and disturbing issues that arose at the meeting.

'In referring to this last Sunday, I mistakenly said that I had spoken to Minister Zappone before her meeting with Sergeant McCabe. That comment was inaccurate, a Leas-Cheann Comhairle,' he added, his speech punctuated by a lone guffaw of protest from the left-wing benches, bringing a scolding and dismissive glare from the Tánaiste. 'The correct sequence was that I was informed through officials in my office that the Minister intended to meet Sergeant McCabe, and last Tuesday she informed me that she *had* met Sergeant McCabe.

'However, as Minister Zappone has confirmed, she did not divulge any of the details of those very serious issues to me, or to anyone else in government. And that was absolutely the correct course of action.'

In short, Kenny had said: all I knew was that she was meeting him. I didn't know the why, where or when; and all I was told last week was that the meeting was now in the past tense. But only four hours earlier, standing in the same spot in the same room, the same man declared that he had been told Zappone and the McCabes 'had discussed allegations that were false in respect of those given to Tusla.'

Which was it? Had Kenny been told about the false information held by Tusla, or hadn't he?

Some in Fine Gael at this point continued to believe the Taoiseach's woolliness on this area was immaterial, because the 'who knew what' discussion was nothing more than a procedural quibble. It didn't matter which members of the Cabinet knew (or didn't know) about the Tusla file when the commission of investigation was being agreed, because Peter Charleton said it would be covered anyway. The bigger picture, as they saw it, was that Kenny and his Cabinet had wasted no time in setting up the highest possible form of public inquiry to get to the truth. Whether public or private, whether a commission or a tribunal, a judge would be given the powers of compellability to get hold of any documents they wanted – and force any relevant witnesses to give evidence under oath.

Given how quickly these rumours had all exploded into the public arena, those loyalists believed Kenny's actions were firm, fair and comprehensive.

Others in the party, and a growing number on other sides of the House, were not quite so forgiving. On a constitutional level, it was difficult to understand why pertinent information would be withheld from ministers when they, collectively, were discussing the scope of a major State inquiry. Could ministers really perform their duties, and be collectively responsible for the running of government, when they were all discussing an investigation but only a few of them knew what was actually being investigated?

Moreover, on a political level, even if this goose chase of 'who knew what and when' was an immaterial distraction, why was the Taoiseach so woolly on this detail? And given the huge embarrassment wrought by Kenny's radio misstep – a completely unforced error – why couldn't the Taoiseach just settle on a story and stick to it? Had his political radar malfunctioned and led him to think this mistake was unimportant? Were his advisors caught napping? Or had Kenny simply fluffed his lines for the second time in three days, just when he needed to be at his sharpest?

Frances Fitzgerald was next called to speak and address the

government's handling of this increasingly complicated and sensitive affair. She too focused on the speed at which the government was responding to the flurry of revelation, rumour and speculation. But she too was forced to address a suggestion that she knew more of the Tusla role than had been let on. Only four days previously, Katherine Zappone (or her spokesperson) had claimed the relevant ministers had been 'kept informed' of her meetings. Surely the Minister for Justice would not only have known if a colleague was meeting a well-known whistleblower, but would also have been informed about this major new development where another State agency had a role in smearing him?

'Suggestions have been made that I had knowledge of Tusla records at the time the matter was before the Government, which would have required me to amend the terms of reference. As I have repeatedly stated, this is not the case,' the Tánaiste stated emphatically. 'I was as taken aback and disturbed, watching the revelations about Tusla that were aired last Thursday, as anyone else was.' Zappone, inspecting her own script as she sat in the next seat, briefly looked up to Fitzgerald in a dispassionate sign of agreement.

Fitzgerald also stuck to her own story when it came to the Zappone/McCabe meeting. Zappone had called her on 25 January to tell her that a meeting was planned and, having previously held Zappone's current position, Fitzgerald understood the need for discretion. If a meeting was being held, it must have been on something sensitive – so if Zappone wanted to keep the content under wraps, Fitzgerald was offering her tacit support. But, she insisted, no information had been shared afterwards – so when she had been asked a week earlier, she had no information to give.

'There is no question of me having misled the Dáil in any way in what I had to say last Thursday,' she said.

This meant Fitzgerald was once again disputing Jim O'Callaghan's claim that he had informed her about the Tusla angle to the McCabe story a day earlier – but knowing that Fianna Fáil could not be kicked around, the Tánaiste made no attempt to stoke any further tensions. Instead, she said their Wednesday evening chat had been a 'constructive' discussion where O'Callaghan had put forward some helpful suggestions for the forthcoming inquiry, which Fitzgerald had accepted and adopted. 'I accept that each of our positions on this aspect of the discussion are genuinely held,' she said. 'I regret that differences have arisen between the two of us as to what exactly was said. I have always found the Deputy honourable and I know he made very helpful suggestions.' Whether Tusla had been discussed was moot, she added, given Charleton's advice that it had already fallen within his terms of reference.

Fitzgerald finished with a defence of the honourable everyday work carried out by most Gardaí and a final doomed attempt to draw a line under the furore. 'We need to get on with addressing the issues that have arisen. Today, the Government agreed in principle to establish a public tribunal of inquiry to establish the truth for all concerned in this situation, and I believe it is incumbent on us all now to get on with that work.'

Katherine Zappone hardly cut an enthusiastic figure, but the speed at which she rose from her seat – before her name had even been fully called – suggested an ambition to lay her cards squarely on the table. As she stood, the vacant seat behind her left a clear eyeline between Fitzgerald and Simon Harris. The justice minister glanced at Harris, almost as if to ask whether she had done well;

the health minister, her one-time parliamentary assistant, gave her a furtive nod.

Without offering a prologue, Zappone set about explaining her meeting with the McCabes three weeks previously – the meeting which had now superseded the Tusla file itself as the chief bone of contention. She said that while many of her Dáil colleagues might have met the McCabes in the past, and all of them would be aware of the torrid time they had endured, the Tusla file and its 'vile, graphic and false allegations' had surpassed it all: 'They told me that the most recent development, involving the information that they had received through the Freedom of Information process from Tusla, was worse than anything else that had already happened to them.'

Zappone's manner of delivery, solemn and wavering, was already emotionally charged. The final words of that paragraph were offered with a musical sigh, a cadence of lament.

The minister accepted that her own failure to share this information with colleagues was now a key grievance and tried to offer an upfront explanation for her silence. 'I was deeply conscious then and since then that it is the State that has almost destroyed this family. I was absolutely determined that, in every action I took, I would try to ensure that through my actions I, as a government minister, did not inadvertently cause them any additional hurt.'

But with only ten minutes to play with, Zappone also had to account for her statutory responsibilities – a ten-minute political defence would leave a bad taste if there were no account of the formalities. She told the Dáil that Tusla had compiled a timeline of its handling of the McCabe case, which she'd arranged to hand over to them three days after the meeting – alongside an invitation to meet its chief executive, Fred McBride, if they wished. The electronic file on McCabe had been deleted, with a single paper copy retained under lock and key, solely for the purpose of assisting the Tribunal. This was all welcome, but not enough – which was why she had asked HIQA, the health services watchdog, to investigate Tusla itself and how it handled allegations of this nature. With that formality out of the way, Zappone could return to a political defence.

The meeting with the McCabes took place on 25 January; Zappone's advisor, Patricia Ryan, had told one of her counterparts at the Taoiseach's office – Kenny's own chief of staff Mark Kennelly – about the meeting a day earlier. 'She told him that it was in relation to a complaint the McCabes had about Tusla,' Zappone said.

This was already a new claim. Kenny's spokespeople (presumably briefed by the man himself) had never said the warning given to Kenny explicitly mentioned Tusla as the topic of the meeting. The Taoiseach himself was already dithering about how much information was shared before the previous week's Cabinet. Zappone was again, nonchalantly, making statements in contradiction of her Taoiseach. But because it was offered in passing – a bland mention, with all the tone of a statement of the obvious – few, if anyone, noticed.

Zappone raced onward, abandoning her wavering delivery. Two weeks later, when it came to telling Kenny in person that the meeting had happened, 'I told him that I had met with the McCabes, that we had discussed false allegations of sexual abuse made against Sergeant McCabe to Tusla. The Taoiseach said that this would be covered by the Commission of Investigation, what we were calling it at the time. I didn't go into the detail of any of the allegations that I was aware of, but I did indicate to him that this was the nature of the conversation.'

Oh? Despite her passive tone, Zappone was peeling away another layer of Enda Kenny's story and stating explicitly that the Taoiseach knew of a false abuse claim held by Tusla about Maurice McCabe in advance of the Cabinet meeting. But more than that: if Kenny had advised that the Tusla file would already fall within the terms of reference, the conversation must have been fairly substantial. They would have had to go into a fair amount of detail in order to determine that the existing terms of reference would cover this new disclosure.

Thinking more deeply, a Pandora's box was now being opened: had Enda Kenny allowed his Tánaiste to propose an inquiry into a matter while he knew something significant and she didn't?

This assurance from Kenny was, it seemed, enough for Zappone to sit on her hands and maintain a prudent silence, even if others now quibbled with her. 'Perhaps I was overly cautious in protecting the details of the information that I had – and if this is the case, then I accept that,' she said, 'but let's be clear that incorrect information circulating about the McCabes is at the root of the horrendous damage done to this couple and their family. I, for one, did not want to risk spreading these false allegations any further.'

Hinting at the discussion with the Independent Alliance earlier in the day, Zappone added: 'In conversations I have had since, the Taoiseach and other ministerial colleagues have accepted the reasoning behind my decision and accept that it was an extremely difficult one … I accept now that some colleagues would have preferred if I had made a contribution at Cabinet. I will learn from that.'

Her dilemma was well founded. Despite the constitutional guarantee of confidential discussion, Cabinet was leaky. Reporters would often learn, within hours of the meeting – and sometimes even sooner – if a minister had broached something sensitive, or raised hell at someone else's proposal. In theory, Cabinet should have been the most leak-proof institution in the country. In practice, it was almost the opposite.

Some ministers had even taken precautions with the Cabinet agenda itself. When a minister tables an item for discussion at the next Cabinet meeting, they usually include a memo so that colleagues can become familiar with the proposal before them. Though intended to give ministers some advance notice of contentious topics, it also means sharing information with talkative colleagues who might leak it into the public domain earlier than the minister would like. To counter this, some ministers – especially those from the Departments of Finance and Justice – had now started bringing memos to Cabinet 'under the arm', where colleagues would only see a proposal a few minutes before being asked to approve it. The unfortunate result of this was that other ministers felt handcuffed, unable to make meaningful contributions (or hold collective responsibility for government actions) if they only had basic information. Zappone suggested this was a bone of contention and wanted it reviewed.

She also touched on her two statements the previous Friday – the botched attempt to add clarity to a delicate situation, which only served to heighten suspicions. The time difference hadn't helped, and while she was sticking by the first statement, she had only issued the second because of the commentary it had generated. 'I wanted to be absolutely clear I had not passed on files and information of confidential, graphic, disturbing and highly sensitive information,' she offered. She thought (rightly or wrongly) that McCabe had mentioned this Tusla file in his protected disclosure, and that she therefore had a duty of confidentiality in handling it. If this were the case, the file would have been so central that the inquiry's terms of reference would literally have been designed around it.

'People can accuse me of being politically naïve,' she added flatly. 'I don't agree, but people are entitled to their opinion. I would prefer that charge, even if I don't agree with it, rather than be the source that spread false allegations of the most horrific type even further.'

***

A few yards away, in the members' bar, the Independent Alliance were agog. 'What the *fuck*?' exclaimed one exasperated member. Faith in the Taoiseach was beginning to fray.

The Alliance five had gathered at the Dáil's main staircase at 6 p.m., intending to head down to the plinth for their 6.15 p.m. press conference, only to realise at that moment that Kenny and his three colleagues were holding court inside in the chamber. Having been absent during Leaders' Questions, the gang simply didn't realise that the impromptu Q&A had been arranged at all.

While Kenny was issuing his 'mea culpa' the Alliance had actually been holed up in Shane Ross's office along the ministerial office corridor in Government Buildings, where all five TDs and the appropriate special advisors were seeking some quiet time to talk. The Alliance had decided to swallow its pride and declare its support for Kenny and company, knowing that its members' individual goals could only be achieved if they collectively kept a grip on the levers of power. The five TDs, plus their collective corps of press advisors, were sequestered, working on a statement to express the Alliance's commitment to the government, though equally venting its annoyance at the muddled stories offered by its colleagues. 'There was a sense that something needed to be done,' one contributor remembered, 'but what was the something that needed to be done?' The statement therefore took on a greater significance, and led to some deep semantic discussions, including a lengthy debate over whether the group should describe itself as 'dismayed' or 'disturbed'.

Alliance sources later revealed that they simply had no idea what had transpired in the Dáil during Leaders' Questions and, because its whip, Kevin 'Boxer' Moran, was too busy to attend the 4 p.m. meeting of the Business Committee, were unaware of the special 6 p.m. Q&A session. 'This is one of the times that we suffer from not having a party structure,' one Alliance source said. 'On a day like that when it was all hands on deck, we had nobody who could stand outside and keep an eye on what was going on in the chamber. We were upstairs in a little bubble in Shane's office, drafting-redrafting-redrafting our statement, while downstairs the sands were shifting and what we were writing about was two-hours-ago's news.'

It was only as the Alliance five, plus handlers, marched down the Dáil staircase that they encountered a journalist who queried their timing, puzzled why the quintet would arrange a schedule clash. Puzzled – and slightly panicked at once again being kept out of the loop – the group slunk into the members' bar to watch the chamber's TV feed uninterrupted. They could enjoy a certain silence there: the bar was almost entirely empty with the rest of their colleagues in the chamber itself. It was a safe spot to sit quietly and wait for the storm to pass.

But that storm would not pass. The group, already harbouring doubts about Kenny's story (and unaware of his 'mea culpa' moment), was now utterly aghast as they watched the statements unfold. The five had no idea Zappone had spoken to Kenny ahead of the Cabinet meeting – and while it was one thing for Zappone to hold her own counsel and keep quiet, it was quite another for Kenny to know *something* and not cough it up. The Alliance had long-running anxieties about Kenny's frankness, or lack of it. This was new territory altogether – and suddenly the nerves were back.

'We always liked Frances, and we had dealt with Frances a lot, but we definitely worried about the Department of Justice at that stage, and whether it was possible for anyone to get a grasp on it at all,' one Alliance TD would later explain. The failure to simply kill the confusion, there and then, was making them very queasy indeed.

'There was already some disgruntlement that we weren't kept in the loop about the special Dáil session, the "star chamber" or whatever you'd call it,' another recalled. 'So for us to spend the day choosing our words so carefully, and then find out Enda wasn't choosing his words carefully at all ... that was rough on us. That clearly wasn't for our benefit, but it felt like a real kick in the balls.'

With a renewed bout of jitters, the five men left the bar to regroup once more. Printed copies of their statement, in which they intended to declare firm but qualified support in Kenny and his administration, were abandoned behind them.

* * *

Simon Harris's brief contribution had little to add. Lorraine McCabe had mistakenly called the Department of Health on 17

January, and the call was returned the following day. The official who spoke to Mrs McCabe realised the complaint was related to Tusla, explained to her that the agency was no longer part of the HSE or under that department's remit, and passed the message to Zappone's department instead.

Harris continued. The previous Friday he had been contacted by the head of the HSE, Tony O'Brien, who had learned that the counsellor behind the copy-and-paste error was an HSE employee at the time. That was why a day later (when Harris was about to go on radio) the HSE had issued its public statement of apology to McCabe – an apology McCabe rejected in a text message to Harris's special advisor on Saturday evening. A formal written apology had been arranged, alongside an invitation for the McCabes to meet with O'Brien in person.

With that, the floor was opened for questions. Jim O'Callaghan, top of the queue, parked any concern about the Taoiseach (or his latest contradiction) and went straight for Frances Fitzgerald. The dispute over the chat in the Dáil's members' bar – 'a quiet area of this house', as he put it – had not been resolved, and he wasn't at all happy about the way in which he had been fobbed off and contradicted. Entering his concerns onto the Dáil record, O'Callaghan put a good question to her: if Fitzgerald had agreed to consider his proposals to tweak the terms of reference, and accepted that he had mentioned a *Prime Time* programme, why wouldn't she have asked what it was about?

'He used the word "documentary",' Fitzgerald replied, addressing her remarks through the chair in the finest parliamentary decorum. 'He said to me that I needed to look at the terms of reference because if what emerged on the *Prime Time* programme – if our terms of reference did not cover it – that it wouldn't be a good place to be. It would leave, I think the phrase he used was, it would leave "egg on our face".'

Fitzgerald claimed the bulk of their twelve-minute conversation had been on the more general theme of making sure the terms of reference covered the full extent of any alleged smear campaign. O'Callaghan had specifically asked for the role of ministers to be investigated – which was why, she said, she had agreed to look at the amendments he was drafting.

'At no time did Deputy O'Callaghan mention Tusla, and if he had mentioned it – or if he had said to me he wanted a particular reference to Tusla – I would have included it. It would have been to my advantage to include it if I had been told about it, and if he had made it clear to me that Tusla – because *Prime Time* were covering it – should be included, I would have included it. It would have been totally to my advantage to come back here into the Dáil and insert Tusla – and,' she concluded, 'Deputy O'Callaghan made no mention the next day about Tusla either when he made his speech here.'

'I disagree with you,' O'Callaghan asserted, politely but firmly. 'I referred to Tusla in my conversation with you ... Is it credible that a Minister for Justice would agree to amend terms of reference, to an important Commission of Investigation, based on a television programme, and wouldn't ask what the programme was about?'

Fitzgerald disagreed, by means of a backhanded compliment that drew some giggles from the press gallery: O'Callaghan, she said, had merely made 'an extremely strong case' that the wording of the Dave Taylor clause was too narrow. Besides: if Jim was so worried about Tusla, why hadn't he mentioned it in the Dáil the following day? Surely, if any TD had feedback about the terms of reference, and a Dáil debate had been arranged specifically to hear it, they should have raised it then? 'You spent most of the time talking to me about how it circumscribed the investigation too much, and how it ought to be broader.'

Fitzgerald was now getting visibly angry. Her earlier hesitant tone had disappeared. 'You wanted to be absolutely clear – which I accepted in full, your bona fides in relation to it! – you wanted the terms of reference changed, so that there was no doubt whatsoever that all of those allegations could be investigated. So what was in, or not in, the programme was not the central point.'

The Tánaiste and her opposition counterpart had engaged in a four-minute tango – both trying to stand their ground, neither truly hoping to fatally trip the other.

However, Gerry Adams, called next to lead the Sinn Féin block of questioning, had no such qualms. If the purpose of the night's proceedings was for ministers to set out what (and when) they knew about the campaign against Maurice McCabe, by any measure Kenny had failed to do so. 'So far the Taoiseach has given three different versions in as many days about what he says *Aire* [Minister] Zappone told him. For her part the minister is very clear about this and what the Taoiseach said to her, and about what her official told an official in the Taoiseach's department. And while giving his contradictory versions, the Taoiseach has refused to say when he first became aware of the false allegation of child abuse against Garda McCabe. And I would like to put that question directly to him now.'

'I've answered this before,' Kenny said, repeating his previous statements in which the question was addressed but not answered. 'I do not deal in rumours, hearsay or allegations' – more hubbub broke out on the opposite benches – 'and your question is irrelevant to the central issue here: how to define and determine the truth of a central issue of senior Gardaí carrying out a deliberate smear.'

The Sinn Féin TDs alongside and behind Adams moaned in anger at what they saw as Kenny being evasive, refusing to address the central point now occupying the public's mind. But politically speaking, the Taoiseach had no scope whatsoever for departing from the official line. Were he to announce now that he might have heard whispers about McCabe on the corridors of Leinster House, or from a Minister for Justice, or from a Garda Commissioner, he would have opened a fresh can of worms. The optics of being hauled back into the Dáil chamber on St Valentine's Day, and suddenly revealing he might have known about these McCabe rumours all along, would have precipitated an even bigger political scandal. There were already grumbles against the media over the possibility that its reporting on McCabe might have been conditioned by the underhand whispering campaign. A sudden concession that the government's own handling of the McCabe story might *also* have been similarly influenced would plunge Kenny into an even deeper crisis from which there would be no escaping.

But many casual observers would not have engaged in this level of political analysis and would not have enjoyed the optics of the scene unfolding before them anyway. On the face of it, the Taoiseach was being asked when he first learned of a smear against Maurice McCabe, and was pointedly refusing to answer. If Kenny were to stick to this tactic for the remainder of the evening – insisting his own knowledge of a smear campaign was irrelevant – it would be a long and testing night for everyone on the government benches.

Adams ceded the floor to his justice spokesman Jonathan O'Brien, who also pointed his questions to Kenny and followed up on Zappone's new information. Was it true that Kenny assured Zappone the Tusla matter was already covered in the inquiry? And if so, how could Kenny know this for certain, when Frances Fitzgerald – the minister responsible for actually drafting the terms of reference – wasn't aware of it herself?

'My assumption was that the terms of reference would cover that,' Kenny conceded, suggesting now he had been a little more equivocal. 'That was actually clarified, also, by the judge appointed at the time to conduct the Commission of Investigation.' The fact that this clarification only came afterwards was omitted.

Mary Lou McDonald, next to speak, prefaced her contribution by thanking Zappone for her frankness – including for revealing that McCabe himself had been talking to the media, thereby implicitly conceding that there was no need for discretion on her own part, before turning to the Taoiseach's stonewalling. McDonald had pieced together various parts of the McCabe jigsaw – and reached the conclusion that Kenny had known about it for years.

In February 2014, as McCabe's complaints began to transcend the penalty points issue and took in broader policing complaints, John McGuinness had instigated a meeting between McCabe and Micheál Martin. McCabe had presented the Fianna Fáil leader with a dossier of his complaints, including botched investigations into serious assaults and even murders. Martin, in a dramatic intervention, then announced details of this dossier in the Dáil and handed it over to Enda Kenny for formal investigation. (The government had handed the documents to barrister Seán Guerin for his scoping inquiry; Guerin's report in May of that year – though contested by Alan Shatter – forced the latter's resignation as Minister for Justice.)

After his party leader had handed over this dossier, McGuinness dropped by Martin's office to thank him for giving a platform to the whistleblower, and told him, by the by, that Martin Callinan had labelled McCabe as a child abuser in a hotel car park a month earlier. Martin would later say he was taken aback by this disclosure. Though he had heard suggestions of child abuse involving McCabe circulating in Leinster House – and some queries had been made to Fianna Fáil's press office about the whistleblower's credibility – he could never pin them down. The idea they would be delivered directly to a TD by the Garda Commissioner was stunning. Nonetheless, faced with hearsay from one source and documentary evidence from another, Martin chose to focus himself on the hard facts available.

Two months later, with Seán Guerin's investigation well underway, Ms D had also taken her case public, giving an interview to Paul Williams of the *Irish Independent*. Although McCabe himself was never named as the alleged aggressor, Ms D's case was presented as another example of failures to investigate serious crimes. She believed the investigation into her own assault was 'a farce' – claiming that not only was it never entered onto the Garda PULSE system, but was not fully investigated at all because the culprit was a Garda. This assault had left a lasting imprint on her; although she had buried the memory as a child, it had re-emerged when she was a teenager, sending her life 'off the rails' and even culminating in two suicide attempts. If a dossier of McCabe's complaints were to be investigated any further, her own grievance should equally be rolled into the inquiry.

Having already been rebuffed by Seán Guerin, who declined to extend his inquiry beyond the terms of reference he was given, Ms D decided to enlist the help of Micheál Martin. Three days after publishing his interview with the young woman, Paul Williams rang Martin's chief of staff, Deirdre Gillane, to ask if the Fianna Fáil leader was prepared to meet with her, and published a follow-up piece the next day to announce the meeting had been agreed. The meeting itself took place in Leinster House at the end of April, after which Martin – conferring with Gillane – agreed that Ms D's complaint over the investigation in her own case, in which McCabe himself was the alleged aggressor, should also be included within Seán Guerin's scoping inquiry, and sent it to the Taoiseach's office. ('There was a sense that this could fall within that [*sic*] parameters, and let's have everything dealt with,' he would later explain.) Kenny decided not to leave the matter in Guerin's hands – but rather sent it, alongside a whole raft of other separate complaints now flooding his office, to an independent panel of barristers being convened by Shatter's successor, Frances Fitzgerald.

All of this meant, Mary Lou McDonald now explained, that Enda Kenny could not have been in the dark about the allegations surrounding Maurice McCabe: Micheál Martin had handed them to him three years previously. 'You were aware from that point, Taoiseach, were you not? Did you in fact instigate an investigation – and why do you persist in a game of make-believe that you didn't know of these allegations? You knew about them going back to May 2014.'

McDonald's forked attack, whether intended or not, prompted a defensive intervention from Micheál Martin, stating for the record that McCabe himself supported having Ms D's complaint investigated by Guerin, and it was Kenny alone who decided against it. Martin, trying to explain how McCabe himself had even contacted Guerin to outline the background of the events, only managed to bring heckles from the Sinn Féin TDs behind

McDonald, who accused him of being equally complicit in some kind of anti-McCabe conspiracy.

When Kenny did finally get a chance to address McDonald, he offered little in reply. 'The letter that Deputy McDonald refers to was a letter in respect of how a case that had been handled by the Gardaí had been dismissed by the DPP. It has nothing to do with the current exposés on the *Prime Time* programme or the so-called Tusla file.' The Taoiseach could not risk breaching the confidentiality of that process by saying any more, but anyone piecing the jigsaw together would again be infuriated by his apparent stonewalling.

Any sense of evasiveness was not helped by the next batch of questions, from Labour's Brendan Howlin. 'I can't understand how it could be the case that you, Taoiseach, have such a flawed recollection of such significant meetings,' he said, pointing out that Kenny's *This Week* interview not only recounted a chat that never took place, but also omitted the pre-Cabinet consultation with Zappone. 'Isn't it the case that had Minister Zappone not insisted on her version of fact, that an entirely incorrect sequencing of events would remain on the public record subsequent to your interview last Sunday?'

The obvious answer was yes: without Zappone having nonchalantly undermined his story, the country would be none the wiser.

With little to offer by way of retort, Kenny simply offered to restate the corrected record, tapping his microphone as he rose to ensure his reply was heard. 'I actually told the truth today in the House here,' he opened (interrupted by Paul Murphy yelling, 'Which time?'), commenting obliquely about the massive volume of information that might cross the Taoiseach's desk on a daily basis.

'I was mistaken in saying I had actually spoken to the minister about her meeting with the McCabes. She did inform me just before the Cabinet meeting began that she had met with the McCabes, and that they had discussed false sexual allegations against the sergeant. She did not make me aware of the existence of a file in Tusla, or any contents of that file' – more interruptions – 'and she did not make me aware of the content of the discussion that she had had with Sergeant McCabe or his wife.'

Here, again, was another seeming contradiction. Only a few minutes earlier Zappone had revealed how Kenny had advised her that Charleton's terms of reference were certain to cover Tusla – thus implying that Tusla had been discussed to begin with. Now Kenny was saying there was no mention of any role for the agency at all. Howlin, picking this up, followed up: so when *exactly* was Kenny informed of the existence of any role for Tusla?

The question had to be put twice before Kenny would answer it. 'As I said to you, before the Cabinet meeting, Minister Zappone said that she had met with the McCabes and that the question of false allegations of sexual abuse had been discussed – had been made to Tusla, and had been discussed with her, or by her, with the McCabes.' The hesitant, self-correcting tones of this answer hid yet another contradiction: once again, Kenny was conceding there *had* been mention of Tusla.

Frances Fitzgerald, in equally reluctant rhythms, told Howlin she knew of no Tusla involvement in the McCabe saga until she saw the *Prime Time* programme – and that Tusla's only involvement in any whistleblower case, that she knew of, was contained in the protected disclosure of a separate Garda, the as-yet-unnamed Keith Harrison. Katherine Zappone added, for the record, that she had not been specifically *advised* to keep quiet during the Cabinet meeting, either by the Taoiseach or by anyone else. Her decision to keep her own counsel, controversial as it was, was entirely her own.

The next block of speaking time fell to the Anti-Austerity Alliance–People Before Profit bloc, led by Paul Murphy. A few hours earlier, on Twitter, Murphy had seized on an apparent contradiction in Enda Kenny's accounts during Leaders' Questions. At 2.16 p.m. he told Micheál Martin that he and Zappone had discussed false allegations held by Tusla – but at 2.32 p.m. he told Murphy he'd had no information about the existence of a Tusla file. (If this were true, it could only have been on a pedantic level: Kenny would be resting his defence on knowing Tusla held the allegations, but not within a 'file'.) Which was it? Did Kenny at least concede he had given Zappone advice about the Tusla file falling within the terms of reference?

Kenny chose to answer a different question entirely. 'No, I was not aware of any of the details of the discussion Minister Zappone had with the McCabe family, and I was not aware of any of the details contained in the Tusla file. What Minister Zappone *did* say to me was that she had met the McCabes, and that they had discussed false allegations of sexual abuse that had been sent to Tusla.'

'Did you say to her that this would be covered by the commission of investigation?'

'The Cabinet was meeting to adopt terms of reference set out by Justice O'Neill in relation to matters that clearly were of a sexual nature. Minister Zappone is the Minister for Tusla. Obviously, she had said that the discussion she had had with the McCabes, without giving me any detail, had been about false allegations of a sexual nature that had been made to Tusla.'

This, again, did not answer the question – causing Ruth Coppinger, sitting beside Murphy, to restate it.

'I had looked at the terms of reference,' the Taoiseach said, 'and I was clear in my mind that anything to do with allegations of a sexual nature would be covered by the terms of reference … I said these would be covered under the terms of reference because they were false allegations of a sexual nature.'

Kenny – still refusing to tell the Dáil when he first heard of the McCabe rumours ('I don't think that nominating a date … would do anything to deal with the central question here') – did offer one extra morsel of fact. Sinn Féin's Caoimhghín Ó Caoláin pressed him on his sloppy wording on radio, when he had claimed Zappone's meeting was 'in a private capacity' instead of 'confidential'. The question, from one of Sinn Féin's more mild-mannered TDs, perhaps offered Kenny a calm, first-hand opportunity to correct the public record. Instead, he offered some new information: Zappone was not alone at the meeting.

'She had personnel with her from her department, and the Secretary of the Department of …' – Kenny was interrupted by some more Sinn Féin heckles, and rebooted his sentence – '… the minister, who's doing a very good job by the way, was quite entitled to meet privately with Sergeant McCabe and his wife, to have a note-taker there, to have an account of the meeting.

'And I might say to you that the secretary general of the Department of Children sent a copy of the note taken at the meeting to the secretary general of my own department yesterday evening.'

Armchair psychologists might have had a field day, hearing Kenny be asked about his ill-fated radio interview and repeating two of the same tropes from the interview itself (the reflexive defence of Zappone and the idea of keeping 'account' of the interactions). For those still paying close attention, the substance of his new contribution was yet another drip in the slow flood of information.

It wasn't all that surprising that a note would be kept of the meeting, or that the note would have found its way to the top civil servant in Zappone's department, given she had discussed the possibility of a formal apology to McCabe by an agency under her remit. Nor was it surprising that, given the ensuing political turmoil, a copy would be shared with his equivalent in Merrion Street. But why had it taken so long? If the notes had germane information of political interest, why hadn't they been shared earlier? The absent Zappone's account of the meeting had caused ructions four days earlier – surely it was in everyone's interests to share those details as quickly as possible?

It was now nearly ninety minutes into the question-and-answer session, and the benches in the Dáil chamber were still fairly full – a tacit indication of just how seriously all sides were taking the present scandal. Some had an obvious reason to stay around: the Dáil's smaller parties and technical groups had not yet been called to contribute, and their smaller populations meant a better chance of individual TDs getting to speak (and even if they weren't due to speak, it was considered poor etiquette to leave a colleague alone in the chamber). On a more cynical level, TDs knew that if they hung around, they might sneak into vision if their colleague appeared on the news.

This cynical analysis could not be applied to the government benches. Only Kenny, Fitzgerald, Zappone and Harris would be called to speak. Other ministers and backbenchers were there, ostensibly to lend their moral support. But the crowds of TDs seated behind the four ministers did not seem to be paying much attention to Dáil business: instead, almost all of them were glued to their phones. Plenty of them were conferring with colleagues about the Taoiseach's ropey defence of his actions.

Kenny's tortured account of events, at this point, was beginning to cause major anxiety on the backbenches behind him. If the Taoiseach was indeed clinging to the Jesuitical distinction between Tusla information and a Tusla file, he was doing an awful job of saying so. In a pre-emptive swipe, Mary Lou McDonald told him: 'The idea that you'd come back and say, "I knew there were allegations but I didn't know there was a file" is a bit far-fetched. I mean, what did you imagine there would be? Of course there would be a file, where there is a complaint, and of course that would be with Tusla.'

All the while, Kenny remained polite, but his air became downbeat, portraying almost a general air of disinterest as more and more TDs lined up to give him a kicking. Beside him, Frances Fitzgerald remained combative, visibly irked at suggestions she might have misled the Dáil when not revealing any knowledge of a Tusla role the previous week. The contrast in their demeanours was stark.

Around thirty hours after Noel Rock had gone on radio and raised questions as to Enda Kenny's longevity, the tenure of the Fine Gael leader was now an open question among even the more loyal soldiers in his ranks.

Doubtless, some of those TDs would have been on the phone to journalists in the press corridor only a few yards away. Print hacks, with one eye on the Dáil and another on their deadlines, were desperately trying to scope out the mood of the Fine Gael ranks and determine whether Kenny could survive the present storm; TV reporters were frantically trying to decide which of the many salient sound bites should be put to air; and radio reporters were scrambling to file the freshest new material for every hour's new bulletin. All of the above, meanwhile, were trying to supply copy for their online operations – platforms that knew no deadline and constantly demanded more material.

***

It was around this time that some of those journalists began to piece together a bigger jigsaw – a sort of proof-by-induction process.

Kenny's account seemed to be that Katherine Zappone had told him of false allegations made around Maurice McCabe and recorded by Tusla; he in turn looked at the terms of reference for the public investigation being planned and told her it was already covered. How could he know this for sure, unless he knew more than he was letting on?

Aside from their sensational contents, the protected disclosures made to Frances Fitzgerald carried a burden of legal confidentiality – a duty that required the Tánaiste not only to keep the documents under lock and key, but even to keep their existence a secret. All Fitzgerald could do with a protected disclosure was refer it to whatever appropriate people could help establish the truth of the claims. There was no scope to share the contents with other ministers, or even the Taoiseach. Given that the law governing such disclosures was introduced almost directly as a result of McCabe's public flogging by Garda HQ during the penalty points affair of 2014, there was no prospect of these laws being ignored when McCabe himself was the source of further claims.

All of this meant that, officially, Frances Fitzgerald could not tell Enda Kenny about anything to do with the protected disclosures on her desk. The Taoiseach should have had no knowledge of the smear campaign that Dave Taylor claimed he was ordered to perpetrate – or which criminal act in McCabe's past he was supposed to highlight. It was those protected disclosures that had been scrutinised by Iarfhlaith O'Neill and that had led to the terms of reference approved by the government a week ago.

Now, separately, Kenny was being presented with a wrongful claim of sex abuse on the part of Maurice McCabe – and, officially, had to treat it as ostensibly an entirely different claim. With legal blinkers applied, Kenny had no discretion to assume the claim before him now was the same claim given to Frances Fitzgerald in the first place. He certainly could not assume that this false allegation was the basis for an organised smear campaign engineered by the country's highest-ranking police officer – which, after all, was exactly what the terms of reference were supposed to examine.

This delicate tour of logic led to a striking proposition: if Kenny believed for certain that the Tusla file would be examined by a public inquiry into a Garda smear campaign, he must have believed that the Tusla file *itself* was at the centre of that campaign. The Tusla file would be off-limits to a public inquiry investigating a smear campaign, unless the file played some crucial role in that campaign. So, by telling Katherine Zappone the file would be covered, Kenny was appearing to confirm that the allegations held by Tusla (albeit completely wrong and referring to another person entirely) *were* the same allegations as the ones that Dave Taylor was supposedly bringing to the attention of the country's journalists.

There was another reason to be uncertain too. Iarfhlaith O'Neill had very little information on which to build his terms of reference. The few facts at his fingertips were drawn from McCabe's and Taylor's disclosures. Those disclosures were written in September 2016, before either man had known of the Tusla file. If McCabe didn't know about it, O'Neill certainly didn't either, and so there was no way he could have set the parameters of an inquiry with the Tusla file in mind.

If this were true, Kenny's on-the-record denial of any knowledge about the Tusla details would unravel – as would his account of when he had first heard of any rumours around Maurice McCabe's past. The foundation stone of the Taoiseach's defence was suddenly looking very shaky.

Already, within the Dáil chamber, Kenny's leap of faith in offering assurances to Zappone was being questioned. Frances Fitzgerald had told Independents4Change's Clare Daly that the protected disclosure 'was to do with a smear campaign', as distinct from the 'child sex abuse allegations' that Tusla had recorded.

Daly was baffled. 'If the allegation was about a smear campaign, why did the terms of reference include reference to an allegation of criminal misconduct? If that criminal misconduct is not alleged child sexual abuse, then you might tell us what it is.'

Fitzgerald shot back. 'The judge decided that any allegation of criminal misconduct that had been made against Sergeant McCabe should be included, clearly, and he has it in the terms of reference. So it would cover sexual allegations.'

Just as the Taoiseach had done a few minutes earlier, Fitzgerald had omitted to state that this advice from Charleton had come after the fact. Kenny's punt might have been vindicated, but only because the man running the inquiry had come along afterwards and decided to interpret his task more widely. He didn't have that same safety net when he made the call in the first place.

As the Dáil questioning went on – with praise for Zappone's nonchalant honesty and little other salient information coming from the government benches – the present author posted a thread to Twitter explaining the nascent logic behind the idea that Kenny *may* just have accidentally spilled the beans on himself. Inside the chamber the thread was spotted by a few TDs idly thumbing their phones scoping the press and public reaction.

As the floor remained opened for members to continue their questioning, Sinn Féin's Pearse Doherty decided to put the logic directly to Kenny himself.

'Obviously, you're not aware of what is in the protected disclosures from David Taylor. You stated there's allegations of criminality – we know that, from the terms of reference – but you said they were of a sexual abuse nature. Perhaps you should clarify it. Are you aware that is what the protected disclosures included? ... How were you able to satisfy [Zappone] that they would be covered in the terms of reference?'

Kenny replied earnestly. 'The judge in question' – meaning Iarfhlaith O'Neill – 'would have had contacts with all of the persons involved in this, and clearly the terms of reference as drafted by him would have covered all of the issues that are relevant there.' And, of course, Peter Charleton believed the file was covered, so what harm?

Sources close to Kenny insisted this was his genuine belief, and grounded on good reason. The government hadn't just asked Iarfhlaith O'Neill to conduct a 'desk review', or some kind of inquiry-on-paper. He had been told to actively approach all the interested parties, hoping to find out whether the claims held any substance. He'd spoken to Maurice McCabe and, presumably, would have been brought up to speed on any extraneous issues that warranted scrutiny.

But Doherty knew the error in this logic, bellowing across at Kenny, 'the judge didn't know that at the time'. Indeed, at the time O'Neill spoke to McCabe, the sergeant knew nothing of the Tusla file. O'Neill had finished his work and sent back his findings in the first week of December; it was only a few weeks later that McCabe received the full file and learned, for the first time, of the horrendous fallout from the copy-and-paste mistake.

A few minutes later, armed with some handwritten notes, the AAA's Mick Barry broached the same logic. For Kenny to assure Zappone the Tusla issue would be covered, he'd have to have known that the allegation within it formed part of the smear campaign. So why didn't Kenny ensure Tusla was explicitly mentioned? Kenny, sticking to his previous position, suddenly grew vocally derisive. 'Are you seriously suggesting that an eminent judge would examine two protected disclosures and draft terms of reference that would not include issues that were relevant?'

This time, Kenny was called out on the error in his logic. Barry's neighbours on the Sinn Féin benches, Doherty and Mary Lou McDonald, could no longer abide what they saw as wilful evasiveness. 'The Taoiseach is entirely wrong in his response,' McDonald announced, cajoling her way back to a live microphone. 'At the time of the protected disclosure, Maurice and Lorraine McCabe were not aware of the particular file. You are not answering the question factually and I think it's essential to point that out.' Doherty chimed in, without the benefit of an active microphone: 'He didn't know what was in the protected disclosure, so how could he reassure the minister? It's impossible, Taoiseach.'

Barry was delighted with the assistance, demanding that Kenny revise his answer in light of this new observation. 'I think given that intervention the Taoiseach needs to respond,' he insisted. But the Taoiseach – once again looking blankly at the opposite corner of the room, stone-faced as well as stonewalling – had managed to beat the clock. Each TD taking the floor had been given a two-minute window in which to ask their question and get their answer. McDonald's intervention had run down the clock on Mick Barry's contribution and attention had to move elsewhere.

Next in the queue was Jan O'Sullivan of Labour, a party which would hardly have been seen as a regular ally of its further-left Dáil colleagues – but while she had her own questions to ask, O'Sullivan understood the sinkhole beginning to emerge and wanted to inspect just how deep it went. She prefixed the same inquiry to her own questions, but it served only to underline that Kenny simply would not move. Again, the Taoiseach simply insisted (wrongly) that Iarfhlaith O'Neill knew of the Tusla file when he wrote up his suggestions for the terms of reference. No amount of cajoling from Mary Lou McDonald ('That is simply wrong … the Taoiseach is simply trying to brazen it out') would change his position.

The other major player in the political crisis – the one outside of Leinster House – was not being forgotten either. Nóirín O'Sullivan enjoyed firm support from the Fine Gael core of government, but elsewhere in Leinster House her future was still up for debate. The suggestion on some corridors was that Fine Gael ministers were being warned not to speculate *at all* about the

Garda Commissioner's future, as any declaration of less-than-100 per cent support could expose the government to a future lawsuit for constructive dismissal. The circumstances of her predecessor's departure had not been forgotten: the commission investigating Martin Callinan's abrupt 'retirement' found that although Enda Kenny did not intend to pressure him into quitting early, his actions (sending a senior civil servant to his home to express 'grave concerns' on some issues) meant Callinan felt that pressure anyway. It was Schrödinger's dismissal: Callinan wasn't being sacked but was entitled to believe he was about to be.

All of this meant Fine Gael ministers were steadfast in their vocal backing for Nóirín O'Sullivan. But was there a similar feeling among the non-Fine Gael ranks – were the independent ministers independent in thought? Richard Boyd Barrett wanted to know. 'Do you believe,' he asked Zappone, 'it is tenable for Nóirín O'Sullivan to stay in situ as Garda Commissioner, notwithstanding her right to due process?' His reasoning was that if the allegations against her were actually true, her remaining in office 'potentially prejudices the ability of any tribunal to get to the truth of the matter. Do you consider that that is a tenable situation?'

Zappone's answer was firm. 'In relation to the Commissioner, I believe in due process,' she said, answering so succinctly that the bottom part of her flip seat had barely returned to its resting position before she was pulling it down again. Frances Fitzgerald and Simon Harris looked on approvingly.

Elsewhere, Kenny's stonewalling remained an open topic of discussion among press circles, where conviction was growing that the explanation given by the Taoiseach on the floor of the Dáil did not hold water.

Sinn Féin's Maurice Quinlivan, though, was distracted by a bigger issue on which Kenny had shed little light. By his estimation, the Taoiseach had been asked ten times when he had first become aware of an allegation against Maurice McCabe – whether it be the one made in error to Tusla, the one handed over by Micheál Martin three years earlier, or the one mentioned surreptitiously in the corridors of Leinster House and Government Buildings. Quinlivan himself wanted to become number eleven on that list.

'My question is simple: when did you first become aware of the false allegations against Maurice McCabe?'

The producers in charge of the Dáil's television coverage did not even have time to switch to a camera view of Kenny before he had offered his reply. 'On the *Prime Time* programme last Thursday night,' he said, out of shot and barely rising from his chair.

Instead the television feed remained on a wider shot of the Sinn Féin benches and captured a slow-burning dawn of apoplexy on the faces of some of the TDs remaining there. Quinlivan suddenly sat forward in bewilderment at what he had just heard. Looking to his right, his eyes met the confused face of Pat Buckley; between them, Peadar Tóibín scrunched his face in bafflement. On the rows ahead of them, Louise O'Reilly rubbed one eye, almost in comical disbelief. Ahead of her, Pearse Doherty and Mary Lou McDonald simply turned towards each other and shook their heads. In the back row of the block, occupied by the smaller parties, Róisín Shortall lunged to the edge of her seat.

Kenny's reply simply made no sense at all. He had already tortured the Dáil with a confusing account about how he and Katherine Zappone had discussed wrongful allegations made to Tusla on the Tuesday morning, sixty hours before they were revealed on TV. The following day, Brendan Howlin had stood in the chamber and given the Taoiseach (and the world) the testimony of a journalist who said McCabe was being accused of 'sexual crimes'. Indeed, Mary Lou McDonald had reminded the House of how Micheál Martin had, quite literally, handed an allegation on paper to Kenny in May 2014. There didn't appear to be *any* plausible way that Kenny could now say he knew nothing before *Prime Time*.

Jonathan O'Brien picked up his own phone, while Donnchadh Ó Laoghaire rose beside him to question the Taoiseach, and ventured on Twitter himself. 'Kenny just said that the first he heard of false allegations of sexual abuse against Maurice McCabe was last Thursday when *Prime Time* aired it ... a blatant lie by Kenny.' The reason for Sinn Féin's incredulity was now explained in full: they believed the Taoiseach had simply lied to the Dáil.

Ó Laoghaire, holding his poise, calmly reasoned that Kenny – quite aside from having discussed the allegations with Zappone two days before the TV reveal – could not have assured Zappone the Tusla file would be investigated, unless he knew the allegations held by Tusla were 'specifically related to a smearing of Sergeant McCabe by members of An Garda Síochána'.

'I've answered this before,' the Taoiseach said – his voice portraying a certain amount of repetitive frustration – before repeating the same explanation that had already frustrated so many others. Iarfhlaith O'Neill had written the terms of reference, and he would have been aware of all the pertinent issues, and so on. 'Clearly, the terms of reference were flexible enough to cover Tusla ...'

It was a telling insight into Merrion Street's frantic response to the political tornado that had torn through the media a few days earlier: journalists had treated the Tusla file as if it was, for definite, part of a whispering campaign. It simply seemed like too much of a coincidence that the allegation would appear at exactly the moment when the supposed aggressor was causing the maximum possible discomfort for the country's top brass. There was always the chance it was a stellar coincidence, but the media would struggle to explain that the two allegations against McCabe were entirely separate. Those at the very heart of government had obviously fallen into the same trap, and while ordering a public inquiry into an alleged smear campaign engineered by Ireland's top Gardaí, had simply *assumed* the allegation given to Tusla was part of the same campaign.

As ever, there were two ways of looking at this. If the allegation that ended up with Tusla was completely unrelated to a smear campaign from Garda headquarters, some would say: What harm? There would be little point in giving the file much thought (apart from the obvious question of 'where did this come from?') if it was a mere coincidence. But equally, if the file on McCabe existed somehow *independently* of a coordinated smear – yet came into existence just at a time when Garda HQ really could have used a stick to beat him with – wasn't there the prospect of an *even bigger* attempt to discredit a police officer who was now approaching the status of public hero?

To some extent, the government seemed to have fallen victim to its own official segregation. The alleged smear campaign was being investigated via the Department of Justice, which legally could not share it with any other wings of the State. But it was the Department of Children that had become aware of the Tusla file, to which the Department of Justice was seemingly completely blind.

In the marathon session of Dáil questioning, it never occurred to anyone to ask why Zappone had gone to Kenny with her anxieties about the terms of reference, but had never discussed the delicacies of the newer Tusla issue with Frances Fitzgerald, who had seen O'Neill's full report and who would know if Tusla had been considered.

In fact, giving it any thought at all, it was actually plainly obvious that O'Neill simply could not have been aware of the Tusla file. If he was, then Frances Fitzgerald would have learned of it when reading his report in December 2016, and not through the journalism of Katie Hannon or Mick Clifford over two months later.

* * *

Back in the Dáil chamber, questions were continuing with an increasing tone of hostility, and a specific focus on Kenny, as the fate of the other three ministers became an increasing political irrelevance. The next contribution was from John McGuinness – the former PAC chairman who always seemed to appear just at the nexus of McCabe's skirmishes with party politics.

As McGuinness was called and rose to his feet, the smattering of journalists perched on the gallery leaned forward – not only in anticipation, but also because McGuinness was seated in the very front row of the chamber, where he was without the benefit of a microphone. 'There's been a mass wringing of hands going on in Leinster House for the last while over this issue,' he said, 'and the fact that we are here now discussing a public inquiry is because Maurice and Lorraine McCabe have absolutely no trust in a private inquiry,' McGuinness began.

Some Sinn Féin TDs interrupted to complain, demanding

that McGuinness move to a seat with a microphone so that he could be heard properly – and which, conveniently, would allow his comments to be recorded for broadcast later. The Kilkenny TD dutifully turned and walked up the nearest steps, searching for a vacant seat. Micheál Martin, in the foremost seat of the Fianna Fáil bloc, motioned to stand up and sidle away so that his party colleague could borrow his seat for his speech – only to be cheekily slapped aside again. 'I'm more in line with Mattie,' McGuinness quipped, snubbing his leader's offer. McGuinness and Martin were colleagues united by a party and very little else. It was fairly symbolic that he instead chose to sit beside the independent Mattie McGrath, a one-time Fianna Fáil TD who left the party over its ban on stag hunting in 2010. 'You're welcome as the flowers of May,' his ex-colleague cheered.

Now amplified – and with everyone else getting a moment to prepare – McGuinness resumed his contribution. 'In relation to the smear campaign, why is it that we cannot admit that for the last number of years, for anyone who wished to stop and listen to what was being said in this House …'

'And in a car park,' interjected colleague Declan Breathnach.

'I'll deal with the car park in a minute … Why is it that when we were told what was happening in relation to Maurice McCabe, anyone who supported him was sold this narrative that he was a sex abuser? That he had abused people, sexually? And that's what they said. And therefore, those that supported him were knocked off of their support by virtue of that gossip, and that innuendo and that accusation.'

The Dáil was now in stony silence.

'The fact of the matter is that while that was going on, the Tusla file existed. So how many Gardaí knew about that Tusla file? How many in this House knew about the allegations that were being made? And when he appeared before the Public Accounts Committee, great efforts were made by this house, and by members within it, to stop him from coming forward. That's why we're here today – because we have ignored Maurice McCabe and the other Maurice McCabes that exist out there. If we're to have any public inquiry into this, then we have to take into consideration the culture that has sent all of those people out sick, some of them struggling now with mental illness, and we cannot ignore those people. And the government cannot ignore them.'

Now he arrived at the crux of his question. 'How many within Government knew about these allegations that were being made, even though it might have been gossip? It was gossip that was spread maliciously to take you off your game, and not to support Maurice McCabe. And all of us in this house knew what was going on.'

Some in government might have claimed to be insulated from those rumours, but others would find it tough to argue with what they had just heard. The McCabe rumours seemed to have touched every corner, every inch of the parliamentary complex and its occupants. McGuinness had seen everyone else dance around this idea for a few hours, and decided to call a halt to the charade.

The Taoiseach, rising carefully, finished scrawling a quick note on his papers before replying in earnest. If McGuinness felt this was an open secret that should be acted on, he had missed his own opportunities to bring it to further attention. 'Am I right or not – did you have a meeting with the former Commissioner of the Gardaí, and did you hear information relevant to a smear campaign against Garda McCabe? And if you did, what did you do about it?'

'You knew about it, Taoiseach!' McGuinness was now furiously jabbing his finger. 'You knew a long time ago about the accusations that were being made against Maurice McCabe. Everyone in this house knew! And great efforts were made to derail Maurice McCabe, and the story that he was telling!'

Fitzgerald and Regina Doherty, who understood the damage of leaving such sensitive claims unchallenged on the Dáil record, immediately challenged McGuinness to prove his claims. With no definitive proof that Kenny knew of the smear campaign all along, he eventually refined his allegation – saying simply that 'those of us who were supporting Maurice McCabe' were fully aware of Garda HQ's underhand tactics. The implication was that the government were not among his supporters.

Not long afterwards, at two minutes to 9 p.m., there was time for only one more TD to contribute. The floor had fallen to Sinn Féin's Jonathan O'Brien, who half an hour earlier had accused Kenny of 'a blatant lie' on Twitter.

'Since this is the final question I'd like to give the Taoiseach the opportunity to clarify the Dáil record, because he just said in response to my Dáil colleague, Deputy Quinlivan,' – turning away from the chairman and facing Kenny – 'that the first you heard of the false allegations being made against Sergeant Maurice McCabe was after the *Prime Time* show on Thursday night. That's what you just said.'

There was an off-mic *mm-hmm* sound from Fitzgerald.

'I'm not sure … well, obviously you're not aware that Deputy Howlin actually raised those allegations earlier that day during Leaders' Questions. Do you honestly expect anyone to believe that you did not hear of those allegations until the airing of the *Prime Time* show, when they were actually aired on the floor of this chamber six to seven hours previous to that show being aired?'

O'Brien had got his sums wrong – Howlin's contribution came the day before and not the day of the TV piece – but the substance was otherwise correct. Kenny's claim didn't make sense, or did it?

'Deputy Howlin raised a matter here in respect of which he was pulled up by the Ceann Comhairle for his actions. Now I don't know had you heard these allegations before, if you know all of this?'

'I'm asking *you* the questions, Taoiseach,' O'Brien frowned.

'Yes, and I'm telling you that I heard it after the *Prime Time* programme ...'

'So you didn't hear Deputy Howlin?'

'Yes, of course I heard him. Of course I heard him. And I also heard the Ceann Comhairle, and I answered Deputy Howlin.'

'He said he heard him!' O'Brien's Cork brogue was thickening.

But the clock was ticking away. Kenny merely had time to say he was of course aware of the previous 1998 allegation against McCabe, and was aware of the DPP ruling on it. (He had known about this after Micheál Martin forwarded Ms D's complaint to him in 2014. This, formally, was a confirmation of Mary Lou McDonald's forked attack earlier: Kenny had known about *some* allegations pertaining to McCabe years ago.)

And that was all the Dáil had time to hear.

***

It had been a marathon session, with little time for respite, to step outside for fresh air, for a toilet break, or even to take a deep breath and gather thoughts.

Kenny neatly folded away his handwritten notes, shared a few words with Fitzgerald and Regina Doherty, and disappeared from the chamber. The other major figures on the government side hung around for momentary chatter with each other, but couldn't stay long, as the emergency three-hour session had merely deferred some other business that was due to be processed. Jonathan O'Brien emerged down the government steps for a brief cordial word with Fitzgerald, appeared to leave satisfied, and that was that.

The session had elucidated some new information, but the impression was that this information had to be pulled and dragged into the open. If the debate had been arranged to allow ministers to completely clear the air – and that was the pretext on which the government had to accept the debate – and if there were facts the ministers wanted to put on record from the outset, the expectation would be that this new information would be included in their opening statements.

Instead, the opening statements had been defensive recitations from Kenny and Fitzgerald, with no new information put into the record. Simon Harris, as merely a minor player in the process, had almost nothing to add. But Katherine Zappone's declaration that the Tusla allegations had been discussed *before* the previous week's Cabinet meeting had served to lay a trail of breadcrumbs that the scandalised opposition TDs were only too happy to gobble up.

The row between Fitzgerald and O'Callaghan appeared to have been buried. After the original skirmish, with the Fianna Fáil man insisting he had raised the Tusla file and the Fine Gael minister insisting he didn't, it seemed O'Callaghan had been mollified by Fitzgerald's olive branch – a recognition that perhaps they were both simply recollecting the conversation in different ways and that no malice was intended in the row. There was, at least, the firm perception that Fianna Fáil would not pull the rug out from under the government in a fit of pique to defend the honour of its justice spokesman.

Beyond that, though, there were plenty of open questions. The open wound in Enda Kenny's logic around his knowledge of the Maurice McCabe allegations was gathering dirt. It was now clearly established he had known of the DPP allegation in April 2014, when Micheál Martin had handed Ms D's allegations directly to him. It was clear that, no matter when or whether he had picked up the rumours elsewhere, the alleged smear campaign by Garda HQ had been announced to him in the Dáil chamber the previous Wednesday. In fact, even when he heard that announcement, it now turned out he had been appraised of a false allegation held by Tusla the previous morning. All in all, his new pronouncement that he had therefore only learned of false allegations surrounding Maurice McCabe through Thursday night's *Prime Time* programme was rubbing salt into the open wound. Put simply, nobody – even Kenny's usual loyalists within Fine Gael – could make any sense of it.

Given his earlier 'mea culpa' moment – which was still leading the evening news bulletins – the mutters of dissent within the Fine Gael ranks about his longevity as party leader, and with the Dáil still to debate a motion of no confidence the following night, it had indeed been a calamitous day for Enda Kenny.

Retiring to the Dáil's members' bar that evening – the same site where Frances Fitzgerald and Jim O'Callaghan had conferred the previous week – TDs reported seeing both Leo Varadkar, jetlagged after his overnight return from Bogotá, and Simon

Coveney. Others in the bar thought this was odd; neither Coveney nor Varadkar were regular visitors to the bar. Seeing either in the members-only venue was rare; seeing the two together, with Varadkar drinking from a bottle of Corona and Coveney supping a pint of Heineken, struck others as almost conspiratorial. The two ministers were the only people to have publicly declared an interest in succeeding Enda Kenny, and if the Taoiseach's future were now a matter of debate, those two would be central to the discussion. The air of intrigue was only added to when the duo was joined by Simon Harris, whose own political rise had been swift and who did not want his age to count against him.

Sources close to all three, however, insist the leadership issue simply was not discussed – and that the conversation was much less substantive, focusing on the unlikely topic of Sikorsky 'Black Hawk' military helicopters. Varadkar had flown in one while accompanying President Higgins to a FARC guerrilla camp in Colombia only two days earlier, while Coveney had previously served as Minister for Defence and maintained a passing interest in military equipment. A source familiar with Varadkar's thinking wryly quipped afterwards: 'If Leo did want to talk about a leadership campaign, in fairness, the two Simons would be the last people he'd want to speak to.'

However fleeting the conversation might have been – and however unlikely the topic – the vision of three aspiring taoisigh sharing a chat in such an unlikely venue caught the attention of many party colleagues. Word was not long making its way back to journalists, who knew the venue was no stranger to a political plot and that Varadkar and Coveney were not often seen there.

The rumour certainly did not help those within Fine Gael who felt uneasy at the breakneck pace of events. Among them was backbencher Jim Daly, who had been incommunicado for some of the night while serving as the Dáil's stand-in chairman, but who found enough time to tell some colleagues: 'The day of the storm is not the day to fix the thatched roof.'

It was in neither Varadkar nor Coveney's interests for the government to have an unruly, disorganised dissolution of Kenny's administration. No matter who the next Fine Gael leader would be, it would be much better for them to inherit a semi-stable government than to be thrust into the job in the midst of a possible election, in which Fine Gael would be forced to set out with a deposed interim and unwilling leader still at the helm.

Enda Kenny could not simply be thrown overboard, but nor could he be allowed to sail on as if there were no storm overhead. Yet Kenny could not simply be talked out of the job either. Damaging as the current crisis was, it would cast only a small dampener on the high esteem in which Kenny was held throughout the party for his fifteen years of leadership, and his general and local election successes. Foisting him out, without grace or ceremony, would be tantamount to regicide.

If Kenny could not simply be thrown out, nor publicly convinced to go, those who wanted him gone would therefore have to find other ways of making Kenny's position untenable. They would have to create circumstances where Kenny would conclude, by himself, that the time was right to go.

***

Elsewhere, the five Independent Alliance TDs were seething. The adjournment of the Cabinet meeting meant there had been no chance to follow up on concerns about Kenny's loyalty to whistleblowers, or their longer-standing frustrations at being generally left out of the loop. There were now added concerns about Kenny's failure to reveal his pre-Cabinet encounter with Zappone, a serious bone of contention that frayed the nerves of the five.

The Alliance understood the optics of the day's earlier delay, and the clouded confusion over whether the government actually had confidence in itself. The whole purpose of the delayed-and-then-abandoned 6.15 p.m. press conference was to put any doubts to bed, only for the calamitous Dáil developments to put that declaration, once again, on ice.

The Alliance now grappled with a bigger concern: was it worth staying in power?

There was, of course, the need to ensure the Tribunal got up and running as soon as possible – a cause which required the government to remain in office. But could Enda Kenny now be trusted to deliver the bigger cultural changes the Alliance was looking for? Some in the group were simply not sure they could take Kenny at his word. The ill-fated radio interview had opened a chasm of doubt. If Kenny was capable of going on the national airwaves and faithfully describing a sensitive chat with a colleague that had never happened, what else might he say that could turn out to be totally untrue? Could some future commitments extracted from Kenny be relied upon?

From the outside it may have seemed deeply uncharitable to portray the Taoiseach as a total conman whose every word could be questioned and whose every gesture could be written off as empty showmanship. But such was the panic and cynicism being endlessly recycled within the Leinster House bubble, and the Alliance wondered if its leader within government was not only a 'political zombie', but in fact a complete charlatan.

'On the one hand Enda had this slightly vague and bumbling attitude to facts, and on the other hand you knew that he would buy you and sell you if he needed to,' one member ventured. 'Enda was just bending the truth in the way he normally would, but this time it caught up with him.'

***

While the various factions of government TDs were conferring, *Prime Time* revealed details of a memo sent by Nóirín O'Sullivan, while still the Deputy Commissioner, in November 2013. O'Sullivan was ordering all of the assistant commissioners beneath her to ensure 'all serious incidents on matters of notoriety [were] brought to their immediate attention' – and to pass on those details to her own office without fail. The memo made no specific mention of any contemporary incidents, but the timing did – maybe by coincidence? – clash with the climax of McCabe's slow rise to notoriety within Garda headquarters.

Elsewhere on the show as a panellist was Pat Rabbitte, the former Labour leader who had always enjoyed media appearances, and had more time for them now that he had retired from the Dáil. Rabbitte had been in Cabinet at the time of Maurice McCabe's run-in with Garda headquarters over the PAC and penalty points – so presenter David McCullagh had an obvious question: had he heard of the rumours around the whistleblower?

In fact, yes, he had. Rabbitte had encountered McCabe in early 2007 when he was still serving as Labour leader, and when McCabe needed guidance on how to raise his concerns about policing difficulty in Cavan–Monaghan. That meant when the penalty points controversy arose in 2014, when asked on TV for his reading of McCabe, he had reason to describe him as an honest and conscientious cop. 'I was approached that night by a friend of mine who is a retired Garda, to say that he didn't know that I had any knowledge of Maurice McCabe and that I better be careful, because did I not know what was going around? And he graphically told me what was going around.'

Rabbitte had not shared this rumour with anyone else, as he did not want to give legs to 'foul gossip', but accepted in hindsight that perhaps he ought to have. 'If this had the weight of senior people in authority you were fearful that there might be some truth in it. In my own case I have no such excuse because I was convinced there was no truth in it.'

Next on the show was a pre-recorded interview with Fine Gael's John Deasy, who served as vice-chair to McGuinness in the previous term's PAC – an item which was thrown into much sharper focus given Rabbitte's comments a few moments earlier.

Deasy revealed that just before Callinan's marathon appearance at the PAC, he too had been approached by a senior Garda bad-mouthing McCabe. (He would not name this senior Garda, other than to say it was *not* Nóirín O'Sullivan.) This senior officer told him McCabe was not to be believed or trusted on anything. 'They were very derogatory … it was a serious attack and very strongly worded.'

A week later, having entertained McCabe in private session at the PAC, Deasy concluded that the whistleblower was indeed a credible witness. 'I think I and others realised that there was a campaign against Maurice McCabe, to undermine his character, [being run by] the Gardaí,' he said.

A couple of weeks later Deasy was in Government Buildings, meeting Enda Kenny on a separate matter. Afterwards he asked to meet Kenny alone for a few minutes, to discuss McCabe and 'the entire affair' – something which should immediately have raised a red flag for the Taoiseach. Deasy and Kenny could never be accused of having a close working relationship. Kenny had given Deasy a high-profile job in his first Fine Gael front bench, making the first-time TD his justice spokesman – but by March 2004 he had been sacked for insistently smoking in the members' bar at Leinster House just a day after the national ban on workplace smoking was introduced. Deasy never regained frontbench status, or any cosiness with his party leader. By the Waterford TD's estimation, the pair had only held one similar private meeting in the previous fifteen years.

'At that meeting I said to him that I believed Maurice McCabe would be vindicated, that he was being treated extremely badly and that he was genuine, and that this needed to be handled completely differently ... He listened, he acknowledged it and the meeting ended.'

'The campaign against Maurice McCabe was extremely effective in hardening opinions with regard to this character. I think that's what we were up against ... He was very badly treated, not just by the political system but also by his colleagues, in my opinion ... I really can't defend anyone in government when it comes to Maurice McCabe.'

Five weeks after his private meeting with Kenny – after Leo Varadkar had broken ranks to declare McCabe and John Wilson as 'distinguished', not disgusting – Deasy had written to Kenny again. 'What I and many of my colleagues don't understand is why Alan [Shatter] would treat these whistleblowers in the manner that he has,' he said. The Garda Inspectorate had just published a report to back up McCabe's complaints about the penalty point system. 'It seems he has had this report in his possession since

January. I believe you should support Leo's position on this, and question Alan's handling of the entire affair.'

***

Fianna Fáil TDs went to bed feeling uneasy. There was no question of throwing the government overboard when the Dáil vote was called the following evening: the party position was settled and would not be abandoned. Collapsing the government would mean a snap general election, and even if the *Sunday Times* poll tempted them to cut and run, there were two practical truths of realpolitik getting in the way: firstly, the party simply wasn't ready for an election, and secondly, it would mean at least a two-month delay in setting up the Tribunal. If an election campaign were to be dominated by the treatment of Maurice McCabe, Fianna Fáil would expect to share the blame for delaying McCabe's access to the truth.

But this did not make their quandary any easier. It was already difficult to voice support for Kenny and his government in the wake of the infamous *This Week* interview, where Kenny had accounted for a conversation that never happened. Now it turned out there was a *separate* conversation with Zappone that Kenny had failed to reveal, a conversation which now seemed to completely unravel the Taoiseach's own account of what he knew, and when. Combine that with the suspicions that maybe Kenny knew more than he had let on, and the more traditional scorpion-and-frog relationship between the two parties, and it was even more difficult to make peace with party policy.

Party headquarters offered briefing notes to TDs making media appearances, telling them to divorce 'the politics' of the situation from 'the policy'. The politics were difficult – and clearly ministers in government were struggling to communicate with each other, let alone the public – but the focus should be on the policy. The Dáil would clear the way for the Tribunal on Thursday, but risked being dissolved only a day early if Sinn Féin's motion were to pass. Fianna Fáil's job, TDs were told, is to get the Tribunal up and running – that was why Micheál Martin had gone to the Taoiseach's office that morning and handed over some suggested terms of reference. It would be left up to Fine Gael to deal with the internal recriminations.

In short, Fianna Fáil told its TDs it was not in the national interest to force a general election. Instead, the short-term interests of Fianna Fáil, Maurice McCabe, Leo Varadkar and Simon Coveney had fallen into crucial alignment. As long as the Independent Alliance remained on board, Enda Kenny would survive the motion of no confidence. The real question was how much longer he might survive beyond that.

DAY 9

Wednesday, 15 February 2017

'Furious Alliance may see coalition collapse', screamed the headline on the *Irish Examiner*. 'Alliance members have demanded a Cabinet meeting today as well as a separate meeting with Taoiseach Enda Kenny to discuss their concerns,' the report claimed. 'They are furious over Mr Kenny's misleading of the public over a story about a conversation with Katherine Zappone, the children's minister. Mr Kenny is under pressure after admitting he was "guilty" of telling the country about a phone call that never actually happened.'

Other papers focused on the internal machinations within Fine Gael. 'Coveney and Varadkar seek to calm backbench alarm at Kenny,' read the *Irish Times* splash, reporting how the two pretenders to the office of Taoiseach were trying to soothe those demanding an urgent change of leader. 'As concern about Mr Kenny's performance has spread, Mr Varadkar and Mr Coveney, the two front-runners to succeed him as Fine Gael leader, have spent recent days trying to assuage the worries of members of the parliamentary party ahead of a meeting tonight.'

The report added that the Independent Alliance had planned to publicly announce its support for Kenny the previous day, only for further differences to emerge in Kenny and Zappone's accounts. Inside, Sarah Bardon had penned analysis: 'If Kenny's chairmanship is his biggest asset, the ongoing Cabinet dispute over McCabe and the Tusla file calls that ability into focus. A senior figure described the predicament Fine Gael finds itself in as "the biggest shit storm".'

The Ireland edition of *The Times* also carried details of fractious exchanges between the Fine Gael and Independent Alliance ministers around the Cabinet table, but the *Irish Independent* provided the most eye-catching headline: 'It's all over for Kenny after his visit to Trump: Final straw as "guilty" Taoiseach changes story on McCabe affair': 'After a week that has rocked Fine Gael, a growing number of TDs and ministers are now briefing against Mr Kenny. There is now a widely held belief in Leinster House that the party leader should get a final chance to step down.' The paper reported on how Coveney, Varadkar and Harris were spotted together in the members' bar the night before, and speculated about a showdown at that evening's weekly meeting of the Fine Gael parliamentary party.

Meanwhile, Fianna Fáil's torture at the current situation was neatly portrayed by Billy Kelleher's uneasy appearance on Radio 1's *Morning Ireland*. Asked to characterise the Taoiseach's performance the previous day, Kelleher continually strove for the words 'shambolic' and 'incoherent' – making it all the more difficult to justify keeping him in power. But then, how would Fianna Fáil justify its stance? How could Fianna Fáil have confidence in a Taoiseach who had given one account in a radio interview on Sunday, and then two different accounts in the Dáil two days later?

Kelleher's explanation was that the party believed that, shambolic as it might be, there was no intent on Kenny's part to mislead, and an incompetent government was better than an unstable one. By taking the position it had, Fianna Fáil had at least secured a stable government. Now its job was to press the government from outside, to ensure competence too. Besides, he said – disregarding the *Sunday Times* poll from the previous weekend – the opinion polls showed that little had changed in the public mind in the year since the last general election. Unless someone had come up with a 'magic formula' for providing an alternative government, he reasoned, a fresh election would simply throw up another fractured and ungovernable Dáil. He had a point: if Fianna Fáil created some distrust with Fine Gael by pulling the plug on the last government, it would be even harder to rebuild that trust second time around. 'New Politics' was so fragile that anyone who damaged it would find it tough to glue back together.

On the same programme, RTÉ's political correspondent Martina Fitzgerald – a reporter not given to hyperbole, or quick to pass hasty judgements – was blunt in her assessment. 'This controversy has caused so much damage to the government, but most of it has been self-inflicted. And really, [since] last Friday we've had clarifications and discrepancies, but you would have expected yesterday – four days on – for them to be on the same page, for them to have clarified their position after a Cabinet meeting, and that no new angle would have emerged.

'And what is frightening, and causing nervousness in Fine Gael: they're really concerned about how the Taoiseach, in particular, has handled this. But their first and foremost priority is to get over this: it's about the government.'

On Newstalk, political editor Shane Coleman was equally blunt. 'There's a moment where every leader, every Taoiseach, every prime minister, where their authority is gone ... I think we reached that moment yesterday. Enda Kenny was at sixes and sevens. It was utterly, utterly hapless. Fair enough, the Taoiseach has dozens of meetings every day – it's understandable he might have gotten mixed up [over] who actually told him something. But for him to relay details of a conversation that never actually existed? It was humiliating to have to clarify that.' The argument that Kenny was a steady hand at the tiller, with Brexit advancing, was shot.

Also on Newstalk was Trevor Collins, solicitor for Keith Harrison, who wanted to make his client's case for being included in the forthcoming Tribunal. Collins argued that Harrison's life had been made hell through brutal and intimidatory treatment by Garda colleagues almost immediately after he had raised concerns about the conduct of a colleague stationed in Athlone.

Collins claimed that after Harrison and his partner, Marisa Simms, moved to Donegal, where Simms had family connections, local Gardaí had pursued her, forcing her to attend the local station for eight hours of questioning in November 2013. Simms was told that her children would be in jeopardy if she did not make a formal complaint about Harrison's domestic conduct. Simms, simply trying to end the ordeal and get home, did so. Almost immediately a senior Garda referred the case to Tusla, where files were created on the Simms children. Although Tusla stated at the time there was 'nothing to see here', four months later it wrote to both Harrison and Simms and invited them to a meeting. Collins said there was little explanation for Tusla's seeming change of heart, but the meeting went ahead. The very next day, Tusla social workers arrived at the couple's home for a formal inspection at which – again – nothing untoward was found.

Collins believed all of this behaviour suggested 'something untoward or abusive on the part of Keith Harrison' even though no formal allegation had ever been laid against him. All of this had 'destroyed' the family. Tusla had descended on them, the family structure was being undermined, their credibility as parents was being attacked, and Simms herself was left to fear the prospect that her children would be taken away. Yet, it seemed, Frances Fitzgerald had largely fobbed off Harrison's numerous letters on the basis that Nóirín O'Sullivan was declaring public support for whistleblowers. This, as the solicitor put it, was a 'misrepresentation of the truth'.

***

At 10 a.m. the Independent Alliance members met to dwell on their own position. The previous day's statement remained in draft form, and though the nerves had settled again overnight, there remained some anxiety about giving Fine Gael a free pass and simply writing off the McCabe–Tusla scandal as an isolated mistake. What would the price be for their complicity in keeping Enda Kenny in power?

The world kept turning while the Alliance was meeting. In Croke Park, attending a conference for carers, Simon Harris issued a public love letter in a bid to keep them on board. 'The participation of the Independent Alliance is crucial to government survival,' he announced. 'They have many people playing a very important role, and I think it's a time for cool heads, it's a time for people to deliberate on the important issues – but ultimately it's a time to put the national interest first. The best thing we can do as a public and as an Oireachtas is set up a full public inquiry to address these very serious allegations.'

Also during their meeting an important clarification emerged from Government Buildings. Senior advisors to Kenny had noticed some confused reporting and wanted to set the record straight.

The failure to include on the Dáil running order the government's own motion of confidence was simply a bureaucratic oversight – and there was no need to fret about the internal health of the administration. Though it was not announced to journalists at the post-Cabinet media briefing, the previous day's truncated Cabinet meeting had, in fact, signed off on the motion of confidence, and the Independent Alliance's grumbling behind closed doors was not going to be fatal – formally, at least. That wasn't to say that the Alliance was completely on board, or happily signed up (at that moment) to Kenny's account of events, but it did at least mean the Alliance wanted the government to remain in office. At that moment, however, it was not something to be taken for granted.

With that in mind, the prospect of a Cabinet meeting had receded. The most vital item of business had been disposed of, so there was no need to rush back into the room – particularly when the Alliance's position was still unclear, and there was every fear that Shane Ross would deliver another furious 'bollocking' (as one witness labelled the previous day's excoriation), whipping himself back into a near-stupor of fury and, in the heat of the moment, convincing himself to walk out of government entirely.

Kenny's diary had little space for a possible Cabinet meeting, anyway. The Taoiseach was due 750 yards away from the office, at the offices of online recruitment firm Indeed, which was opening a new headquarters and creating 500 jobs. Ordinarily it was the sort of occasion Kenny would love – a typical 'good news' story where a more upbeat Taoiseach would happily chirp away to the waiting media, even if unplanned. (Kenny would sometimes talk to reporters on the way in to work on Tuesday mornings before Cabinet meetings, but otherwise would not usually entertain the media on Tuesdays or Wednesdays, on the premise that reporters would hear from him at Leaders' Questions in the Dáil anyway.)

On this occasion, however, there was no conviviality. Kenny gave a formulaic speech from the podium and kept a wide berth from the hacks. One reporter said they were 'almost manhandled' away from Kenny as they tried to raise inquiries. His only contribution to the media was to sit on a stage beneath Indeed's corporate slogan ('We help people find jobs'), allowing some creative photographers to get photographs of the Taoiseach with the word 'help' over his head. One such snap, with Kenny looking into the air as the word hovered over him, would feature heavily in the following morning's newspapers. Ministers were aggrieved at the relative lack of coverage for the event itself: only a few days ago Mary Mitchell O'Connor was being pilloried for the loss of 500 jobs in HP in Leixlip; now the creation of the same number of roles in the city centre was barely remarked on.

Kenny did not have much time on his hands anyway. He had scheduled fifteen minutes to shoot videos for MerrionStreet.ie, the government's PR website, before having to prepare for another bout of Leaders' Questions. At least there would be little scope for nasty shocks: often the worst possible outcome in Leaders' Questions would be that an opposition leader would raise a topic on which Kenny had not been drilled in advance.

There was little chance of that today.

***

Micheál Martin rounded on the gap in the Taoiseach's explanation that had gathered wind the previous evening, when extra scrutiny had fallen on his assurances to Zappone. Fianna Fáil had been quiet throughout that passage of the Q&A session, but would not hold fire now. 'How could you know that the Commission of Investigation would cover the allegations if you knew nothing about the allegations themselves?'

Kenny's languid reply did not address this question. Instead he set about recapping the timetable of events thus far – including how, on 24 January, Zappone's advisor had contacted one of his own to notify him about the forthcoming meeting, and how Zappone had followed up with him in person on 7 February in 'a brief informal conversation', where he claimed she had not gone into the specific detail of the allegations or Tusla's mishandling of them.

Eventually he turned to Martin's question, but retained his flat and phlegmatic tone. The previous evening he had been animated, sometimes even snarky, when left-wing opponents had raised the same issue. With his tenure dependent on Fianna Fáil's cooperation that night, there was no such bravado now. 'It was absolutely clear to me that these allegations, of a false nature, would be fully covered by Justice O'Neill's draft terms of reference as allegations of criminal misconduct against Sergeant McCabe are at the very core of the proposed constitution's [*sic*] remit.' Once again, he said, Peter Charleton had agreed with him.

'But Judge Charleton's conclusion is retrospective,' Martin countered. 'You don't know the details of the allegation at the time, is what you're saying, in the Tusla file. So it therefore begs the question: how did anyone in the Cabinet know? … It seems an extraordinary display of Cabinet telepathy at work – that each individual minister deduced for themselves, individually, that this was somehow going to cover something that nobody knew anything about.'

The choice of words had elegantly underlined the logical gymnastics on show.

Gerry Adams was next in line, taking issue with both of the larger parties and defending the motion of no confidence being discussed that night. While some in Fianna Fáil had accused him of trying to collapse the Dáil before McCabe got his answers, Adams claimed it was the government itself withholding those answers – before turning to read the text of the Government's counter-motion from the Dáil order paper. '"Dáil Éireann reaffirms its confidence in the Government",' he read, pointing out that its only signatory was the Taoiseach himself. 'How could that be? Could the Taoiseach not get the support of anyone else in Fine Gael or the so-called Independents in government? Could he not get a dig out from his friends and partners in Fianna Fáil?' Kenny, again wearing his parliamentary earpiece, smiled. It was simple parliamentary routine that ministers were the sole sponsors of their motions, nothing more.

Eventually Adams arrived at his question, and pre-guarded against an *ad hominem* attack from Kenny – the same sort of Máiría Cahill-themed reply he had received only a day earlier, which already seemed like a lifetime ago. 'You clearly won't want to answer my question, and indeed you may wish to attack me personally. You can do it again and again and again,' – turning his attention away from Kenny and back towards the chairman – 'but that, as part of his mock feigned anger, will not get anyone, in particular the McCabe family, any answers.'

The question, ultimately, was the same as Micheál Martin's. The only way Kenny could know this Tusla allegation would be covered by an inquiry into a smear campaign was if he knew it was the same allegation Dave Taylor had relied upon. But that would require him to have seen Taylor's protected disclosure. '*Sin an fhírinne*,' Adams declared, '– that's the truth'. So had Kenny actually been briefed on the contents of Taylor's disclosure – a document he wasn't supposed to know anything about?

Kenny had three minutes to reply but, with the party political route closed off to him, needed only thirty-seven seconds. Of course he hadn't seen them – he was forbidden from seeing the documents or even from inquiring into their contents. But the terms of reference mentioned an allegation of criminal misconduct, he said, and that seemed enough.

'But "criminal misconduct" could have been anything – anything at all,' said Adams, who completely dismissed Kenny's reply as being legally prescribed. As he saw it, the Taoiseach simply couldn't admit to the apparently obvious – that he *had* been aware of Taylor's allegation – because doing so would confirm that the allegations were illegally shared with him in the first place. But that also sidestepped the possibility that Kenny had heard the original rumours swirling around Leinster House years earlier. 'That's why this question is entirely relevant – that's why your motion of confidence in yourself should be rejected by the Dáil, and that's why you should give us a definitive, definite, conclusive answer to this totally relevant question. When did you first become aware of the false allegation against Maurice McCabe?'

It was a question Kenny didn't answer, instead reciting his logic that the terms of reference were self-evidently wide enough to include whatever allegations had made their way to Tusla.

The Taoiseach was granted some brief respite by Mattie McGrath, who deployed his usual mile-a-minute delivery to raise concern about shortages of school places for children with autism in Tipperary. The Greens' Eamon Ryan, concluding the session, returned to the topic of the day and raised other concerns. How did nobody sit up and take notice when Zappone's aides had approached Kenny's staff, notifying them of the plans to meet McCabe? From his own time in Cabinet, Ryan knew this ought to have set off some alarm bells straight away. The system was set up almost precisely so that special advisors could raise concerns about issues in advance of escalating them to ministerial level. 'All the red lights would be going, in my mind, in any functioning government, that that would be an issue that would have to be discussed at cabinet.'

While again telling the absent Independent Alliance that they worked well in government, Kenny could only reply: 'Yes, it's true that one learns lessons on these things all the time, on how business has to be conducted.'

This was new territory for everyone. Only a handful of independents had ever served in Cabinet before, and rarely at the same time. The improvised coalition with a group of five, and the formal acquiescence of two more, meant everyone was on a learning curve.

* * *

Kenny had more places to be. He was detained in the chamber for a further hour, however, taking scripted questions about meetings with the ECB governor Mario Draghi and Brexit. The latter theme was one he would get a chance to elaborate on: when finished in the chamber, there was just enough time for lunch before Kenny was due at the Mansion House to address the Institute of International and European Affairs (IIEA). It was holding a major symposium to discuss the forthcoming Brexit process – the 'Article 50' notification to set the ball rolling was imminent – and Kenny had been asked to recap on Ireland's broad negotiating tactics.

The occasion would have justified a large media presence by itself, but the Taoiseach's extra travails meant the press area was packed to capacity. Indeed, a sizeable media scrum politely waited outside the building – on the rational premise that Kenny would make the 600-metre journey on foot – but Kenny was driven to the event instead, and shepherded through a side door. The media then filed inside to hear Kenny outline a plan for seeking European aid for Irish business damaged by the UK's departure, all while making no comment around the role he would personally play.

While Kenny was speaking, a statement landed from Denis Naughten, one of the non-alliance independents in Cabinet. He and Dr Michael Harty had met directly with the Taoiseach earlier in the morning, 'to hear personally from the Taoiseach about the events that have unfolded since late last week and to bring clarity to their understanding of the sequence'.

Naughten echoed Katherine Zappone's complaint from the previous evening, when she bemoaned the prevalence of 'under-the-arm' memos being brought to Cabinet that did not give other ministers the chance to study them before decisions were needed. Kenny, he said, had agreed to ensure Naughten and Zappone would receive advance briefing on those sensitive memos in future. That, it seemed, was enough to guarantee Naughten's ongoing support.

There was no question of needing to secure Katherine Zappone's support for the government – she was never likely to abscond from the government in the midst of a crisis that was partly, albeit accidentally, of her own making. But Zappone still had meetings of her own to attend to, including hosting Keith Harrison in Leinster House to hear his own account of his perceived mistreatment by Tusla. Afterwards Harrison was appreciative of the chance to be heard. 'To be fair to Minister Zappone, we did receive an apology after she saw the Tusla file and she gave us an assurance the matter would be investigated promptly,' Harrison told *The Sunday Times*. He and Marisa Simms had sent 'one letter to her, and she met us. We sent fourteen to the Tánaiste and she continues to ignore us.'

Word meanwhile came through from the Independent Alliance, which sought a meeting with Kenny and the same negotiating team that had sealed its own participation in government. Unsure of exactly what to make of this request, Kenny gathered the entire team of negotiators – Frances Fitzgerald, Simon Coveney, Paschal Donohoe, Michael Noonan and Simon Harris – in his office to appraise the situation. Leo Varadkar was also invited, but his invite came only after journalists got wind of the meeting, and the social protection minister was visibly annoyed when he showed up at Kenny's office to find that his colleagues had begun strategising without him.

Though formally labelled as 'a genuine oversight', Varadkar's belated invitation might have been a deliberate measure. Varadkar had not quite endeared himself to the Alliance during the talks on government formation, taking a languid back-seat role and leaving Fitzgerald and Coveney to do the bulk of the talking, before suddenly swooping in with the role of 'bad cop' at moments of dispute and threatening the collapse of talks unless the Alliance gave way. Varadkar, irked by the failure to invite him on time, opted not to attend the Independent Alliance meeting at all. Whether by accident or design, however, his absence from the room was taken by the Alliance as a sign it was being treated seriously.

There was good reason for Fine Gael to put on a show. The

Alliance's desperation to keep its government in power was matched by its own devastation at the handling of the previous few days. Some of the Fine Gael attendees were seeing the meeting as if it were a date with an executioner, and dared not predict its outcome. 'You could see the toll it was having on Enda,' one Alliance TD later told *The Sunday Times*. 'Normally, his hair is brushed to perfection but it was standing on his head – a mess. You couldn't help but feel sorry for him.'

The nervousness of the Fine Gael side manifested in a cautious tone to their contributions – except, according to another Alliance TD, when it came to the role of the Gardaí themselves. 'They wanted to resolve it and give [the government] a lifeline, but they were also very defensive. It's in their gene pool, it's in their DNA, to be defensive on the whole issue of law and order.'

Kenny and his lieutenants sought to assure the Alliance that there was, despite the level of political furore, very little to see. There was no conspiracy, they said; no Deep State at play in trying to undermine an inconvenient Garda. Yes, the entire Cabinet should have been better informed about the whole matter, but that was spilt milk and could not now be cried over. The best thing to do would be to ensure that, when sensitive matters were being broached in future, every minister would be given the full picture.

It did not take long for the Fine Gael ministers to conclude that the Alliance was staying put and fears of a government collapse were overblown. The group of five simply wanted to be taken seriously, and their colleagues on Kenny's side of the table offered ample assurance that their participation was valued. One Fine Gael participant, contrary to the earlier fears, recounted the meeting as being surprisingly cordial. 'You know how they operate,' they later quipped. 'They have a tendency to demand these crunch meetings, as they're entitled to do as a part of government, and then generally the meeting is little more than a cup of coffee, where they say their piece.'

So calm was the meeting that most participants, on both sides of the table, have little recollection of it (which, one later explained, 'probably means there was nothing to remember'). One recalled, despite his panic while watching Kenny fluff his lines from the members' bar the previous night, the belief that John Halligan was especially conciliatory.

Though the Alliance was happy with the assurance of closer Cabinet collaboration in future, it could not accept an assurance alone. Members had already had their fingers burned with false dawns on their pet constituency projects; Halligan had already come close to walking out over the failure to provide even a temporary Waterford cath lab. A simple oral guarantee that things would change, to borrow the old quip, was not worth the paper it was written on.

'It sounds a bit crass, but there had to be something in it for us,' one Alliance TD recalled. 'There had to be a reason to stay, beyond just supporting our coalition partner.'

The Fine Gael team did not have much of a breather between that meeting with the Independent Alliance and the weekly get-together of the parliamentary party, which was getting underway at 5.30 p.m. Many were only making their way towards the fifth floor of the Leinster House southern wing, when the Independent Alliance's press handlers sent word around: the Alliance would address the media on the plinth at 5.45 p.m. The motion of confidence was due within the hour, and despite everything, nobody could be 100 per cent sure that the Alliance would back it.

***

In this case, a week had certainly been a long time in politics. At the previous Fine Gael parliamentary party meeting, there had been only scant discussion on the future of Nóirín O'Sullivan, especially following that day's Dáil intervention by Brendan Howlin. Otherwise, the most notable issue had been a complaint from Kilkenny TD John Paul Phelan to Simon Coveney about a purported plan to transfer some land from south Kilkenny into Waterford. That was the meeting during which Frances Fitzgerald got the call from Jim O'Callaghan, after which they met and did-or-didn't discuss the Tusla file on McCabe. Now, seven days on, the continued tenure of the Taoiseach was a matter of live discussion.

Or was it? Kenny was (typically) a few minutes late, and party chairman Martin Heydon declined to start the meeting without him (leaving even less time, critics moaned, to discuss the party leadership). The Taoiseach eventually arrived ten minutes behind schedule, upon which Heydon invited him to make an opening speech.

Kenny spoke, but not for terribly long. As with any other week, he accounted for his activities of the last few days and offered a general overview of government activity. He concluded by informing his troops that the previous week 'had not been easy' and that he accepted 'responsibility' for the political tumult that followed his botched radio appearance – but TDs needed to divert their attention to the motion of confidence facing them tonight. If everyone would only focus on that near-term issue, they would give Kenny 'an opportunity to talk with the parliamentary party at a different time' about the 'pressures and frustration' that were now arising.

There was, by all accounts, 'not a word' explicitly acknowledging the frailty of his position as leader. The reference to a future talk was clearly a shielded reference to his own political mortality, but Kenny hadn't given a tangible indication on when this chat might happen. In truth, the talk had already begun – there were precious few loyalists within the party who had not already been chatting behind the Taoiseach's back, and Kenny knew it. His refusal to broach the topic more explicitly might have been seen as a sign that he was knuckling down.

As Kenny concluded, Heydon briefly commented on the need to avoid deep and damaging divisions. 'United we stand, divided we fall,' he said. Backbencher Alan Farrell suggested the meeting be adjourned. 'Let's get down to the chamber,' he offered, urging everyone to unite behind Kenny for the coming hours at least.

Heydon deferred that decision so that Michael Noonan could have his say. Not only was the Minister for Finance Kenny's predecessor as leader, but he also held one of the three Cabinet jobs with a specific name-check in the Constitution of Ireland. What's more, he had served in governments going back as far as the early 1980s. He might have been dumped as party leader without ceremony in 2002, but he had navigated his way back to the top table of Irish politics and was now a bona fide political heavyweight. Noonan had become one of Kenny's most senior lieutenants, without ever seeming like one of his loyalists. When he spoke, people listened.

Noonan's other major asset was a soothing, calm demeanour. Many journalists had stories of times when they had bumped into him around Leinster House, where Noonan would hunch forward and lower his voice, giving the impression that he was about to share some sensitive or juicy information ... only to state something blithely obvious. ('I'll tell you one thing,' the hurling fan might whisper, 'Limerick have a long way to go before they win the All-Ireland.')

This baritone delivery was deployed once more now. The finance minister went into lengthy, almost excruciating, detail about how the economy had dramatically rebounded during Fine Gael's tenure. 'Practically every objective we have set has been achieved,' he said. The Troika had been kicked out; Ireland was free to pursue its own economic objectives; unemployment had sunk from over fifteen per cent to under six; two million people were at work. Fine Gael (and he and Enda Kenny) had taken Ireland from the doldrums and put it back on a sound footing from which it could thrive once more.

Noonan spoke at such length that, although there were no explicit references to the party leadership dilemma, some in the room believed he might be mounting a filibuster. The Dáil motion of confidence was to be debated at 6.45 p.m., which offered a natural deadline for the Fine Gael meeting to conclude. Noonan's speech seemed to be dragging on for an interminable length. Every minute he spoke was a minute taken away from others who wanted to use the opportunity to vent their concerns.

On the face of it, Noonan's speech was all-purpose: it bought time, calmed nerves and reminded everyone present that they should have no reservations about trooping into the division lobbies of Dáil Éireann that night and reaffirming their confidence in the Government of Ireland as led by Enda Kenny. Under the surface, however, it deprived Kenny's critics of an opportunity to take aim at the party leader.

Those critics in the room grew twitchy. The anticipated showdown was turning into a washout.

***

While Noonan continued his soliloquy, going on for almost fifteen minutes, the Independent Alliance were marching to the plinth. Shane Ross took the lead, reading from a statement – a tweaked version of the same statement that been abandoned the previous evening – outlining the group's contact with Maurice McCabe and the determination not only to establish the truth, but to tackle the cultures that might have led the smear campaign to be pursued.

'We have been dismayed and, frankly, disturbed by contradictory versions of events which have emerged this week,' Ross read (including both of the words over which members had dithered a day earlier). 'Some aspects of Cabinet communications are not working effectively or appropriately. This is not how we wish to do business.

'We went into Government in good faith in order to implement the commitments we secured in the Programme for Government after protracted negotiations. We went into Government to provide a voice for the marginalised in Irish society, to ensure that those who have been hit hardest by the years of recession will be cared for. We went into Government to end cronyism and that insider culture which can prove so corrupting to society.'

Where was this going – was the Alliance about to walk?

'A Government is greater than any individual or personality within it and we are committed to delivering on the promises we made when we took office …'

Then the punchline: 'Our continued participation in Government will be conditional on a comprehensive resolution of what are, by any standards, extremely worrying allegations of malpractice within areas of An Garda Síochána in relation to Sergeant McCabe, in relation to other whistleblowers, and more generally…

'We in the Independent Alliance have therefore secured a commitment from the Minister for Justice today to appoint without delay an independent, international policing expert to carry out a thorough investigation into the wider and more fundamental issues of public concern which have emerged ...'

That was it. The group had extracted the concession it needed. The Independent Alliance was on board. The government was safe. But how uneasy was the marriage? Journalists jumped in with questions. What exactly had Ross and his band of brothers said to Kenny?

'We said that we were very disappointed with a lot of the confusion that had occurred within government in recent days, and that we found it unacceptable, and we hoped it wouldn't happen in future.'

Had withdrawal from government been an option?

'We considered it.'

Finian McGrath interrupted. The appointment of an international policing expert to examine the cultural issues should not be overlooked, he said. 'We're going to weed out people that are involved in any bad practices in any situations, and that's where we've given a commitment today.'

Has the Taoiseach clarified for you his account of events?

'I think there is still confusion. I think the truth is that there is still confusion about what happened at that stage, and we've made it quite clear it is something which we found very, very difficult to understand. No, I'm not very clear about that yet, and I don't think anybody else is.'

So do you actually have confidence in him?

'What we've said about that is this: we are upset and very distressed by what has happened, both with the Taoiseach and with other members of government in the last few days. We do not think it would be appropriate, in this situation where we're putting down a motion of confidence in the government, to suggest that we have no confidence in the Taoiseach.'

What about the future of Nóirín O'Sullivan as Commissioner?

'The issue of the Commissioner is a completely and utterly separate one, and it's one which we believe that it would be absolutely wrong – as it would have been with the McCabes – to prejudge anything at all.'

'But can you believe Enda Kenny when he says things?' There was no answer to that question: the five TDs were already walking away and back inside the off-the-record safety of Leinster House.

The group of five seemed happy with its achievement, but not all the journalists shared their enthusiasm. The slew of Garda and justice reforms in the previous years had already resulted in an independent Garda Inspectorate that examined broader issues around Garda culture and performance. At that time it was chaired by Robert Olson, a former chief of police in Minneapolis. Surely he was the very definition of an independent, international policing expert? They could be forgiven for thinking that Frances Fitzgerald's 'concession' was simply to set up a new body that had already existed.

Certainly the Fine Gael negotiators – who shared the appetite for a major overhaul of justice administration – were happy to allow a certain amount of overlap. The Alliance, though, was assured that the new review's mandate would exceed that of any previous body. The review granted to them would even consider whether An Garda Síochána ought to be split up, broken into separate bodies dealing with specific intelligence or security functions in line with the global norm.

* * *

Five floors above, Noonan was wrapping up his contribution to the Fine Gael meeting while the Independent Alliance was wrapping up its press conference outside. Taking the two events in aggregate, it suddenly seemed an attack on Enda Kenny was not going to materialise. If all sides – Fine Gael, independents, Fianna Fáil – were focusing on surviving the motion of confidence, it gave everyone a united cause behind which to rally.

Then Leo Varadkar got to his feet. The social protection minister, who had spent the week texting colleagues (from Lima, Bogotá and mid-air) telling them to remain calm, would now intervene first hand.

He began by outlining the impact of the last week's drama on Maurice McCabe, the man whose public popularity had largely mirrored his own – the 'distinguished, not disgusting' remark in 2014 had attracted wide public support and garnished Varadkar's public reputation as a straight talker. McCabe was now described as a 'hero' who deserved, at the very least, a swift tribunal to restore his reputation.

Varadkar's penchant for straight talking would now return. The wild unpredictability of the last week had only highlighted the precarious footing on which the government was placed. It might not happen tonight, but it was plainly obvious now that some other scandal could come along in the not-too-distant future that would cause either Fianna Fáil or the independents to withdraw their support and end the government. 'We must be ready,' he said, 'for an election.' Varadkar even suggested the parliamentary party should bring forward its meeting the next week to specifically discuss those preparations.

This contribution had not come with much fanfare or hysteria – it 'wasn't that dramatic,' one TD texted – but behind the matter-of-fact delivery of anodyne words, the deeper meaning was clear. Kenny had ruled himself out of leading a further election campaign, so if Fine Gael was to be ready for a surprise election, it needed to have a leader who was prepared to lead it. Varadkar, an aspiring leader, was asking for that conversation to begin.

Perhaps wanting to underline the arguments the social protection minister was making behind closed doors – and knowing an account of his speech would get out anyway – Varadkar's press officer sent journalists a copy of the minister's speech for the Dáil's 'motion of confidence' debate, without an embargo, at almost the exact moment he was speaking. In a debate where sympathetic TDs could cite any reason they wished as grounds to keep the government in office, Varadkar's prepared speech conspicuously did not offer *any* defence of the government's record. It referred to Maurice McCabe as 'heroic', but made no mention of the Taoiseach for whom the Dáil's backing was now being sought.

Next came Simon Coveney, the housing minister and Varadkar's likely opponent in the leadership stakes. As a second-generation Fine Gael minister from one of Cork's 'merchant prince' families, Coveney did not enjoy bashing his own party. But he too felt the need to underline the government's frailty. While stressing the need for 'unity' within the party, he declared that the party needed to be ready for a snap election outside of its own control or timing. (The call for 'unity' might have been twofold: to stop the party tearing itself asunder from within, but also a coded call to Kenny not to resist the clear tide of opinion.) The 'future of the party' therefore needed to be addressed, he said.

The symbolism could not be understated. Those in the room with longer memories could recall how, seven years earlier, the same two frontbenchers were among those declaring a lack of confidence in Enda Kenny as party leader. The resulting heave, in which Kenny comprehensively defeated the challenge of Richard Bruton, was often thought of as being the moment Kenny truly came of age. Now the same two men – pretenders to Kenny's throne – were concluding that Kenny needed to be nudged along. The Taoiseach's opening speech had suggested he would not read the tea leaves himself, and both men felt the point needed to be made. Reports at the time suggested the intervention from the same two men were coordinated, a claim contested by both camps afterwards.

Coordinated or not, the dam was broken. Paschal Donohoe, a minister who had often enjoyed Kenny's preferment, made a similar contribution, stressing the volatility of the marriage to Fianna Fáil and the need to be prepared for a short-notice divorce. Simon Harris declared that the country needed Fine Gael to be ready to restate its case, and that Fine Gael in turn could not be caught unawares by an election. Even the Tánaiste herself, Frances Fitzgerald, warned of how ill-prepared Fine Gael would be if the Dáil were suddenly to be dissolved. Five of the Fine Gael ministers who had taken part in the government formation talks were now warning that the party's grip on power was tenuous enough to warrant a serious intervention.

'We all wanted him – and when I say "we", I mean a significant majority of the parliamentary party – wanted Enda to be able to leave on his own terms,' said one critic. 'We trusted him to do that and to get it right. But the fright this gave us made it very clear that this is not a majority government, and therefore the timing might be out of your hands.'

Each of the five ministers had been careful to phrase their words delicately. None had pointedly demanded the Taoiseach's resignation – all had, rather, simply inferred the need to prepare the party for a worst-case scenario. One witness said the true message was delivered through 'nuance and implication, as much as what was said by anyone and everyone'. Nobody would have been in any doubt, however, over exactly what was being implied.

With ministers having opened fire, more junior members were free to take aim. Seán Kyne, the junior minister responsible for Gaeltacht affairs, and backbenchers Michael D'Arcy and Pat Deering all chipped in to the conversation, making more explicit links between Fine Gael's election preparation and Kenny's future. For those who had tried to choose their words carefully, some of the later speeches came across as crass, even 'brutal'. The more pointed tone drew some animated defences from two of Kenny's loyalists, long-standing Kildare TD Bernard Durkan and Kerry Senator Paul Coghlan.

With energies now stirred, some (including, briefly, Varadkar) even suggested that the parliamentary party should meet again the following day, when both the motion of confidence and the Tribunal technicalities would be disposed of – clearing the decks for a more open discussion about the future of Kenny's leadership. Heydon was having none of it, saying more notice would have to be given, but leaving open the prospect of perhaps bringing forward the following week's meeting.

It was a somewhat sour, but pointed, note on which the meeting disbanded. Kenny could have been in no doubt about where his lieutenants stood.

'It wasn't a heave,' one participant said. 'There were no nasty divisions, or at least there weren't intended to be. Instead it was a genuine realisation by practising politicians that the game was up, whether we wanted it or not. We had a choice: we could either be humiliated by Fianna Fáil at a time of its choosing, or we could resolve that never again would we find ourselves on the cusp of a general election not knowing who was going to be on the posters.'

Below the radar, Fianna Fáil's parliamentary party had also held its own weekly meeting at around the same time, where Micheál Martin wanted to ensure his members were all fully squared with the voting policy for later in the night – a policy which, in truth, was implemented unilaterally by the party leader himself. The only vocal opponent was John McGuinness, who said he would struggle to renew the mandate of a government in which he, personally, had no confidence. The rest accepted they would have to abstain, albeit with heavy hearts.

Martin used the opportunity to tell the party's TDs that they were no longer to question the position of Nóirín O'Sullivan. Only two days earlier, Martin had gone on local radio in Cork and called on the Garda Commissioner to consider whether her role was still tenable. Now, the instruction was she was to be left in situ while the Tribunal made sense of her future. 'Innocent until proven guilty,' Martin said, more than once.

* * *

Enda Kenny and Frances Fitzgerald emerged together from the corridor joining the ministerial offices to the Dáil chamber, but there were striking differences in their demeanour. The Tánaiste bounced down the stairs and straight to the dais for a twenty-second chit-chat with Pat 'the Cope' Gallagher, the Leas-Cheann Comhairle, seeking clarity on whether she would get to speak immediately after the Taoiseach, or whether opposition leaders would get to go first.

Kenny, though, did not show the same vim. He ambled

carefully down the steps, eyes fixed on his notes. After sitting, he did not pass words or even make eye contact with a single other TD. One colleague later mentioned that, so sour was his mood, Kenny had simply walked away from a backbencher who had met him en route into the chamber and who wanted to stress the absence of any ill will.

'The Taoiseach will have ten minutes,' Gallagher announced. 'In your own time, Taoiseach …'

Kenny's microphone, already active, amplified the heavy sound of his pen being dropped on the heavy wooden desk and his notebook being dropped to the carpet beside him.

'… to move the motion?' Gallagher prompted. The Taoiseach's preparation seemed so languid and unhurried that nobody could be sure he had even heard his name being called. But Kenny had heard him – he simply didn't want to be rushed. Gathering and organising the A4 sheets of his script, he took one final sip of water before rising to his feet and fastening one button on his suit jacket. Perhaps it was his way of avoiding the same rushed demeanour that had prefaced his disastrous radio interview three days earlier.

'I'm pleased to have this opportunity to report to the House about the important work being undertaken by the government, the major challenges that face the country, and how the government intends to meet those challenges,' he opened. Of all the occasions on which Kenny could be accused of misleading the Dáil, the first six words were perhaps the most apparent: he didn't look, or sound, at all pleased with his opportunity.

Other ministers had now all taken their seats – a rare occasion in which almost the entire Cabinet was present for a Dáil debate, highlighting a minor deficiency in the chamber's furniture. The block inhabited by the Taoiseach only had eight seats on its front row, but Fine Gael had ten Cabinet-rank ministers and some would have to sit physically removed from their colleagues.

Three opted to sit elsewhere: Simon Coveney, Leo Varadkar and Simon Harris. An hour earlier that triad had implicitly demanded that Fine Gael prepare for life without Enda Kenny. The optics of the same trio now sitting physically removed from their colleagues was stark.

'This debate is also an opportunity to expose the political opportunism that has resulted in this motion,' Kenny continued. 'Sinn Féin, not content with collapsing the power-sharing arrangements in Northern Ireland, now want to cause similar chaos down here.'

'That didn't take long,' grumbled Sinn Féin's David Cullinane from across the floor, unmoved by the partisan attack.

'By their actions, Sinn Féin have deprived the people of Northern Ireland' – he was now looking up, directly across at Cullinane and his comrades on the Sinn Féin benches – 'a representation at this crucial time in the Brexit process, and I am not going to let them do the same in this state.'

The Taoiseach had evidently decided that attack would be the best form of defence. 'When one reflects on the history of that party's relationship with An Garda Síochána over the years, and their shameful handling of sexual abuse claims within their own movement, they have a brass neck to call for a general election on these issues.'

Ordinarily that kind of partisan barb would elicit some raucous cheers from his party faithful. This time, there was barely a smirk.

Before Kenny could go any further down that road, there was some important housekeeping to attend to. 'The false allegations against Sergeant Maurice McCabe are simply appalling. Sexual abuse is the worst crime that a person could be accused of. He and his family deserve the truth, as do all against whom allegations have been made. I therefore offer a full apology to Maurice McCabe and his family for the treatment meted out to them as exposed in recent programmes.'

Kenny denied that McCabe's treatment was the by-product of government policy, outlining for posterity the actions taken at every stage to investigate and vindicate McCabe's complaints over several years, before nodding to his government partners. 'I recognise the long-term commitment of Independent Alliance colleagues acting in the interests of the McCabe family and the cause of whistleblowers ... I hope the work of the Tribunal of Inquiry will also contribute to the ongoing process of policing reform, which is absolutely necessary in the public interest.' From there it was once again a recap of his encounters with Katherine Zappone and the mistaken recollections, for which he had already apologised.

'An election is the last thing the country needs less than a year after the last one. At a time of huge international uncertainty we need stability, and in a few short weeks the formal negotiations on Brexit will begin. Ireland is well prepared for this process but we do need to hit the ground running as soon as Article 50 is triggered. Our Programme for Government is based on a clear principle to use the fruits of a strong and well-managed economy to improve the daily lives of our people. That plan is working ...'

With a final quick tour of the work still to do, to put the final fix to the construction collapse, and to ensure the public finances did not succumb to another crash, Kenny concluded. 'The delivery of these and other initiatives in the programme for government is what the country needs to meet the very real challenges ahead, not political stunts by the Sinn Féin party. I commend the motion to the House.'

Returning to his seat, Kenny fixed his gaze at the ceiling. Nobody on the ministerial benches beside him sought to make eye contact, or even look directly at the Taoiseach. The only sign of any life on the benches at all was from Dara Murphy, seated a few yards away from Kenny, who made an unrecorded quip that drew smiles from Seán Kyne and Eoghan Murphy alongside him. But that was all.

In the final fight of his political life, a landmark speech from the Taoiseach failed to elicit even as much as a sole 'hear, hear' from anyone sitting near him. The demeanour of the Fine Gael group as a whole suggested its members had simply lost interest in Enda Kenny.

Kenny might at least have appreciated one consolation prize. Micheál Martin had chosen to adopt the same Shinner-bashing stance, opening with a barb against Sinn Féin's 'legion of online trolls' while Fianna Fáil had sought not to play politics with the crisis of the previous week.

'There's no question but that the government has, especially over the past week, handled this matter in a casual and an incompetent manner. The Taoiseach and his Ministers failed to react with appropriate concern when deeply disturbing information was brought to their attention concerning the possible use of a State agency to terrorise an honourable servant of the State. Their complacency in relation to ensuring this matter would be fully investigated by the proposed inquiry is appalling and is clearly at the heart of their ongoing failure to respond to any of the many ways in which they were informed about the Tusla file.' Martin's words cut like a scalpel: even the most fervent or partisan Fine Gael supporter could not deny their truth.

There was, too, a final barb at Frances Fitzgerald and her unresolved dispute with Jim O'Callaghan, now relegated far down the pecking order. 'We have no doubt whatsoever about the fact that the Tánaiste knew from multiple sources, including a direct conversation with Deputy O'Callaghan, that requests to broaden the inquiry's terms of reference were specifically founded on the need to include the Tusla file.' Frances Fitzgerald bowed her own head, shaking it slightly, as Martin continued. 'Just as when they met each other, members of the government may have talked but they appear never to have listened.'

Looking to the press gallery – as Martin often did, especially when a punchline was coming – he added: 'May I say, [on] news coming from the Fine Gael parliamentary party: it's great to hear that Fine Gael ministers have rediscovered their voices, having been running from journalists for the last three days.'

All of that left Martin to explain how his party would act now. 'We do want a change of government,' he elaborated, 'but we also believe that this Dáil has not yet fulfilled its obligations to the people, who we are elected to serve. My party's priorities are to address this scandal, and to help our country overcome the many challenges it faces. There is no evidence that an immediate election will do this. We will abide by our agreement.'

That is why Fianna Fáil would abstain in the motion – a stance that, he jibed, Sinn Féin would criticise now. But only two months previously, when Stormont discussed a motion of confidence in Arlene Foster as Northern Ireland's First Minister, Sinn Féin – one of her government partners at the time – had taken a similar tack.

But it wasn't all sunshine and endless patience. 'However,' he added, 'there is a point after which all good faith efforts to make this Dáil work will have failed, and there will be no alternative but to have an election. That point is much closer today than it was last week: it may well be reached if there are further revelations which suggest that the government has been acting in bad faith in this matter, or if it fails to honour both the spirit and the detail of its agreements.'

The implication of Martin's speech was that the confidence and supply arrangement would not survive many more crises of this scale. It was effectively a final warning, akin to a jilted lover's ultimatum: if you pull this stunt one more time, I'm taking the kids and I'm gone. If anything underlined for Fine Gael the need to stop shipping any more losses, it was that prospect – now stated explicitly for the first time by the leader of Fianna Fáil – of an unplanned election.

By now, of course, the outcome of the motion was already assured. With each integral part of government happy to vote in favour, and with Fianna Fáil content to sit on its hands, the remainder of the debate allowed TDs a captive media audience and the opportunity for a free hit on anyone, or any topic, they liked. It was, effectively, open season. Gerry Adams claimed the two major parties were responsible for 'a culture of insiderism, strokes, cronyism, corruption, graft, cute-hoorism, brown envelopes, dig-outs and whatever-you're-having-yourself, Micheál.'

Brendan Howlin had already sought to carve a niche by lambasting the unproductivity of the current arrangement as a 'Do-Nothing Dáil' – but 'over the last week or so, things have gotten more serious. From doing nothing, the government has actually begun to do harm.' Howlin, complaining that collective

Cabinet responsibility had been virtually abolished in the previous weeks, had one other salient contribution: as the author of the law on whistleblowers, Howlin had included a clause allowing the content of protected disclosures to be shared where it was necessary to allow an investigation, or where it was in the public interest. The constitutional duty of ministers to reach their decisions collectively ought to have been reason enough to share the details with other ministers, even if some could be gossipy.

It was a sobering idea. The notion that ministers *could* legally speak to each other after all, and break down the silos of different Cabinets – avoiding this whole political calamity – was one that hurt some ministers deeply.

And still the hits kept coming. Paul Murphy accused Kenny of 'studious and wilful misunderstanding' after four different TDs had pursued his advice to Katherine Zappone, about how the Tusla file would fall within the terms of reference, when he didn't know either what Tusla had held on file or what Taylor claimed to have said. Murphy's party colleague Ruth Coppinger remarked that if Ireland had 'even a pretence of being a *bourgeoisie* democracy, the Taoiseach and Tánaiste would be gone and an election would be called.' Kerry independent Michael Healy-Rae channelled the words of his late father, Jackie: 'The person that never made a mistake never made anything … but my goodness, how could ye make so many mistakes in the handling of the aftermath of this issue?' Mattie McGrath was less forgiving, saying that while everyone deserved a second chance, the electorate had already cast its verdict once on Enda Kenny's government and the second chance now looked to have been squandered.

There was scant comfort from anywhere else on the opposition benches, as TDs widened their net of complaints. The Social

Democrats' Catherine Murphy said the previous *Prime Time* documentary on scoliosis ought not to be forgotten as another sign of a dysfunctional State; Independents4Change's Joan Collins belittled the government's *laissez-faire* attitude to a forthcoming Bus Éireann strike, which would leave many communities isolated; the Tipperary socialist Seamus Healy noted newspaper reports that Michael Noonan would shortly be accused of acting inappropriately over the sale of a €1bn NAMA portfolio, meeting the winning bidders on the day before the deadline for submissions.

Kenny sat through an hour-long barrage of opposition fire and fury, barely stirring. The business before the House was too serious to justify any jovial or jocular tone, but the Taoiseach had not registered any reaction at all. Other ministers seemed to pass comment to each other, but the leader of the country remained unmoved. One backbencher, with a certain amount of black humour, later compared Kenny's demeanour to an out-of-towner attending a funeral: attending dutifully, looking around and taking note of his surroundings, but not daring to open his mouth or make small talk with strangers, instead sitting silently and regretting having to be there at all.

***

With each opposition group having now spoken, the baton was returned to Fine Gael, where other frontbenchers would have a chance to rally the troops – but it seemed that the leader was the troop who most needed perking up. Frances Fitzgerald went first, following up on one of the Taoiseach's themes – Sinn Féin's woolly support for justice and security forces – before restating a summary of her own actions in the past weeks: her scrupulous handling of the protected disclosures, her work with the Policing Authority and Garda Inspectorates to tackle deeper malaises in the force, and her own ambitious legislative programme.

But there was, again, no cheering or hear-hear from the benches behind – there was barely even a quip from the opposition. On the far side of the chamber Mary Lou McDonald and Pearse Doherty were buried in their phones, and Micheál Martin had left entirely. Much like in the meeting of the Fine Gael parliamentary party, the landmark debate that had hung over the government for four days now seemed all set to become a damp squib.

With Paschal Donohoe next to speak, and given the reputation of Howlin's ministerial successor as a mild-mannered technocrat, there did not seem to be much prospect of a fight. 'I will respond back,' he said, deploying one of his favourite redundant turns of phrase, 'in relation to this motion, to address some of the points made by opposition speakers tonight – we have a motion in front of us here tonight that is motivated only by political objective, only with the aim of destabilising the government …'

That seemed to awaken the Sinn Féin benches. 'It's a government motion!' heckled Pearse Doherty, correctly.

Donohoe's remarks seemed to have been prepared in response to the original Sinn Féin motion of no confidence, rather than the government's affirmative counter-motion, but Donohoe had already extracted the sort of reaction that neither Kenny or Fitzgerald had managed. Harris, Coveney and Varadkar had relocated to the central bloc of seats and now sat alongside as Donohoe continued.

While Fine Gael's actions were always motivated by 'the national interest', Donohoe turned his attention to Ruth Coppinger and Catherine Murphy in particular, punctuating his remarks with the gentle shakes of his lightly closed fist. 'I think there's a special place in hypocrisy heaven for the kinds of claims you have made here tonight. Two Deputies who have stood up on so many occasions asking our citizens to break the law, now stand up here tonight ...'

'Unjust law,' hailed Coppinger, as Richard Boyd Barrett folded his arms in an unimpressed sulk. Coppinger and Murphy had both suggested a boycott of water charges, citing ideological concerns with how they had been introduced. That was a mortal sin under Fine Gael's constitutional law-and-order ideology.

'... purporting to be champions of those who enforce and implement our laws, on behalf of our State,' Donohoe rallied on. 'For you to stand up, who have asked the public – called upon your supporters – to break the law that An Garda Síochána are asked to force and implement, shows the contempt that you have for the institutions of the Gardaí ...'

Boyd Barrett piped up. 'Civil disobedience is slightly different from a smear campaign,' he jibed, as Sinn Féin's TDs murmured nearby.

'That leads me to Sinn Féin and its behaviour here tonight ... there is *nobody* in this House who believes the newfound interest of Sinn Féin in the integrity of An Garda Síochána ...'

The Fine Gael front bench was now beginning to rouse.

'... an institution that has suffered at the hands of your associates, an institution that you have sought to frustrate for decades in this country ... there's nobody here in this House who's buying your newfound interest in whistleblowers, given the way your party, you treated the former senator Máiría Cahill, and given the blatant and ongoing denial of the truth regarding the handling of cases of sexual abuses within the IRA ...'

Mentions of Sinn Féin's intermingled history with republican paramilitarism were common, and nothing that its TDs hadn't heard before. But Donohoe kept pushing, poking, prodding. 'Their antics, their behaviour have debased Dáil Éireann …'

And now there was unhappy chatter on the Sinn Féin benches.

'You have been left politically stranded by an economic change, by a change in our prospects that you said would never happen – that you challenged at every stage. Your lack of vision is masked by an abundance of vitriol. And while others in this House looked to put forward real answers to real problems …'

There were outright giggles now from Adams and McDonald, the latter a constituency rival of Donohoe. At the very least they were enjoying the show. So too were the Fine Gael backbenches: junior ministers were openly smirking. Frances Fitzgerald even offered a 'hear, hear' of approval.

'… your inability to do all of this is masked by an anger, masked by a fake anger, that masks the political vacuum that is at the heart of modern Sinn Féin – and what is this? It's this: it's that they fear stability. You fear progress. They fear that there will ever be any light at the end of the tunnel …'

The Sinn Féin din grew louder. 'We wouldn't mind a bit of stability,' quipped Pat Buckley.

'Fine Gael's thinking of itself here,' analysed Seán Crowe. Mary Lou McDonald put her hands to her chest in an ostentatious display of parody anguish, feigning a mortal wound at Donohoe's offensive. The Ceann Comhairle watched with a mixture of amusement and perplexity: Donohoe was usually one of the chamber's more softly spoken characters, and never prone to partisan tirades like this. Was this *really* Paschal Donohoe?

'Any issue that is raised is an opportunity for division. Any matter that is raised is an opportunity for political advance. They challenge the presumption of good faith of nearly anybody in Dáil Éireann apart from yourselves. That is why the motion, and that is why your efforts here tonight … they are malicious, nakedly political, and they are aimed at destabilising a government that is doing its best to make progress on behalf of those that we are privileged to serve.'

With that final flourish, Donohoe resumed his seat to a chattering of supportive commentary from colleagues. Gerry Adams applauded sarcastically and enthusiastically. 'That was his speech for the leadership,' summarised his colleague Johnny Brady. The ice had been broken: suddenly there was life in the chamber, a nervous energy among TDs on both sides of the House. The fact it had been sparked by the likes of Donohoe, a man hardly famed for partisan diatribes, only seemed to underline the earlier stony silence.

Donohoe's monologue had stretched ninety seconds into the time allotted for his successor Simon Coveney, but the housing minister was vocally glad to donate it. 'He was making so much sense – so much sense that he has, in fact, got a response and a bit of a life out of this motion, or the motion that we're responding to from the opposition.'

'What will you leave for Leo?' yelled Dara Calleary from the Fianna Fáil benches in the opposite corner, prompting vocal giggles from Varadkar.

'If ye were successful in your efforts to bring down this government, there'd be no party more surprised than yourselves this evening,' Coveney continued. (An unknown Shinner interrupted with an 'oooo' sound.) 'You have, in my view, no intention of trying to bring about an election here – this is simply yet another negative stunt that comes from a party that offers nothing constructive or positive.'

'Test us!' begged Sinn Féin whip Aengus Ó Snodaigh. 'Go for an election.'

Coveney bulldozed on. 'The reality is that our job in government is to actually deliver for people who rely on the government to solve problems across this country, whether it's in healthcare, whether it's in housing, whether it's in education ...'

The Sinn Féin din grew louder again. 'Ah, come on,' drawled Pearse Doherty. 'Failure, failure, failure,' as Coveney elaborated, accusing Doherty and his colleagues of abdicating any chance to claim power while Fine Gael and Fianna Fáil had struck a deal following a 'complex result' that neither was truly comfortable about.

'Who's sitting on the pin cushion?' inquired Mattie McGrath, suddenly, invoking a metaphor that nobody could quite understand, but doing enough to momentarily derail Coveney's delivery.

'Mattie, with all due respect, you would have hopped into government quite comfortably,' the housing minister quipped back, 'if you were given the jobs you were asking for.' His role in the government formation team meant Coveney was fully aware of the deals other independents had tried to strike.

'True!' bellowed Donohoe to his side. 'He's on his way in!'

'He wanted to be a minister,' echoed Simon Harris on the other.

'The grass isn't that long yet,' McGrath sulked.

With the chamber now bustling with partisan energy, Coveney resumed his original train of thought, insisting that retaining the government was the only way to make progress. 'My job in government,' he said, 'is to deal with one of those big problems ...'

'Enda,' chimed Jonathan O'Brien from afar, sending Gerry Adams into barely controlled hysterics. Mary Lou McDonald held her nose in an effort to stifle a laughing fit. Even the junior ministers behind Kenny cracked a smile.

It was an ingenious quip with a damning conclusion. At the end of yet another long day, the latest in a week of long days, Fine Gael's most successful ever leader was now the butt of the joke.

'He was absolutely ridiculed,' one bashful critic would later concede. 'This whole thing, how he could think he had a conversation that he didn't ... Everyone has the occasional off-day, or gets wrong-footed by events, but this was on another level entirely. And he was absolutely crucified for it. The Dáil tore him apart.'

The remainder of the debate largely proceeded to form, with the government and pseudo-government TDs lobbing grenades at Sinn Féin for mischief-making, looking to collapse the only government the current Dáil could muster; and Sinn Féin and others in turn condemning Fine Gael's perceived hands-off approach to tackling not only Garda corruption, but also the country's larger social ills.

Enda Kenny sat unmoved. For at least two hours, he simply sat, listened and looked around wearily. 'He was shell-shocked,' one colleague said. 'He looked like he hadn't slept a wink in days. To be honest, after what happened at the PP [the parliamentary party meeting], he mightn't have slept much that night either.' It was a fair analysis: Leinster House's regular inhabitants agreed that they hadn't seen Kenny look so exhausted since the tail end of the difficult, stuttering 2016 election campaign.

For hours, his only interaction with any colleague was to exchange nods of approval with Simon Harris at the end of the latter's contribution. The health minister had drawn parallels between Sinn Féin's current support of 'Garda McCabe', and the IRA's 1996 murder of another Garda McCabe, Detective Garda Jerry McCabe. The Taoiseach seemed to appreciate the reference. Slowly, as Frances Fitzgerald occasionally invited his comment on various matters, he seemed to warm back into life. By the time the debate was wrapping up – with the junior sports minister, Patrick O'Donovan, and Sinn Féin TD Dessie Ellis tearing strips off one another amid all sorts of IRA references – he almost seemed to be enjoying the show.

The show was all there was to enjoy. Each Fine Gael minister contributing to the debate obviously had their own role to defend, their own record to stand over. With the survival of the government notionally at stake, each minister had to play their part in defending their collective right to retain office. But, tellingly, not a single one offered an olive branch to the leader whose clumsy response had prompted the very debate.

Leo Varadkar was the last to speak and brought the debate to an end, sticking to the script that had been circulated a few hours earlier – one which addressed the mammoth Garda scandal of the past nine days and which made no reference, even a passing one, to the incumbent Taoiseach whose motion was being debated. Party political point-scoring, he said, was 'not what people at home want to hear about'.

'I've absolutely no doubt in my mind, from what I know and what I have heard, that Sergeant McCabe was subject to a scurrilous whispering campaign to discredit him. What I don't know is who was involved and the extent to which it was organised. The inquiry must find that out. What is evident is that the aim was not only to intimidate him, but also to scare people off from supporting his claims, and for a time that was successful. We now need to know if similar campaigns were organised against other Gardaí, against public figures and private citizens.'

Varadkar quoted from the very first Garda Commissioner, Michael Staines, a close ally of Michael Collins. 'He said that An Garda Síochána would succeed not by force of arms or numbers, but on their moral authority as a servant of the people. If they are not to be seen as servants, but masters, they will lose their moral authority. The government can't and won't allow that to happen because the security of the State and the liberty of our citizens depends on it.'

As a speech from the self-described party of law and order, it could easily have been seen as a stump speech on the party leadership campaign – an attempt to stir the soul of a partisan loyalist.

'We need to bring an end to a culture where wrong is done but nobody is held to account,' Varadkar ended. 'Systems failures, administrative errors, endless reviews and prevarications, lost records, putting on the green jersey, alleged lack of resources … all too often these things have been used to justify and make excuses for wrongdoing. This should no longer be the case. Our Republic can and must stand for something better. The government proposes this motion: let us get down to the business of doing that.'

There was no applause, but a definite murmur of approval from Varadkar's colleagues as the debate drew to a close and the Ceann Comhairle formally called the vote.

Enda Kenny seemed to have warmed back into something of his usual humour by this point. Frances Fitzgerald managed to nudge some words from him, and by the time the division bells rang around Leinster House at 10.39 p.m. – summoning absent TDs to the chamber for the climactic vote – the Taoiseach seemed to have overcome the mortal shock of the open rebellion he had witnessed a few hours earlier.

Fitzgerald, Flanagan and Varadkar all took turns chatting with him as the absent TDs slowly returned. Michael Healy-Rae wandered over for a minute to chew the fat, as did Kevin 'Boxer' Moran, who hunkered down on the shallow stairwell beside the Taoiseach's seat, until Paschal Donohoe came along a few minutes later to occupy the same spot. Another TD, Marcella Corcoran Kennedy, visited to shake his hand and lift his spirits.

Elsewhere on the floor Fitzgerald and Mick Wallace were in deep and civil conversation. Colleagues patted Patrick O'Donovan on the back, literally, for his colourful but off-topic excoriation of IRA paramilitarism. Even John McGuinness wandered over to the Fine Gael benches to share a joke with him.

The vote began, with TDs reminded that electronic voting could not be used on a matter of such gravity, and that they would have to vote the old-fashioned way, walking through either of two lobbies at the rear of the chamber – a process which would take close to ten minutes. Ministers, one by one, peeled away to perform their duty, leaving Kenny momentarily alone to make a phone call. The Fianna Fáil TDs, abstaining in the vote, had no lobby through which to walk, and so sidled over to the clerk's desk to register their official ambivalence. Eventually the Taoiseach laid down the phone and squeezed sideways through an aisle of seats to walk towards the voting lobbies himself.

The vote was narrow, but conclusive. Fifty-seven TDs voted in favour of the motion of confidence, only a little over one-third of the House. It was enough: only fifty-two had voted against, and thanks to the abstentions of Fianna Fáil's forty-four deputies, the government had a majority of five. All that was left for Kenny was to return to his seat and retrieve his earlier-abandoned notebook, stopping for a moment to chat convivially with Shane Ross, the transport minister who only a few hours earlier had told the press he had considered collapsing the government entirely.

Officially speaking, the parliament of Ireland had once again affirmed the right of Enda Kenny and his government to hold power. But in practice, it was merely a stay of execution. Fine Gael's TDs, fresh from filing through the lobbies to legitimise Kenny's tenure, retreated to their own quarters and immediately resumed plotting his demise.

The clock was striking 11 p.m. and several TDs ventured back to the members' bar, seeking to unwind after another long and arduous day. Among Fine Gael deputies – and, indeed, among the others who dropped by for a nightcap – there was only one topic of conversation. Most agreed that Enda Kenny surely now knew the writing was on the wall.

Eventually Kenny himself appeared in the bar for a drink, though some believed the wounded Taoiseach was actually on a scouting mission to determine how openly his future was being questioned. Procuring a pint, Kenny took a seat at a table in the central area with one or two loyalists, but further sympathy was hard to find. Onlookers said the Taoiseach cut a doleful figure – and that far from self-policing any chat about his political fate, colleagues had simply turned their backs and continued their gossiping. On the few occasions that fellow TDs (of all hues) would venture to his table, the chatter was strained and uneasy. Even sympathisers who offered to chat felt the discussion was monosyllabic and superficial.

'He was broken that night,' said one opposition member who witnessed the scene. 'Absolutely broken. People were going to lengths not to be seen near him. Here he was, leading the country for six years, and now all these first-timer Young Turks were looking for his head on a plate. He must have just thought, "What the hell am I at? Do I really need all this?"'

Enda Kenny may have remained a central figure in the Dáil bar that night, but in the minds of Fine Gael he had already been sidelined. The plot to unseat him as party leader and Taoiseach was already afoot.

One minister, texting colleagues, simply declared: 'Game on.'

AFTERMATH

The Tribunal and the Taoiseach

Maurice McCabe did not get immediate answers to his six questions, but he did get a public forum for them to be answered. The day after its fate was secured by Dáil Éireann, the government won unanimous approval to establish a tribunal of inquiry into the protected disclosures of McCabe and Dave Taylor. The original terms of reference were significantly widened: Peter Charleton would now be asked to specifically find out what Martin Callinan and Nóirín O'Sullivan knew of the previous allegation of sex assault against Maurice McCabe, and to examine the call logs between Taylor and his two bosses by way of proving any collaboration between them. The Tribunal would also examine contacts between Gardaí and Tusla, ministers, the HSE, the media and anybody else who might turn out to be relevant in a coordinated national attempt to blacken McCabe's name.

The infamous Tusla file would also get an explicit investigation. The Tribunal would investigate whether Gardaí had embraced a convenient mistake concerning an inconvenient man, or even whether the file might have been created through more sinister means than a clerical copy-and-paste error. It would also ask whether Garda HQ had unfairly relied on the details of the Tusla file during the previous O'Higgins Commission, with the effect of trying to undermine the key witness.

The door was opened to other whistleblowers too: Keith Harrison, the other Garda who said his internal complaint resulted in a referral to Tusla, also fell within the net – as did any other Garda who felt their whistleblowing incurred the wrath of the force.

'What is required,' Frances Fitzgerald told TDs, 'is that the issue of how whistleblowers in An Garda Síochána have been treated is examined independently, fairly and publicly. For the first time, we will hear in public all sides of the story.'

As was the case with the previous O'Higgins Commission, Maurice McCabe found himself being represented by Michael McDowell – the former Attorney General, the former Minister for Justice, the now-independent senator, the still-senior counsel, and the man who had once proposed a limit on the amount of free legal aid a tribunal witness could claim from the State.

***

The last item on Charleton's hit list turned out to be the easiest one to dispose of. Harrison had claimed he was also slighted for causing internal hassle for the force, and had also been the subject of a malicious referral to Tusla designed at slurring his good name. The Supreme Court judge put Harrison at the front of the queue for investigation, and demolished his accusations in an interim report after only a few weeks of hearings – almost as if he was determined to clear the decks.

Harrison and his partner Marisa Simms testified to having a troubled and sometimes strained relationship; an extra complication was that Simms' brother had been charged with the homicide of a Garda based in the very station Harrison had been moved to. Charleton had no time for his claims of harsh mistreatment: the call to Tusla was entirely justified, he said, because of Harrison's intimidatory domestic behaviour, which may have put his partner's children at risk. He found that

Harrison's sense of persecution was entirely unjustified because he had actually been a difficult employee. 'No order given and no action taken by Gardaí in relation to this matter was illegal or morally wrong; yet so very many reasonable and ordinary commands were routinely questioned,' Charleton's report stated. 'No police force can serve the public in this way.'

Not only did Charleton refuse to accept Harrison's claims – he rejected them outright. 'All of the allegations of Garda Keith Harrison and Marisa Simms examined by the tribunal are entirely without validity,' the interim report found, consoling the accused parties for the 'considerable emotional toll' that the unfounded claims had placed on those against whom Harrison's complaints were made. The Tusla employees were singled out for particular praise, for acting with integrity and pride.

The Tusla file on McCabe turned out to be a tragic, but honest, error. The counsellor responsible, Laura Brophy, had been holding referrals with Ms D in mid-2013. McCabe's name was beginning to be raised in Garda and media circles, and Ms D was having trouble dealing with the attention being afforded to him. She repeated the original 1998 allegation to Brophy, who did not know the allegation had been investigated by Gardaí or the DPP, and wanted to forward it to the official channels.

At the time she was seeing Ms D, Brophy was also dealing with an entirely separate client ('Ms Y'), who had reported being digitally penetrated by an entirely different abuser. The copy-and-paste error was of an atypical variety: rather than pasting Ms Y's allegations into Ms D's document, Brophy had made a copy of her electronic report on Ms Y, and used it as a template to complete her paperwork on Ms D, amending the original document to reflect the different circumstances of the case.

Her error – which had caused such distress for the McCabe family when they eventually found out – was that she had simply neglected to delete the specific paragraph describing how Ms Y claimed she was abused. As a result, seemingly by pure fluke, the crimes perpetrated by Ms Y's alleged abuser were attributed to the man connected to Ms D, and that man just happened to be Sergeant Maurice McCabe, the country's most high-profile whistleblower.

The first she learned of it was the following year, when Ms D called her in tears – the wrongful report had made its way back to Bailieborough Garda Station, which was now investigating the claim that she had been raped. Brophy immediately recognised the error and made arrangements to correct the file.

Brophy had submitted the wrongful paperwork in July 2013, but it seemed not to have prompted an investigation by Gardaí until May the following year – months after McCabe's name had finally ventured into the broader public arena. Why had it taken so long? Why was this false allegation allowed to sit on file for ten months, just at a time when it would do most damage? It seemed to be a total fluke it was caught at all: a social worker was processing a batch of files, pulled McCabe's, and only then was the error addressed. Having sat within the vaults of the HSE and Tusla until that time, the repeated wrongful allegation had not made its way to the Gardaí – or, at least, not through the vehicle of Tusla itself.

But the existence of the Tusla file – despite its massive political significance – largely appeared immaterial. Plenty of Tribunal witnesses gave the distinct impression that the allegation did not need to fall into their laps in order for the original 2006 allegation to sit in their minds. Nóirín O'Sullivan said she was already aware of the allegation, owing to her time in the force's HR division in

2008–09; there was a passing reference to it in the first internal Garda report into McCabe's complaints of wrongful policing in Cavan–Monaghan. Martin Callinan said he had also read this passing reference and given no further consideration to it. The fact that the Tusla file had come into existence around the same time, to all intents and purposes, seemed merely coincidental – at least, when it came to the force's senior staff.

Dave Taylor told the Tribunal he only became aware of the historic allegation against McCabe in the middle of 2013 when the penalty points affair was beginning to cause concerns in Garda HQ. Martin Callinan, he said, was sitting in his office and was 'deeply frustrated' that McCabe's allegations about the wrongful deleting of penalty points were gaining traction, when top brass felt they had no currency at all.

'I could physically see him being deeply, deeply frustrated that this issue was being raised again and again,' Taylor told the Tribunal in May 2018. 'It was causing discomfort to senior Garda management, it was causing discomfort to him, and he felt that he was hamstrung in relation to how he could respond … he said to me on a number of occasions that, "If people only knew what I've to put up with."'

Taylor said Callinan therefore decided to invoke extreme measures to try and dampen the flames of McCabe's campaign. 'He told me that Sergeant McCabe had been investigated a number of years previously for an alleged sexual offence, had been fully investigated, had gone to the DPP, [that] the DPP had directed no prosecution and this was the epicentre and the core of why he [McCabe] was now engaged in this campaign.'

The press officer claimed he was told to raise this alleged motive with journalists whenever a McCabe story might arise – if his claims were raised in the Dáil, for example, and journalists would contact Garda HQ for a comment or reaction. The months thereafter gave plenty of opportunities to do so, as the PAC tried to investigate a dossier of McCabe's complaints and Callinan threatened legal action to stop them in their tracks.

Taylor further testified that Nóirín O'Sullivan, though not directing this campaign, was purportedly aware of it throughout. He said the two occupied next-door offices at headquarters, and the second-in-command would often sit in on meetings in the Commissioner's office where they would discuss the force's reaction (official and unofficial) to McCabe-themed stories. Taylor also claimed he would regularly report back on his activities to both Callinan and O'Sullivan, and that the latter would sometimes reply with a single-word text message: 'Perfect'. O'Sullivan dismissed any significance to this, saying it was a stock reply, a mere acknowledgement of the text she had just received.

Nonetheless, any political fallout on Nóirín O'Sullivan by this point was moot; though the Commissioner had endured the opening phases of the Tribunal, she had abruptly quit in September 2017, after separate complaints had been raised about irregular bookkeeping at the Garda training college in Templemore and about a falsified number of breath tests. O'Sullivan complained she could not do the job while fending off so many external inquiries and simply walked away.

So too did Frances Fitzgerald. The Tribunal was long underway before questions emerged about Fitzgerald's knowledge of matters at the O'Higgins Commission – and a claim that O'Sullivan's lawyers were trying to challenge McCabe's integrity and motivation. Having told the Dáil three times that Fitzgerald was unaware of any such business, the Department of Justice eventually produced emails showing she had been informed of the exchanges and had 'noted' her briefings. Another political firestorm suddenly exploded: Sinn Féin insisted Fitzgerald should have intervened to correct the Garda legal strategy, even though she herself was the ministerial sponsor of O'Higgins; Fianna Fáil felt the misleading of the Dáil was a fatal sin. Both tabled motions of no confidence in her and, in November 2017, she reluctantly resigned to avoid a general election.

* * *

Seeking to prove his case, Taylor named twelve different journalists across a series of print and broadcast outlets who had been the direct recipient of his briefings – but not a single one would corroborate his claims. Some simply testified that Taylor had never briefed them about McCabe at all; others cited journalistic privilege as a basis to avoid the question, even though Taylor himself had waived any privilege he might enjoy as their source. Charleton was quite clearly annoyed at this tactic, but opted against going to the High Court to challenge it.

This left Taylor in the sorry state of being unable to prove any of his major allegations. His mobile phones, having been seized by O'Sullivan's husband in the course of a separate investigation, had been retained by Garda HQ after the investigation and were no longer available to him. The innuendo of this being a deliberate ruse was diluted when it turned out that Taylor had actually kept one of his broken phones, giving it to his daughter to use for a while before it was eventually binned for good. McCabe, in turn, was left with little first-hand evidence of a smear campaign.

Taylor's story also appeared to unravel in other aspects. One example was the alleged use of text messages. McCabe's protected disclosure included a claim – coming seemingly from Taylor himself – that the press officer had done some of his briefing via texts. Taylor himself told the Tribunal this wasn't the case.

These various contradictions led Garda lawyers to argue that the former press officer's claims were, in fact, 'essentially a work of fiction': 'There is no substantiated evidence that Callinan or O'Sullivan instructed or directed any such effort on Superintendent Taylor's part to malign Sergeant McCabe, or that either were aware of any such effort,' the Garda counsel told Charleton during the closing submissions.

Taylor's own counsel sought to play down this rejection. While no journalist would go on the record to name him as a source, almost all testified to having known about the McCabe allegation, or having heard it as being used against him. It must have been an incredible coincidence, his legal team said, that none of these people heard the news from Taylor but they all managed to hear it anyway. 'If he was a fantasist who just wanted to throw a spanner in the works, he was a very fortunate fantasist and he was a very lucky spanner thrower.'

* * *

This unravelling did not mean the Garda establishment emerged free from any controversy. Martin Callinan – who of course denied ever instructing Dave Taylor to smear McCabe – saw his reputation systematically destroyed by a litany of witnesses.

A few days in January 2014 stood out. On the Thursday of one particular week, Callinan gave five hours of testimony at the PAC, the infamous meeting in which the Commissioner described the actions of whistleblowers McCabe and John Wilson as 'disgusting'.

John Deasy – having first revealed an approach by a senior Garda on *Prime Time* – named the senior Garda as Callinan himself. Deasy had met him at the coffee dock of Leinster House's LH2000 wing, on the way into that five-hour meeting. Callinan, Deasy said, gave a pre-emptive warning that McCabe was 'not to be trusted'.

One of the people attending that PAC meeting was Seamus McCarthy, the Comptroller and Auditor General whose work is closely linked to that of the committee. McCarthy testified that when he met the Commissioner at the bottom of the staircase leading into the committee rooms, Callinan 'raised Sergeant McCabe's name in the conversation, along the lines that [he] is not to be trusted, that he had questions to answer, and that there were sexual offence allegations against him'.

After the five-hour meeting had concluded, PAC chairman John McGuinness approached Callinan to exchange formalities, thanking him for his evidence. McGuinness told the Tribunal that the Commissioner was already mid-critique of the two whistleblowers – dismissing John Wilson as a malcontent who had once taken a horse from 'a knacker' on Grafton Street and returned to Pearse Street Station on horseback. McCabe, Callinan then purportedly added, 'fiddles with kids. And that is the kind of fucking headbangers I'm dealing with.' (Dave Taylor, who was also present at the PAC hearing, testified similarly.)

A day later, with the PAC considering a hearing with Maurice McCabe, Callinan called McGuinness to ask for a meeting – the same meeting McGuinness had revealed to the Dáil two years later – in which Callinan suggested that McCabe 'had sexually abused family, and an individual; that he was not to be trusted; that I [McGuinness] had made a grave error in relation to the

PAC and the public hearings because of this; [and that] I would find myself in serious trouble.'

The next day, Saturday, the Garda press office got a call from Gerald Kean, a talkative 'celebrity solicitor' who was due to appear on *The Marian Finucane Show* on Radio 1 a day later. The query was routed to Taylor and eventually to Callinan, who repeated 'the Garda line' to Kean, including what turned out to be wrongful claims about McCabe's non-cooperation with an internal probe into the penalty points affair. Kean later told the Tribunal that Callinan had asked not to be identified as his source – which turned out to be a useful condition, given that McCabe immediately called RTÉ to complain about Kean's on-air recitation of those 'facts', and later initiated legal action over them. Kean even revealed to the Tribunal that he had sought Callinan's input in his further correspondence to McCabe.

There was also a separate claim from Philip Boucher-Hayes, the presenter of RTÉ's *Crimecall*, who said he had been briefed by Callinan in December 2013 ahead of a set-piece TV interview, to the effect that McCabe had 'psychiatric issues' and had been responsible for crimes so unspeakable that he could not even repeat them.

Callinan denied every single one of these claims. He dismissed any negative briefing to John Deasy. He insisted Seamus McCarthy himself had raised the subject of McCabe's allegations, not him. He flatly denied knowing the phrase 'kiddie-fiddler', let alone using it in the PAC room after the meeting. He claimed John McGuinness had broached the subject of McCabe's sex allegations in the car park, before he could ever do so himself. He completely denied telling Gerald Kean not to name him as a source for his radio appearance. He dismissed Boucher-Hayes's claims, saying he would never discuss a fellow Garda in such a manner. The former Garda Commissioner earnestly insisted he simply didn't know why all these people were independently making claims against him. At an inquiry in which he was accused, somehow Callinan had found a tactic to cultivate sympathy.

It didn't work. When Charleton issued his conclusive report in October 2018, he accepted the evidence of McGuinness, Deasy, McCarthy and Boucher-Hayes – and sided with them over Callinan at each moment of conflict. The former Garda Commissioner, he found, had spoken in 'the most derogatory way' about Maurice McCabe as part of an overall 'campaign of calumny'.

The nation's highest form of inquiry had concluded that the head of An Garda Síochána had set out to smear a member of his own force … but that he had not acted alone.

Taylor, far from being a passive vehicle for Callinan's campaign, appeared to be its co-creator. Callinan's press officer was found to have 'pursued a scheme that somehow evolved out of his cheek-by-jowl working relationship with Commissioner Callinan'. He was, in effect, a co-author of the plan – not acting on instructions, but rather acting on his own initiative with Callinan's backing.

An inquiry prompted by a protected disclosure from Dave Taylor had concluded in his complete excoriation. Two days after the Tribunal reporting its findings, Taylor was told he would be once again suspended from duty; only a day later, he applied for early retirement.

The other alleged author of the campaign, Nóirín O'Sullivan, was completely vindicated. For starters, she had not been the officer responsible for assigning her husband to investigate Taylor for alleged leaking of sensitive data. It was not her fault that the investigation (lauded for its 'brilliance') had resulted in some of Taylor's phones being seized.

What O'Sullivan *had* done was remove Taylor from his role as press officer, a move which had clearly punctured his self-regard. Taylor, Charleton concluded, was bitter: about losing his press office job, about being investigated over the Roma leaks, about being arrested, about having his phones seized. That bitterness led him to 'set out to destroy people', by placing himself on the side of Maurice McCabe and undermining O'Sullivan instead. This all made Taylor 'a witness whose credibility was completely undermined by his own bitterness and by the untruthful nature of his affidavit'.

There was, in short, 'no credible evidence that Deputy Commissioner Nóirín O'Sullivan played any hand act or part in any campaign conducted by Commissioner Martin Callinan and by Superintendent David Taylor'. Even on other matters where O'Sullivan stood accused – such as instructing her legal team to pursue McCabe's historical abuse allegation at the O'Higgins Commission, or otherwise challenging his integrity and motivation, or even engineering an RTÉ report about O'Higgins before its formal publication – the departed Commissioner came out with a clean record.

So too did Frances Fitzgerald. The Tribunal did not investigate the political circumstances of her departure, but supported her unequivocally in refusing to intervene in the O'Higgins Commission once the legal skirmishes were made known to her. It was completely correct of her to leave Justice Kevin O'Higgins to sort out the dispute by himself. Fitzgerald, having originally told the Dáil she knew nothing of the row, then made a virtue of her inaction – and won Charleton's approval for doing so. Charleton even lamented her resignation, saying it was necessary to avoid a calamitous election in the midst of crucial Brexit negotiations, and bemoaned the seeming absence of fair procedure in her case.

But the one vindicated most of all was Maurice McCabe. The emergence of a Tusla file carrying false allegations against him was a 'hideous coincidence' – but there had, throughout it all, been a plan conceived at the highest levels of An Garda Síochána to do him down and to blacken his name ... simply for trying to serve the public good.

'What has been unnerving,' Charleton summarised, was that 'a person who stood up for better standards in our national police force, Sgt Maurice McCabe, and who exemplified hard work in his own calling, was repulsively denigrated for being no more than a good citizen and police officer.'

No higher inquiry could possibly question his vindication. After twelve years of struggling against the system, Maurice McCabe had finally come out on top.

But after such a lengthy fight, and such a sustained period in the public eye, it would be impossible to return to normality. After a meeting with O'Sullivan's successor, Drew Harris, to discuss the Tribunal's findings and the future of policing, McCabe decided it was time to conclude his three decades of service in uniform.

'I am happy with the findings of the Charleton Tribunal but I think it is in the best interest of my family to retire from policing,' he told the *Irish Independent*.

As the clock struck midnight on 31 October 2018, Maurice McCabe formally retired from An Garda Síochána.

***

After largely keeping himself to himself in the Dáil members' bar following the events of the Fine Gael meeting and the vote of no confidence, Enda Kenny remained coy about his immediate response to the naked dissent now on show within his party. Sympathisers texting him with well-wishes received non-committal replies. 'Let's see what happens,' he replied to one. 'We've been around here before.' To another he simply said: 'I've learned a lot in the last three days.'

Looking only a smidgeon more refreshed, Kenny made a rare appearance in the committee room bowels of Leinster House on Thursday 16 February 2017, the morning after winning the motion of confidence, as he was required by law to visit annually and account for spending within his own Department of the Taoiseach. John McGuinness – hardly a sympathiser – chaired the meeting and offered an olive branch of sympathy at its end. 'These are difficult times, and I wish you well.'

'*C'est la vie*,' came the reply, and a brief flash of his usual smile.

Outside, some opportunistic journalists asked him how he was doing. 'I haven't slept in weeks,' Kenny told him, appearing to confirm the bleeding obvious. 'But then,' he added, 'I only need four or five hours a night.' And with that, he breezed up the stairs and away.

Kenny's first reaction to a power struggle appeared to be the adoption of the Sun Tzu philosophy: simply sit, exploit the advantage of incumbency and wait for someone else to make the first move. Nonetheless, he spent a few days soliciting counsel from his nearest and dearest. They advised him of what he already knew: if he wanted to leave on his own terms, and not go down in history books as having been hounded out of office, he would have to leave fairly soon. The only question was how much time it would take for the McCabe story to move off the agenda and for his retirement to seem like a more managed transition.

Importantly, they counselled, Kenny could not publicly outline any intention of giving way. Part of the trouble Kenny had got himself into was to declare he would not seek a third term as Taoiseach. Had he simply kept to himself on that note, the *putsch* against him now would be far less urgent – if it had existed at all. The lesson to learn was not, now, to fob off the leadership challenge by announcing a departure in two weeks, or four, or eight or twelve: it would merely render everything done in the interim as illegitimate. Such a move would be tantamount to scheduling a rainstorm.

The temptations were there. There had been talk that Kenny might want to stay for a couple of months, in order to surpass John A. Costello as Fine Gael's longest-serving leader of all time. That, many TDs felt, would be going too far. The party's vice-chairman, Carlow TD Pat Deering, told Today FM's *The Last Word* that it was time for Kenny to 'reassess his position'. While nobody wanted an uneasy ouster, he could not be allowed to cling on forever.

In the bowels of Sheriff Youth Club that night, making a community visit to Dublin's north inner city, Kenny was asked specifically: when are you leaving?

'Well, politics is a vocation,' he chirped. 'It draws you into stormy waters as well as calm, as the late James Dillon used to say. Today for me was a very ordinary working day …' Kenny proceeded to rattle off the full day's business he had just gone through – beginning with a 7.30 a.m. Cabinet meeting to conclude the terms of reference for the Charleton Tribunal. 'I'm focused on my job and my responsibility as leader of the country, to continue in a very challenging time to deal with the preparations for what will be exceptionally difficult and challenging negotiations in respect of Brexit.'

It was no surprise that Kenny might remain defiant, but some were worried he was *too* defiant. His reference to the Brexit process raised particular alarm: that entire process would take two full years. That simply wasn't tenable. That night one minister noted: 'We want to let him do this with dignity, but there is no long term here. This is a matter of weeks.'

Others were unsure whether the State could afford to dispose of Kenny. Kenny was one of the longest-serving leaders at the European Council table and it made little sense to dispose of him at a time when his experience was needed most. Separately, the scheduled visit to the White House was only a month away, when the Taoiseach would have his annual meeting with the President of the United States. Nobody wanted to deny Kenny that perception of a victory lap in Washington; equally, nobody wanted a newly elected successor to be sent straight into the lion's den.

On 22 February – seven days after his TDs voted confidence in his government – Enda Kenny returned to the Fine Gael parliamentary party and hinted at his plans. Beginning his speech with a certain amount of snark (urging party secretary Noel Rock to take accurate notes of the speech, a quip at Rock's public challenge of his position), Kenny said he would deal with the question of his future 'effectively and conclusively' after St Patrick's Day, and had no time for ultimatums or deadlines. His brief speech was met with a standing ovation, and nobody else offered any commentary.

The often-leaky Fine Gael parliamentary party was unusually quiet; it was even suggested that TDs might be asked to leave their mobile phones in a basket outside the door to stop them from recounting the story. The initial reports leaking into the media suggested it was an assertive, powerful performance from Kenny, almost as if he were staring down his challengers, baiting them to prise him out of his office. Later accounts seemed to challenge this view. 'He was emotional and nervous. This "played a blinder" and "stared down people" is bullshit,' one attendee reported.

'He had scripted remarks which he never has, written on flash cards. That's not the fighting Enda I've seen before,' recounted another.

The mood within the Fine Gael ranks was that, with Kenny now implicitly recognising his time was up, nobody wished to rush the process. At the very least, Kenny would be allowed to remain in office until the annual trip to the White House. In the meantime, the machinery to replace him was already moving into gear. 'That's the timeline we wanted,' said one member itching for a change. 'The contest begins the week after Paddy's Day.'

* * *

The Washington visit went off almost completely without a hitch. Enda impressed his host sufficiently to become Trump's 'new friend'; his wife Fionnuala, joining the formal presentation of the bowl of shamrock, proved a consummate charmer. The only speed bump came when the travelling journalists, desperate for a news line from the encounter, asked Trump in the Oval Office if he'd be coming to Ireland, and effectively bounced the Irish party into formalising an invitation on the spot. Otherwise, Trump was so intoxicated with flattery that he seemed unbothered by Kenny standing in the east room of his house and implicitly excoriating his ban on immigrants from mostly Muslim countries, in a speech that went viral in the following days. (Kenny's entourage were aggrieved that these bold comments did not garner much praise in the Irish media; explanations of time differences and healthy coverage on non-RTÉ airwaves fell on deaf ears.)

The timeline suddenly seemed to switch immediately afterwards. The next day, on the side of Fifth Avenue as the St Patrick's Day parade rolled by, Kenny suddenly announced that he could not contemplate leaving government just yet. 'I have a number of immediate priorities tomorrow morning when I land back on my desk at ten o'clock,' he declared to reporters. One was Brexit, for which the formal Article 50 notification was now imminent, with a major summit pending soon afterwards. Another was the political impasse in Stormont, where snap elections had not yet produced a new Northern Ireland Executive.

The former argument was difficult to argue with. Kenny's European clout would be important in ensuring Irish concerns were central to Europe's negotiating agenda. The latter was a bolt from the blue. Nobody in Kenny's inner circle had ever cited the future of Northern Ireland as a political imperative. Declaring it as a red line issue now, to some, sounded like a U-turn – a spurious attempt to portray himself as engaged and indispensable.

'It was bullshit, plain and simple,' grumbled one backbencher summarising the mood of most colleagues. 'Enda was the least interested Taoiseach in Northern Ireland for donkey's years. He didn't give a shite about Stormont or cash-for-ash or anything else. It was pure desperation on his part, one final crisis to cling to, or to insert himself into some row that made him too important to get rid of.'

The criticism, quiet but clear, seemed to settle. Only four days later – both in the Dáil and the parliamentary party rooms

– Kenny had dropped the Stormont clause entirely, announcing he would attend the Brexit summit at the end of April as Taoiseach, but assuring his party there would be no 'leadership vacuum' thereafter. The storm clouds again seemed to dissipate – Kenny's cryptic remarks had again been interpreted as an implicit acknowledgement that his time was running out.

Moving the deadline until after the European Council summit bought Kenny not only some more time, but also an added accolade: a week before heading to Brussels, he marked his 2,233rd day as Taoiseach. In doing so, he surpassed John A. Costello's record of service and became Fine Gael's longest-serving Taoiseach.

***

There was to be one final attempt at lingering on. At only a few days' notice in early May, Kenny took up an invite to visit Canada's Prime Minister, Justin Trudeau – sending newsrooms into a hasty scramble deploying reporters to follow him. Kenny's Twitter account trumpeted on arrival about his 'first visit to Canada as Taoiseach', prompting even more anxieties among itchy challengers. (The fact that Kenny rarely took first-hand control of his account, which was managed almost exclusively by press officers and handlers, was forgotten.) The travelling hacks, sent at major expense by newsrooms still nursing the cost of the Washington trip, agreed the leadership question was one worth asking.

But there would be only one opportunity to do so: Kenny's bilateral post-meeting press conference with Trudeau, at which the scope for questioning would be limited. Protocol dictated that the Irish and Canadian media troupes would be granted two questions each, with RTÉ awarded one as national broadcaster.

The travelling media were in full agreement that the leadership issue was a justified topic, and nominated *Irish Examiner* political editor Daniel McConnell to go first and raise it. RTÉ's Washington correspondent Caitríona Perry would go second with a shopping list of other topics.

Called for his question, McConnell was polite but blunt. 'Can we get such clarity and certainty from you,' he asked Kenny, 'as to when you intend departing from your own position, and do you intend doing so at your own parliamentary party next week?'

'I can't believe, actually, that you've travelled this distance to ask me a question like that,' Kenny scolded. 'I've come here to speak to the Canadian prime minister and Canadian business about opportunities that exist across the Atlantic ...'

Trudeau looked around, unflinching and unbothered, as Kenny launched a soliloquy about the no-doubt important business to be conducted.

'But actually, with respect, Taoiseach ...' McConnell tried to interject.

'Next question,' Kenny scolded, his eyes scanning the opposite side of the room.

'Taoiseach,' McConnell continued, refusing to yield his microphone. 'You haven't actually answered the question. I asked you specifically would you deal with it next Wednesday at the parliamentary party meeting?'

'As I said to you, Daniel, I can't actually believe you've travelled this distance to ask a question like that.'

'I'm actually asking on behalf of all the Irish media, Taoiseach.'

'My function here ...'

'All the Irish media have asked me to ask this question, Taoiseach. Just to be clear on that.'

'My function here is a discussion with the Prime Minister of Canada, to discuss the opportunities that present themselves for investment and job creation on either side of the Atlantic. Thank you.'

The remarks went down like a lead balloon among the travelling press corps, who insisted the question was a legitimate one, raised in the only available forum. Some back in Leinster House believed the timing of the question was regrettable, but the substance was fair. Within Fine Gael, mood was split. 'It was an outrageous thing to ask a travelling head of government, when a counterpart is standing beside him,' huffed one supporter. Others were less sympathetic. 'No matter what the circumstances, you can't do the job if you don't have the media onside,' one wiser TD noted. 'He's on a hiding to nothing if he's going to start giving grief to hacks for asking a fair question.'

Kenny and his closest handlers defended the hostile tone of the Taoiseach's answer, but the terse encounter did crystallise a belief that the jig was up. If Kenny undertook any other novel-but-routine business, the reporters would ask the same questions. *Why are you getting involved in this now? Isn't this a ruse to cling on?* Any attempt to simply pretend it was business as usual would fail pretty quickly.

No matter what direction he might turn, or path he might take, Enda Kenny would keep running into questions about when he would resign. This was a *cul-de-sac* with no room for a U-turn.

* * *

Kenny returned and bought himself one final week, telling colleagues on 10 May he had seen the speculation in the newspapers, and wanted to address the issue conclusively so that 'the texters' (another snipe at gossipy colleagues) would know exactly where he stood. 'All party colleagues will be clear where I stand then,' he said.

Despite having now effectively set his own deadline, Kenny remained coy, both publicly and privately. If the only card left in his hand was the element of surprise, he would not allow someone else to play it on his behalf. Right up to the end, the Taoiseach refused to publicly countenance his own political mortality.

One example was on the evening of 16 May – the day before the 'conclusive' statement – at the launch of the latest *Nealon's Guide*, the *de facto* Dáil handbook produced after each election. The book's cover photo offered a poetic illustration of Kenny's state: whereas the previous edition carried a happy smiling photograph of an Enda Kenny–Eamon Gilmore double act, the new one captured Kenny walking down a cold and unforgiving concrete staircase, completely alone.

The isolated tone of the picture was juxtaposed with a more assertive comment from Kenny himself, who had written the foreword, which concluded: 'The political climate in Ireland today, though unprecedented and challenging, also presents great opportunity and I carry the honour of being re-elected Taoiseach last year with great pride, great humility and an abiding sense of duty. My enduring belief in the potential of this country is boundless, and my determination to see that potential realised remains unyielding.'

Journalists would have no chance to ask the Taoiseach precisely what he meant by 'unyielding'. Leaving the launch, Kenny politely shrugged off any questions ('Now now,' he playfully scolded) as he unexpectedly eschewed his car and driver, walking away into the Merrion Square evening sunshine.

A few hours later Kenny and an aide wandered into Smyth's pub a few minutes' walk away on Haddington Road – a popular spot among political elders, sufficiently removed from Leinster House for discretion – for a quiet Guinness. The visit became a session, as Kenny was joined by other luminaries leaving the book launch and hunting for a nightcap.

Eventually someone in the troupe invited suggestions for a sing-song. Possibly in a nostalgic mood, Kenny requested 'On Raglan Road', the Patrick Kavanagh poem made famous as a song by The Dubliners, written about the Ballsbridge thoroughfare only ten minutes from the present venue. Liam Collins, a veteran columnist of the *Sunday Independent*, led the tune, with Kenny personally joining in – the melody escaping out as far, as the lyrics go, as the quiet street where old ghosts meet.

* * *

Dáil business the following day, 17 May, came and went without any mention of Kenny's future, so journalists packed into the Italian Room of Government Buildings for his only other public event of the day – the launch of an ironically titled report from Senator Marie Louise O'Donnell (a Kenny appointee) about end-of-life care named 'Finite Lives'. The same journalists traipsed out later without having heard Kenny address his own political mortality – held politely, but firmly, at arm's length as the Taoiseach left the room. All they had learned, via chatter with politicians, was that the Fine Gael meeting had been brought forward by an hour: the party leader had unilaterally moved the 5.30 p.m. fixture to 4.30 p.m.

Stepping out of that event for a moment, this author bumped into Leo Varadkar. It turned out the Minister for Social Protection was going to miss the meeting: he had been taking a civil service course in Irish (a fairly clear indication of his political aspirations, most people thought) and might be late to the Fine Gael meeting because he was on his way to a *scrúdú béile*, an oral language exam.

Varadkar turned out to be one of the very few absentees as the Fine Gael parliamentary party – TDs, senators and even MEPs – piled into the party rooms on the fifth floor of the southern wing of the Oireachtas. As ever, Kenny arrived late, having gathered his advisors in his office for a few minutes beforehand.

At 4.35 p.m. the chairman, Martin Heydon, opened the meeting and invited Kenny to address his ranks. Rising from his seat, Kenny pressed 'send' on a text to Jack O'Donnell, his assistant government press secretary, with a single thumbs-up emoji. Within seconds, a statement – drafted earlier by the Taoiseach himself, alone in his office – was posted to Kenny's Twitter account. An email with the same statement had also been drafted, and the party's head of communications, Barry Duggan, was in the room with his laptop open, ready to distribute it as soon as Kenny had concluded. Kenny had come to despise the uncontrolled media leaks emanating from the party meeting room. This was his news and he would control it. The statement opened:

> Last year I indicated that I would not lead the FG Party into the next general election. I have decided to implement that decision today. Therefore I will retire as Leader of Fine Gael effective from midnight tonight 17th May 2017.

While Kenny would remain in a caretaker role, the party's national executive had been asked to arrange a leadership election to conclude on Friday 2 June. The Dáil was in recess for the following week, which left his successor with an eleven-day period to nail down the support of Fianna Fáil and the Independent Alliance before asking the Dáil to nominate them as the new head of government.

> I would like to stress the huge honour and privilege it has been for me to lead our party for the past 15 years, in opposition and into Government on two successive occasions.
>
> I thank all our members, past and present for that privilege.
>
> I thank all my local constituents and supporters in Mayo for their unstinting loyalty since 1975, and for their support for my family previously in Dáil Éireann since 1954.
>
> I thank my personal staff for their commitment over many years to my duties.
>
> I especially want to thank my wife Fionnuala, our children, my siblings and their families for their understanding of my work, and indeed for accepting the many intrusions of politics into family life in the interest of building our Country. I could not have engaged as I did without that base.
>
> Thank you.

Concluding the same statement in the Fine Gael party rooms, Kenny looked up at his followers. Many, like him, were struggling to keep their composure. Some were in tears. All were applauding.

Heydon attempted to lead some tributes, thanking Kenny for his service to party and country, but the Taoiseach was in little mood to hear it. 'Mind if I go?' he asked, before gathering his papers and bolting for the door with a final message to the room: 'Let the games begin.'

'It was the most graceful case of a leader standing down I can imagine,' one witness recalled. 'If I was ever doing that, that's how I'd want to do it. There was a brilliant dignity to it: instead of having hypocrites standing up and *plamásing* him after trying to get him out, he just gathered his things and puffed out his chest.' So speedy was the departure that a small number believed he had actually walked out in a huff, all but slamming the door behind him. In truth, after six years as Taoiseach and fifteen years as leader of Fine Gael, Enda Kenny was simply close to tears.

Nobody was in any mood to continue the meeting after that. Heydon adjourned the meeting at 4.42 p.m. Leo Varadkar, detained at his Irish test, missed the whole thing. The Fine Gael parliamentary party descended to the plinth of Leinster House to speak to the waiting media, while Kenny quietly slipped out through Government Buildings. He and a small team of confidants slunk away for dinner around the corner in Marcel's restaurant on Merrion Row, and later to the beer garden of O'Donoghue's pub.

***

Fine Gael had not conducted a leadership election since 2002, when only the members of the parliamentary party had been given a vote. 'More than ever, Fine Gael needs to consult members and councillors across the country about the future of the party and its leadership,' read one letter printed in *The Irish Times* after Kenny's win. 'The decision of the parliamentary party to decide the future of Fine Gael alone and behind closed doors is a disgrace and demonstrates their contempt both for the loyal Fine Gael membership and the 400,000 or so electors who voted for them. Shame on you all.'

The letter was authored by Lucinda Creighton, the vice-president of Young Fine Gael, and her Trinity College pal Leo Varadkar. The two had been part of a move to change the party's electoral system following Michael Noonan's 2001 victory, but the change had not taken effect in time for 2002. Neither could have known that their changes would not truly take effect until 2017 – or that one of them would be a participant in the contest.

The overall contest was weighted so that the votes of parliamentary party members were worth sixty-five per cent of the vote, with ordinary members worth twenty-five per cent and councillors accounting for the remaining ten per cent. The changes meant everyday members of Fine Gael did get their say – but their voices would be massively outweighed by those of TDs, senators and MEPs. As there were seventy-three members of the Fine Gael parliamentary party, this meant that each of their votes was worth 0.9% of the final national total. In effect, the most popular candidate among the parliamentary party would likely be the victor. Candidates needed the backing of eight of those parliamentary colleagues to contest the job, meaning only Leo Varadkar and Simon Coveney had the popular clout to put their names forward.

Varadkar and Eoghan Murphy, now acting as a formal campaign manager, understood the blunt arithmetic and immediately set about locking down the support of the all-important parliamentary votes, even encouraging them to choreograph their declarations, timing their public announcements in order to give the impression of momentum. The plan worked: the election quickly became a runaway train, with Varadkar claiming an insurmountable lead. TDs who may have been on the fence about his candidacy were left with almost no choice but to support him, in case their reluctance cost them a ministerial job later.

Kenny was one of the few who did not publicly declare support for either candidate – largely out of a sense of decorum, needing to ensure that the new leader was successful on their own account and not because they were a designated *dauphin*. Some felt, however, that this clause offered useful cover. The suspicion, widely held within the parliamentary party, was that Kenny would have preferred for a third candidate to enter the field and claim his office. Paschal Donohoe had become the intellectual heavyweight of Cabinet, elevated to the prized junior ministry of European Affairs by Kenny only two years into his Dáil career, and promoted to senior ministerial ranks after a further twelve months in a 2014 reshuffle. The same reshuffle saw Simon Harris given the junior ministry at the Department of Finance, before his surprise appointment as Minister for Health in the minority government. Both men were seen as Kenny's favoured sons, and had he served for longer, either could have been more heavily backed to challenge for the leadership themselves.

But with Kenny leaving so soon and so suddenly, neither was seen as comparably senior to Varadkar or Coveney – both of whom had been chosen to join Kenny in his first government in March 2011, despite taking the opposite side in Richard Bruton's failed leadership heave only eight months earlier. Varadkar had been one of Bruton's most vocal supporters, and had continued to rock the boat inside government, including through his vocal support of Maurice McCabe. But Coveney's bib was not deemed entirely clean either: he had also backed Bruton in the 2010 heave, and had been accused of deliberately exploiting the resulting internal ructions by offering himself as a compromise candidate. The only comparably senior candidate with Kenny's likely blessing was Frances Fitzgerald, but she had opted against running and given assertive backing to Varadkar.

Many now believed that Kenny's grumpiness at being foisted out was compounded by the choice of candidates on offer to succeed him.

When the votes were finally counted in the Mansion House on 2 June, Varadkar claimed fifty-one of the parliamentary party votes, to Simon Coveney's twenty-two, while also winning over councillors by a margin of 123 to 100. The combined margins suggested that both current and aspiring parliamentarians felt Varadkar possessed an electoral stardust Coveney could not match. Ironically, the rank-and-file membership – who only had a vote because of Varadkar's efforts – rejected him. Varadkar was backed by 3,772 of them, but 7,051 opted for Coveney's steadier predictability. It mattered little: under the weighted voting system, Varadkar claimed almost sixty per cent of the final vote and the job was his. Leo Eric Varadkar, a thirty-eight-year-old mixed-race gay bachelor, became the eleventh leader of Fine Gael.

Enda Kenny did not attend the appointment of his successor and limited his contribution to another Twitter statement. 'I want to extend my heartiest congratulations to Leo Varadkar on his election as leader of the Fine Gael party. This is a tremendous honour for him and I know he will devote his life to improving the lives of people across our country. He has my full support now for the work that lies ahead.'

The outgoing Taoiseach, now to be replaced by a man twenty-eight years his junior, chose instead to visit the Laura Lynn children's hospice in Leopardstown. Observers concluded that Kenny was on something of a farewell tour, visiting causes close to his heart, perhaps looking for proof that the country was in better shape now than it had been in those dire days of 2011. Maybe, one colleague suggested, he needed assurance that the labours of the office had borne fruit – that the long days, short nights and personal sacrifice had really been worth it.

His successor certainly believed it was. At his post-victory press conference, this author pointed out that Varadkar's leadership manifesto (rewarding 'people who get up early in the morning', a platform that sounded like it excluded those who could not help themselves) was constrained by the Programme for Partnership Government agreed with the independents, and the confidence and supply agreement reached with Fianna Fáil. With that in mind, how would ordinary people know the era of Leo Varadkar had arrived and the era of Enda Kenny was over?

'You know, the important thing to say is we are the same party. I was a member of a government led by Enda Kenny for the past six years – a government that has turned this country around economically. Just look where we were six years ago and look where we are now, and look where countries like Greece and others that chose a different course are now. So my election now, as leader – and hopefully as Taoiseach in the next couple of weeks – isn't an abrogation of Enda Kenny's period in office. I would be proud and honoured to continue the work he has done, and if I can be as good a Taoiseach as he has been, and as good a leader as he has been, I'll be very happy if I can match that level.'

The Round Room of the Mansion House, still mostly populated by members of Fine Gael, broke into spontaneous applause.

***

There remains a cohort within Fine Gael that, despite ultimately overthrowing him, believes Enda Kenny had secretly sacrificed himself for the benefit of others.

Kenny's downfall was, on its face, precipitated by Fine Gael's need to be prepared for an unexpected general election. The risk of such an instant election had been highlighted by the way in which the Taoiseach was savaged – firstly by the Dáil and then by his own colleagues – after the botched radio interview where he 'recalled' with specific detail how he had spoken to Katherine Zappone before her meeting with the McCabes. When that account was later written off as untrue, Kenny's trustworthiness took a hit from which he never recovered.

But what if, in the contradictions between Kenny and Zappone, Kenny was in the clear? Some of his former colleagues still cling to the belief that Kenny's account on radio – anecdotes and all – was, in fact, totally correct. Their theory is that when theatrically addressing reporters on the plinth, it was Zappone whose memory was at fault. Her story simply didn't seem to make sense: why would she personally tell Frances Fitzgerald about her proposed meeting, but only leave it up to advisors to inform Enda Kenny? It was plausible that Zappone and Kenny may truly have spoken in person, as Kenny described – perhaps in a fleeting encounter on a corridor, or at the fringes of a Cabinet meeting. If that was the case, Zappone's appearance on the plinth, for all of its theatrical earnest delivery, might have got the story completely backwards. The theory is linked to the fact that Zappone addressed reporters on the plinth, on that dramatic Monday afternoon, without speaking to either Kenny or Fitzgerald first (an 'extraordinarily selfish' decision, as labelled by one colleague). Had she done so, perhaps her memory might have been refreshed and the whole scandal would have concluded differently.

Faced with the prospect of a minister wrongly contradicting him, what was Kenny to do? Was he supposed to fan the flames by going into the Dáil chamber, and doubling down on his story? The arithmetic of the minority government meant every vote was crucial: if Katherine Zappone was pressurised any further, there was a chance she would simply walk away, withdrawing from government and collapsing the entire house of cards.

The theory of some in Fine Gael – albeit one for which there can be no hard evidence – is that, faced with a teetering administration and a minister wrongly contradicting him, Kenny simply chose to take the bullet himself with his 'mea culpa', instead of inviting a further barrage on his colleague.

Perhaps, those colleagues surmise, Enda Kenny simply didn't expect the wound to be fatal.

* * *

As ever, Enda Kenny was late. His tardy timekeeping was the butt of many jokes among journalists – a Twitter account had even been set up to log his persistent lateness. The previous evening he had been back in O'Donoghue's, letting off some steam with advisors, only to end up spending an hour and a half chatting to two American tourists about the speeches of JFK, the poetry of Yeats and the music of The Beatles. But he had left at an appropriate hour, and that wasn't the reason Kenny was now late for Dáil business. For the day that was in it, though, nobody would chide him too much.

Kenny's final Cabinet meeting on the morning of Tuesday 13 June had been more formal than usual, but still a warm occasion. Some routine government business had been disposed of: ministers approved Frances Fitzgerald's plan to draft a law allowing pubs to open on Good Friday, and Paschal Donohoe briefed his colleagues on some ongoing pay talks. There were appreciative words for Michael Noonan, the veteran Minister for Finance who had announced he would follow Kenny to the backbenches and bow out of any future Cabinets.

There were some departing gifts too. The Attorney General Máire Whelan – originally appointed at Labour's behest in 2011, and who stood little chance of being retained by Leo Varadkar – was nominated for appointment as a judge on the Court of Appeal. This ought to have brought ire from Shane Ross, who had personally demanded an overhaul of judicial appointments as a *quid pro quo* for entering government – but Ross left the meeting with good news too. After being asked to identify six closed Garda stations for reopening, Gardaí were recommending Ross's favoured Stepaside as their first candidate. (Both decisions would provide future controversy: Whelan's appointment, at a Cabinet meeting at which she herself was present, seemed to flout the usual best practice; senior Gardaí would later describe the Stepaside process as effectively being rigged, so that Ross's favoured station was almost literally the only valid option within Dublin.)

The meeting concluded with Kenny going around the table, asking each of his colleagues in turn for an overview of how their department was faring and offering his thanks for their respective efforts. His colleagues applauded as he adjourned a meeting of the Government of Ireland for the final time and made his final private preparations, before entering the Dáil chamber at 2.03 p.m. – bounding down the steps with handshakes aplenty – for a session that was supposed to begin at two o'clock. Only when the Taoiseach had taken his seat and shaken hands politely with the clerk of the Dáil, did the clerk retreat from the chamber to summon the Ceann Comhairle so that the formal business of the day could begin.

The outgoing Taoiseach appeared to be in giddy form. During the moment of prescribed silence between the opening prayer and the start of business, Kenny grinned up at the press gallery, motioning to lazier hacks encouraging them to stand up straight. Then, as the Ceann Comhairle invited him to make an announcement for the information of the House, he sat and grinned one more time – as if he didn't realise this was his curtain call – before suddenly arising and telling the Dáil *as Gaeilge* that he would be visiting Áras an Úachtaráin at the conclusion of business with a letter of resignation.

'I was hoping that having said that much, that I could leave quickly and quietly,' he offered – his rushed, heavy breathing had returned once more – 'but the business of the Dáil is such that I no longer have any control over how it is to be conducted in full. And the prospect of making a speech, or listening to them – either of glorification or flagellation – is not something that I really relish, because this has never been about me. It has always been, a Cheann Comhairle, about the problems and challenges our people and country face.

'It was Teddy Roosevelt who said, "Far and away the best prize that life has to offer is the chance to work hard at work worth doing." I have been truly blessed I have had that chance, and I am eternally grateful to the Irish people and particularly the people of Mayo for repeatedly giving me that opportunity.'

Offering brief words of thanks to his colleagues in Fianna Fáil, his former partners in Labour and his lieutenants in Fine Gael, he concluded with a reference to another man from Mayo.

'Actually Ceann Comhairle, I passed through Strade recently, which is the birthplace and final resting place of Michael Davitt.' A scoff could be heard from the Solidarity benches across the chamber at the invocation of the Land League leader by a man whose tenure coincided with a wave of home repossessions.

'To paraphrase what he said in his will to the Irish people: he said, to all my friends I leave kind thoughts; to others I express my fullest forgiveness; and to Ireland, my undying prayer for absolute freedom and independence, which it has always been my ambition to achieve for her. I hope, a Cheann Comhairle, that in the two governments I have led, we have made a modest contribution towards that ambition. *Go raibh maith agat.*'

Most of the chamber applauded as the departing Taoiseach resumed his seat, visibly pained. Smiling briefly at Frances Fitzgerald beside him, and raising his hand to the public gallery where his wife and children were seated, in the same way a tenor directs applause towards his orchestra, Enda Kenny was otherwise ashen-faced and morbid. He was obviously uncomfortable at the prospect of hearing his political obituary being read to him from the far corners of Dáil Éireann, but sat dutifully through it anyway.

The final speech of the lot was from Shane Ross, his unlikely government colleague – the man who spent the previous Dáil term eviscerating Kenny's first government from the opposition backbench, who eleven months earlier had described the Taoiseach as a 'political zombie', and who now found himself putting the coda to the tributes.

'The Taoiseach is doing something unique today: he's not only departing with dignity, but he's also departing at a high point in his career,' Ross opened. The dark nights of the Maurice McCabe–

Tusla scandal seemed a long way away now. Indeed, not a single speech to mark Enda Kenny's departure as Taoiseach thought to mention the particular issue on which his party lost its faith.

'It is undoubtedly true that the morale of the country is higher now than it was when he took office … overall, the nation is in a better place. Those people who are in a bad place are in a better place than they were when he took office. What Enda Kenny and Michael Noonan leave this country is a country with a morale and confidence which it didn't have when they took office.'

It was a polite moment of solidarity. From the outset there had been little trust between Kenny and Ross, borne largely from the 'political zombie' debacle, but some genuine rapport had developed between them over time. There was, however, a certain degree of excitement within the Independent Alliance at the prospect of Kenny giving way. 'To be honest we were privately looking forward to a bit of change of attitude,' one said. 'The way Leo is, he won't throw you under a bus. Kenny would throw us under a bus in two minutes to survive, like he did with Alan Shatter.'

When business concluded – with further applause, no small amount of handshakes and a playful thump of Michael Noonan's shoulder – Kenny took one final detour on his road to the Áras, heading to Dublin's north inner city to meet with community leaders. The welfare of the underprivileged area had become a pet project of Kenny's since a high-profile gangland murder in the middle of the 2016 election campaign, and the departing Taoiseach wanted to make one final visit before ceding his office. Maybe he was again seeking assurance that his efforts had not been in vain.

***

The new regime was formally installed a day later. The falling of the Dáil timetable meant that if TDs had reconvened to elect a new Taoiseach on the same day as Kenny's departure, the formalities of appointing a Cabinet would not have been completed until well after midnight. It made happier sense for Enda Kenny to be given a full day of plaudits and to delay his replacement until the following day.

Leo Varadkar strode calmly onto the Dáil floor at noon, but his predecessor was three minutes late. One last time, Enda Kenny kept them waiting. 'We have some business to conduct,' he laughed, standing in the leaders' spot of the government benches for the final time, announcing to Dáil Éireann that he had resigned as Taoiseach and formally proposing Leo Varadkar to become his successor.

'As the country's youngest holder of this office, he speaks for a new generation of Irishwomen and Irishmen. He represents a modern, diverse and inclusive Ireland and speaks for them like no other – an Ireland in which each person can fulfil their potential and live their dreams.'

It was doubtless true, but some of Kenny's loyalists saw it as an unfair reflection of the outgoing Taoiseach. Objectively, as they saw it, Kenny himself had perhaps been Ireland's most socially liberal leader ever. A lifelong Mass-goer had stood in the Dáil and brutalised the Catholic Church's systematic cover-ups of child abuse scandals. A conservative man of rural western Ireland had overseen a referendum on same-sex marriage, and passed one of the world's most progressive laws on transgender identity. He had also set up an initiative that, in time, caused a referendum overturning the near-total ban on abortion. All of the above could have been written off as Labour's influence, but as one Kenny follower said, you can't get blood from a stone.

'I wish Leo Varadkar and his team every success in the challenges that lie ahead. I have no doubt but that he will build on the solid foundations on which our country now stands, and that he will see that it is managed carefully in the people's interests and that the decisions his government will make will always hold the people as central to those decisions. I therefore commend his name to the House for selection as Taoiseach of Ireland.'

TDs filed through the lobbies at the back of the chamber to vote. Returning to the front bench, Kenny moved into the second seat in the row, usually occupied by the Tánaiste. Leo Varadkar jumped into the now vacant seat beside him just as the Ceann Comhairle announced the result: fifty-seven TDs in favour, fifty opposed, forty-five abstaining. Ten years to the day after first stepping into the same chamber as a rookie member of Dáil Éireann, Leo Varadkar was elected Taoiseach.

The new man immediately set about lauding his predecessor, for paving the way both formally and politically. 'I've no doubt that only for him, this country as we know it would not be here today. On a personal note, I would like to add that were it not for Enda Kenny, I have no doubt that I would not be standing here in this seat today. Because of his stewardship of our party, I was able to regain the seat for our party, first on the council and then in the Dáil.' Kenny, seeming unaccustomed to his new seat or to arching his neck up at a speaker to his right, looked less uplifted by the occasion than his frontbench colleagues.

'His leadership also enabled me to become an equal citizen in my own country only two short years ago, and to aspire to hold this office – an aspiration which I once thought was beyond my reach, at least if I chose to be myself. And so I'd like the outgoing Taoiseach to know that those of us who take on the torch of leadership here today will protect all that he has achieved, and make him proud of us by building on all that he has done for the country.'

* * *

If Leo Varadkar had learned anything from his predecessor, it was to shake every hand offered to him. The Dáil adjourned just after 2.30 p.m. but it took Varadkar almost half an hour to make his way to the car in front of Leinster House and take the ceremonial journey to Áras an Úachtaráin. Along the way he was flanked by well-wishers, political staff of almost every hue, and Leinster House civil servants and hangers-on who simply wanted to bear first-hand experience to the transition of power. Every single one wanted a handshake.

It seemed everyone who wasn't outside Leinster House, waiting patiently behind a barrier to greet the new Taoiseach, was in the canteen. The small self-service restaurant ('the canner' to its regulars) was always busy during the Dáil's lunchtime recess, but it was now nearly 3 p.m. and nobody wanted to leave for lunch until the historic formalities had concluded in the chamber.

Among the hungry hordes was Enda Kenny. This wasn't unusual; Kenny was no stranger to the canner and was usually seen getting a hot lunch there once a week, often on a Friday when the Dáil wasn't sitting and the occupancy rate was lower. Given the occasion, however, it took far longer for him to make his way to the counter to order his meal. Party supporters, clerks, journalists and civil servants – many of whom were filtering in after seeing Leo Varadkar's motorcade leaving through the front gates – were among those now lining up to offer their congratulations, thanks and best wishes to the man taking his bow from the main stage.

Almost all of them were strangers, but, ever the politician, Kenny never let it show. 'Thank you,' he'd say to one.

Or, 'You're very kind.'

Or, 'Not at all.'

Or, 'All in a day's work.'

Eventually one of his aides, realising Kenny would never get to eat at all otherwise, ordered his dinner for him and politely nudged him towards his seat, at a table with his personal secretary and a few other close staff.

At 3.18 p.m., in front of the fireplace at the State Reception Room in Áras an Úachtaráin, Michael D. Higgins and Leo Varadkar signed the warrant of appointment. The inevitable became official and Leo Varadkar became Taoiseach na hÉireann, the fourteenth Prime Minister of an independent Ireland; at thirty-eight, its youngest ever, showered in applause and flash bulbs.

Enda Kenny formally ceded Ireland's most powerful office while sitting in the everyday canteen of Leinster House, his workplace of forty-one years, tucking into a €6 meat-and-veg dinner as he laughed with his closest confidants.

NOTE ON SOURCES

The second and third interim reports of the Disclosures Tribunal – dealing with the treatment of Keith Harrison and Maurice McCabe respectively – are available at that Tribunal's own website, www.disclosurestribunal.ie. That site also contains transcripts of Tribunal proceedings, which form the basis of much of the 'Aftermath' chapter.

Transcripts of Dáil proceedings are published by the Houses of the Oireachtas and are available at www.oireachtas.ie/debates.

Archive recordings of the TV and radio programmes mentioned in this book are available on the respective websites of RTÉ, Today FM and Newstalk. Transcripts from press conferences, and from similar 'doorstep' interviews, are made from the author's own archive of contemporary recordings.

Newspaper extracts cited in this book are drawn from *The Irish Times*, the *Irish Independent*, the *Irish Examiner*, the Ireland edition of *The Times*, the *Irish Daily Mail*, and *The Sun*; and from their respective websites, where appropriate.

ACKNOWLEDGEMENTS

This is not the book I originally set out to write. Having agreed to produce a separate book entirely – and simply to get some words onto the blank page – I set about writing the story of Enda Kenny's downfall, hoping it might contribute a couple of thousand to the final word count. It was only when I had written nearly 9,000 words that I realised I was barely scraping the surface of the story – and that I should get back to the publisher to ask if this alternative tale might just be worth telling instead.

For commissioning one book in the first place, and then for showing remarkable patience and encouragement when I suggested changing tack entirely, I am hugely grateful to Patrick O'Donoghue of Mercier Press.

Turning that improvised draft into a legible final product was the work of an eternally patient editor in Noel O'Regan, who made the whole process far less arduous than it could have been. Thanks also to the rest of the Mercier team – Wendy Logue, Deirdre Roberts, Aileen Ferris and Alice Coleman – and to the proofreader, Monica Strina, for their efforts in putting this work into your hands.

The story of Enda Kenny's downfall, and of Maurice McCabe's redemption, could not have been told without the work of my fellow journalists in Leinster House and beyond. I am grateful for their comprehensive work in chronicling the tumult of the time – in particular Katie Hannon and Michael Clifford, who so consistently broke new ground – but, especially, for their moral support in pulling me through the book-writing process. For the latter, my special thanks to Christina Finn, Jennifer Bray, Sean Defoe, Senan Molony, Hugh O'Connell, Niall O'Connor and Páraic Gallagher.

I also owe thanks to my bosses at Virgin Media News, especially Mick McCaffrey and Joe Walsh, who understood the time this book would take and allowed it without hesitation; and my former colleagues at Today FM, especially Sinead Spain, who were actually paying my wages while I was doing the work I've summarised on these pages.

This story obviously could not have been told without the enthusiastic input of the dozens of people who granted interviews for my book. I am hugely grateful for their willingness to speak to me, and for the illumination they cast into the darker corners of this story.

The process of getting the first draft over the line was made all the easier thanks to the invaluable feedback of early readers Sarah Bardon, Kenneth Barrett and Killian Woods. Their honest appraisals of what worked, and what didn't, were priceless – thanks, you guys.

Thanks to the wider Reilly, Maguire and Brennan families who, if they have ever had any doubts in me, never let them show.

Finally, to my wife, Ciara, who gently nudged me through the regular moments of self-doubt; who read the first draft more dutifully and attentively than anyone could ask; who encouraged me to do what I thought I couldn't; and who kept me on schedule when my own instincts were to shelve the whole thing. You are the only person I have ever truly wanted to impress. I hope I have: this book is for you.

Gavan Reilly

May 2019

ABOUT THE AUTHOR

© Nathalie Marquez Courtney

Gavan Reilly is political correspondent with Virgin Media News (formerly TV3) and the host of Newstalk's Sunday morning show *On The Record*. He is one of Ireland's best-recognised current affairs journalists, and a prominent contributor to current affairs programmes on TV and radio across Ireland and Europe. He is also a columnist with the *Meath Chronicle* and a former political correspondent with Today FM, where he regularly served as a guest presenter on *The Last Word*. Originally from Meath, he lives in Dublin with his wife, Ciara. This is his first book.